BASIC PRACTICE IN COURTS AND TRIBUNALS

BASIC PRACTICE IN COURTS AND TRIBUNALS

by
NICHOLAS FRIDD, MA (Oxon), Barrister of the Inner Temple
and
STEVEN WEDDLE, BA, Barrister of Grays Inn

WATERLOW PUBLISHERS

First edition 1989
© Nicholas Fridd and Steven Weddle 1989

Waterlow Publishers
Paulton House
8 Shepherdess Walk
London
N1 7LB

A division of Pergamon Professional and Financial Services PLC

ISBN 0 08 036901 4

British Library Cataloguing in Publication Data

Fridd, Nicholas
  Basic practice in courts and tribunals.
  1. England. Civil courts. Procedure
  I. Title II. Weddle, Steven
  344. 207'5

Typeset by Type Out, Graphics House, Station Approach, Streatham, London SW16 1LB

Printed and bound by Biddles Limited, Walnut Tree House, Woodbridge Park, Guildford, Surrey GU1 1DA

Foreword

BY THE RT HON LORD HAVERS OF EDMUNDSBURY

This is a remarkable book – it takes the reader by the hand through practically any court he may visit and tells him exactly what to do and warns the unwary of the pitfalls.

I would have been an avid reader if it had been available when I started at the Bar.

In my view there should be a copy in every set of Chambers and solicitors' office.

If there is there can be no excuse for not getting everything right.

The scope is enormous; it covers all the ordinary courts and the Coroner's Court and even a Consistory Court.

I cannot praise it too highly.

MH
14.11.89

Contents

Introduction

The Purpose of the Book

This book is designed to assist an advocate in an unfamiliar court or tribunal.

It offers general advice in respect of each court and tribunal and then gives the advocate a step by step guide to the practice of the court or tribunal.

The book tells the advocate what usually happens in any court, tribunal or enquiry.

The Art of Advocacy

It is upon this basic foundation that the advocate will gain the confidence to enable him to use his skills as an advocate to their best advantage.

This book is therefore about the form rather than the art of advocacy. If any advice about the art of advocacy can be given, it is summed up in the words of Lord Birkett:

The primary rules are not many and they are easily mastered.

They are to seek simplicity, to avoid verbiage, to use familiar words of plain meaning and to be natural.

It is lucidity that makes speech enjoyable to the hearer; it is grace of speech that makes the spoken word memorable; and grace and lucidity come only from the observance of the primary rules and the willingness to take pains.

The Chapters and Sections in the Book

As a general rule, the preparation for a hearing in the civil courts is more structured than the actual hearing of the case whereas the opposite applies in the criminal courts. This book concentrates on the structure of usual forms of preparation and practice.

Practice in Courts and Tribunals

Although the book is self-explanatory, the advocate should note that practice varies between different courts or tribunals and, although allowances have been made for this in the book, the number of variations cannot be exhaustive. The book is as correct as it can be where the variations of practice will be as many as the courts and tribunals or, indeed, the advocates appearing before them.

Addressing the Court or Tribunal

The book also omits references to the court (for example, **My Lord** or **Your Worships** and sometimes refers to the court as **you**) for ease of use. The advocate should always use the correct references (usually set out at the beginning of each chapter or section) as a matter of courtesy.

The Preparation of the Book

The method of work adopted in the preparation of the book was that Nicholas Fridd was responsible for the research and writing of the chapters on criminal practice, general practice and practice in tribunals; and, Steven Weddle for the research and first draft of the chapters on civil practice. These chapters and the chapters for which there are acknowledgements were then re-written by Nicholas Fridd in order to achieve uniformity of style.

The typing was shared by Fiona Fridd, to whom many thanks.

The Temple   **Nicholas Fridd**

September 1989   **Steven Weddle**

Acknowledgements

The authors would like to thank the following persons, who are practising barristers unless otherwise stated, who provided the first draft of, or wrote, the following chapters (or sections) either in whole or in part:

Chapter 5: High Court   Section 7: Winding Up

> Peter Mullen, BA (Cantab)

Chapter 9: Tribunals   Section 1: Industrial Tribunal

> Guy Prichard, MA (Oxon)

Chapter 10:Enquiries

> A Derwin Hope, BSc (Lond)

Chapter 11:Coroner's Court

> John Wilson, BA (Cantab)

Chapter 13:Consistory Court

> Nigel Seed, BA (Dunelm)

Chapter 14:General Practice   Section 3: Etiquette

> James Bullen, LLB (Lond)

The authors would also like to thank the following people who are practising barristers unless otherwise stated, who have checked and added their comments to the following chapters (or sections):

Chapter 1: Magistrates' Court, and Chapter 2: Juvenile Court

> David Speed, MA (Oxon)
> Clerk to the Makerfield and Wigan Justices

Chapter 3: Crown Court

> His Honour Judge Butler QC
(although without approval of the practice of **Seeing the Judge**, see **3.03.03**).

> Alan Brown
> Court Clerk at Southwark Crown Court

Section 3: Seeing the Judge   David Gibson-Lee, LLB (Lond)

Chapter 4: Sentencing and Bail   David Speed, (as above)

> Alan Brown, (as above)

CHAPTER 1

Magistrates' Court

SECTION 1: INTRODUCTION

INTRODUCTION

1.01.01   Mode of Address

Lay bench: (Justices)	Sir or Madam to the chairman (Your Worship(s) is sometimes used).
Stipendiary magistrate:	Sir or Madam.

1.01.02   The Hearing

Unless otherwise stated, the hearing of any matter in the magistrates' court takes place in open court.

1.01.03   Rights of Audience

Barrister.

Solicitor.

Authorised official (for example: local authority employee).

Defendant in person.

Other person, sometimes called next-friend or McKenzie adviser, rarely, with the leave of the court, for example:

With your permission, I would like to represent the defendant in these proceedings.

1.01.04   Dress

Barristers and solicitors should be respectably dressed.

Defendants in person and other persons may appear in their normal everyday wear.

1.01.05 Burden of Proof

The prosecution/applicant/complainant has the burden of proving, in any contested matter, the case against the defendant.

1.01.06 Standard of Proof

Criminal cases: Beyond reasonable doubt.

Civil cases: On the balance of probabilities.

1.01.07 Seating in Court

Criminal cases:

Where the dock is at the side of the court the defence will usually sit in the rows and/or seats closer to the dock. Otherwise, the defence may sit in the rows, and/or seats, on the right hand side of court facing the bench.

Civil cases:

The applicant may sit in the rows and/or seats on the left hand side of the court facing the Bench.

1.01.08 Addressing the Court

Any party addressing the court should do so standing.

1.01.09 Witnesses

Criminal cases:

Witnesses should remain outside court until called to give evidence. The witness should then remain in court until the conclusion of the case or until he is given permission to leave by the court.

Civil cases:

Witnesses should remain outside court until called to give evidence. The witness should leave court after having given evidence.

1.01.10 Appeal

In practice, appeal is to the crown court. For appeal by case stated to the Divisional Court, see **8.03.41-56** and the common practitioners' handbooks.

SECTION 2:
ATTENDANCE OF THE PARTIES

ATTENDANCE OF THE PROSECUTION/APPLICANT/COMPLAINANT

1.02.01   If the prosecution/applicant/complainant and/or witness(es) essential to the proof of that party's case fail to attend court, the defence may apply for the case to be dismissed for want of prosecution for example:

The prosecution/applicant/complainant and/or (name of witness(es)) **does not attend.**

I have/The court has been offered no adequate explanation for his failure to attend.

I therefore apply for this matter to be dismissed for want of prosecution.

ATTENDANCE OF THE DEFENDANT (CHARGE)

1.02.02   If the defendant has been charged and bailed in criminal proceedings he must attend court. If he does not do so, a warrant may be issued or bail may be enlarged in his absence.

1.02.03   Warrant Without Bail

A warrant without bail will be issued where the defendant has given either no explanation or no reasonable explanation for his non-attendance.

1.02.04   The defence should not make an application for bail if no explanation has been given for the defendant's non-attendance.

The prosecution may say:

The defendant does not appear. I ask for a warrant.

The defence may say:

I can give the court no explanation for the defendant's failure to appear.

1.02.05   Warrant With Bail

A warrant backed for bail may be issued where the defendant has given a reasonable explanation for his non-attendance but the court is not necessarily satisfied that, if true, the explanation would excuse the defendant from attending court, for example:

(a)   The defence produce a medical certificate which shows that the defendant has a broken arm.

(b)   The defendant has telephoned the court to say that his car has broken down.

1.02.06   Enlarging Bail

Bail will be enlarged in the absence of the defendant where the defendant has given a reasonable explanation for his non- attendance and where there is evidence (from either the prosecution or the defence) to show that the defendant is unable to attend court, for example:

(a)   The defendant is in hospital and a medical certificate is produced.

(b)   The defendant is in custody on another matter.

ATTENDANCE OF THE DEFENDANT/RESPONDENT (SUMMONS)

1.02.07   If the defendant/respondent has been summonsed, he should attend court except (in criminal proceedings) where he has been invited to plead guilty by letter.

If the defendant/respondent does not attend court

1.02.08   Where the defendant/respondent has given no explanation or no reasonable explanation for his non-attendance, and the prosecution/applicant/ complainant can prove that the summons has been served

(a)   The case may be heard in the defendant's/ respondent's absence, or

(b)   A warrant (with or without bail) may be issued where the information is substantiated on oath.

1.02.09   Where the defendant/respondent has given a reasonable explanation for his non-attendance, the summons may be adjourned.

1.02.10   Where the prosecution/applicant/complainant is unable to prove that the summons has been served, the summons will be marked *not served* and may be re-issued marked *for personal service.*

SECTION 3:
NON-EFFECTIVE HEARING

INTRODUCTION

1.03.01 Criminal Proceedings

Criminal proceedings in the magistrates' court are commenced by charge or summons. As a general rule, non-imprisonable offences only are commenced by summons (see **1.04.03**).

1.03.02   Where a defendant appears on charge and the case is adjourned, the defendant is remanded either on bail or in custody to the adjourned date (see **4.02: Bail Applications**). The date must be fixed.

1.03.03   Where a defendant appears on summons, the case is adjourned. There is no need to fix a date for the next hearing, although this is usually done, or the case may be adjourned for a date to be fixed or *sine die.*
   In some circumstances the defendant is remanded even if he has appeared on summons.

1.03.04   Civil Proceedings

Civil proceedings in the magistrates' court are usually commenced by summons (see **1.03.03**).

PRACTICE

1.03.05   Identification of the Defendant and/or Parties

The defendant and/or parties are usually identified by name, date of birth and/or address.

The clerk may say:

Are you (name)? **What is your date of birth? And do you live at** (address)?

1.03.06   Introduction of the Parties

Either party (but usually the party making the application for the remand/adjournment) or the clerk may introduce the parties to the court, for example:

The Prosecution/Applicant/Complainant may say:

I appear on behalf of the prosecution/applicant/complainant.

The defendant/respondent is represented by Mr (name).

This is the prosecution's/applicant's/complainant's application for a remand/adjournment.

The defence/respondent may say:

I appear on behalf of the defendant/respondent. I apply for a remand/adjournment.

1.03.07   Application for Remand/Adjournment

The party making the application then gives reasons for the application (see **1.03.08** and **1.03.09**).

1.03.08 Specimen Reasons in Criminal Proceedings

(a)   First appearance

This is the defendant's first appearance. The defence is asking for (-) **weeks to take instructions.**

(b) Advance disclosure

In indictable offences and either way offences, the defence has the right to advance disclosure of the prosecution case:

The defence is asking for advance disclosure. I believe that (-) weeks is appropriate.

See **1.04: Mode of Trial.**

(c) For a date to be fixed

The defendant is pleading not guilty and a date will need to be fixed for trial. The time estimate is (-) hours.

See **1.06: Summary Trial.**

(d) Committal to crown court

The defence is seeking committal to the crown court.
Mode of trial will usually be determined at this stage.

See **1.04: Mode of Trial.**

(e) Remand for old style/read committal

The defence will be seeking an old style/read committal and a date will need to be fixed. The time estimate is (-) hours.

Mode of trial will usually be determined at this stage.

See **1.04:   Mode of Trial.**

The advocate should remember that the evidence in an old style committal is written down by the clerk (see **1.05.19-21**) and the time estimate should take account of this.

(f) Lack of time

There is insufficient time for the case to be heard today. Could a new date be fixed?

(g) Lack of preparation

The prosecution/defence has not had time to prepare the case because (state reason).

(h) Non attendance of witness(es)

A witness essential to the prosecution/defence is unable to attend court because (state reason).

(i) Non attendance of defendant

See **1.02: Attendance of Parties.**

Summons only:

The defendant does not appear but nevertheless wishes to contest the summons.

1.03.09   Specimen Reasons in Domestic or Civil Proceedings

(a) First appearance

This is the respondent's first appearance. I am asking for (-) weeks to take instructions.

(b) Legal aid

An application for legal aid often takes longer to be considered in civil proceedings than in criminal proceedings.

The respondent has made/will be making an application for legal aid. I am asking for (-) weeks for this to be considered.

(c) For a date to be fixed

The respondent is contesting the summons and a date will need to be fixed for a hearing. The time estimate is (-) hours.

(d) Reconciliation

The complainant and respondent are attempting a reconciliation. The parties would therefore wish this matter to be adjourned (usually) *sine die*.

See **1.09.09.**

(e) Blood tests

The complainant/respondent is seeking a direction for blood tests/DNA fingerprinting.

See **1.09.07.**

(f) Lack of time

There is insufficient time for the case to be heard today. Could a new date be fixed?

(g) Lack of preparation

The complainant/respondent has not had time to prepare the case because (state reason).

(h) Non Attendance of witness(es)

A witness essential to the complainant/respondent is unable to attend court because (state reason).

1.03.10   Argument

If the application is opposed the court may wish to hear argument on the merits of the application. The order of submissions is usually as follows:

(a) Party making the application for remand/adjournment.

(b) Party opposing the application.

(c) Reply by party (a) on any new matters only, raised by party (b) or the court.

1.03.11   Decision

The magistrates' announce their decision:

We are/are not prepared to grant this application.

1.03.12   Remand or Adjournment of Case

The magistrates determine the next date of hearing (if appropriate):

This case will be remanded/adjourned to (date and time).

The defendant will be on bail/in custody.

SECTION 4: MODE OF TRIAL

INTRODUCTION

1.04.01   Mode of trial proceedings are conducted in either way offences only.

1.04.02   *Classification of Offences*   *Court of Trial*

Summary offences   Magistrates' court

Indictable offences   Crown court

Either way offences   Either magistrates'
(Schedule 1, MCA 1980)   court or crown court

1.04.03   As a general rule, a defendant appearing before the magistrates' court on summons will not be able to elect crown court trial although practice varies, and in some areas either way offences are often summonsed, for example: reckless driving, fraudulent use of vehicle excise license, shop-lifting (depending upon the age and sex of the offender) (see **1.03.01**).

1.04.04   Mode of trial will usually be determined at a non- effective hearing (see **1.03.08(d)-(e)**).

The decision will determine whether, at the effective hearing, the magistrates' court hears the evidence in a summary trial (see **1.06: Summary Trial**) or in committal proceedings (see **1.05: Committal Proceedings**).

1.04.05   Factors to be taken into consideration

When deciding which court is the appropriate court in which the case should be heard, the magistrates' court shall have regard to:

(a)   The nature of the case.

(b)   Whether the circumstances make the offence one of serious character.

(c)   Whether the punishment which a magistrates' court would have power to inflict would be adequate. (The court must assume that the defendant is of good character).

(d) Any other circumstances which make the case more suitable for one method of trial rather than the other. (For example, the complexity of the case).

PRACTICE

1.04.06   The charge or summons is read to the defendant by the clerk:

Mr (name)**, you appear before the magistrates today charged that** (the clerk will read from the charge sheet or summons)**.**

1.04.07 Mode of trial proceedings are not usually conducted unless the defence has had the opportunity of considering a summary of the evidence against the defendant (see **1.03.08(b)**).

However, mode of trial may be considered at the defendant's first appearance (where, for example, the defendant intends to elect summary trial, plead guilty and 'get it over with').

After the charge or summons has been read to the defendant, the clerk may say:

Has the defendant been informed of his right to advance disclosure?

The defence may say:

He does not require advance disclosure.

1.04.08   Representations as to Mode of Trial

The clerk may say (to either party):

Are there any representations as to mode of trial?

1.04.09   Prosecution Representations

The prosecution ask for summary trial/trial on indictment for the following reasons (state reasons)**.**

See **1.04.05**.

1.04.10   If the prosecution takes the view that the court may be assisted in its decision to accept or decline jurisdiction, the prosecution should briefly outline the facts of the case and draw the court's attention to the factors to be taken into consideration, for example:

The application is for:

(a) **Trial on indictment. This is a serious assault involving the use of a weapon.**

(b) **Trial on indictment. There are a substantial number of documents in this case and if it were tried before this court would last** (state length of time).

(c) **Summary trial. Although the charge alleges theft of a substantial amount of** (state nature of goods), **full compensation has been made voluntarily by the defendant.**

1.04.11 Where there is unlikely to be any real dispute, the prosecution need not give reasons, for example:

This is a charge of theft (state nature of goods and value) **by shoplifting. The application is for summary trial.**

1.04.12 Defence Representations

Where there is argument over mode of trial, the defence will address the court as follows:

The defence would say that summary trial/trial on indictment is more appropriate for the following reasons (state reasons).

The defence may then outline the reasons for the application and draw the court's attention to the factors to be taken into consideration (see **1.04.05**).

1.04.13 The defence will usually only address the court where the prosecution are asking for trial on indictment, for example (see **1.04.10(a) and (b)**):

The defence application is for:

(a) **Summary trial. Although the assault involved the use of a weapon, the victim sustained minimal injuries.**

(b) **Summary trial. The defence do not agree that this case would last** (state length of time). **Most of the documents are agreed.**

1.04.14 Where there is no argument over Mode of Trial and the defence support the prosecution's application, the defence may say:

No representations.

1.04.15   The Defendant's Right to Trial on Indictment

The determination of Mode of Trial does not in any way affect the defendant's right to elect Trial on Indictment (see **1.04.17**).

1.04.16   Determination of Mode of Trial

The court determines mode of trial:

The clerk will usually say (to magistrates):

Do you accept jurisdiction?

The court announces its decision:

We find that this case is suitable for summary trial, or

We find that this case should be tried on indictment (see **1.05: Committal Proceedings**).

1.04.17   The clerk will then say to defendant:

The magistrates have determined that this case is more suitable for summary trial. If you consent, you may be tried by the magistrates, or you may, if you wish, be tried by a judge and jury at the crown court. However, I must warn you that if you are tried at this court and are found guilty or plead guilty, you may be committed to the crown court for sentence if the magistrates, after hearing about your character and antecedents, and previous convictions, if any, are of the opinion that greater punishment should be inflicted upon you than this court has the power to impose.

Do you understand that?

Where do you wish to be tried?

The defendant will say:

Either:	**This court**
	The defendant will then usually be asked whether he pleads guilty or not guilty, (see **1.06: Summary Trial**).
Or:	**The crown court** (see **1.05: Committal Proceedings, 1.03: Non-Effective Hearings**).

CHANGE OF ELECTION

1.04.18   The magistrates' court will usually permit a defendant to change his election from trial on indictment to summary trial.

1.04.19   The magistrates' court will usually only permit a defendant to change his election from summary trial to trial on indictment after consideration of the following:

(a) Whether the defendant obtained or was able to obtain legal advice before making his election.

(b) The length of time before the application to change his election.

(c) The age of defendant.

(d) The mental ability of defendant.

1.04.20   The defence may say:

> **I apply for the defendant to be permitted to change his election, for the following reasons** (state reasons, if **1.04.19** applies).

If the court grants the application, the defence may say:

> **Could the election be put again?**

1.04.21 Repeat **1.04.17**.

SECTION 5: COMMITTAL PROCEEDINGS

INTRODUCTION

1.05.01   The function of committal proceedings is for the magistrates' court to determine whether the prosecution can adduce sufficient evidence (a *prima facie* case) for the court to commit the defendant for trial to the crown court.

If, after consideration of the evidence and any submissions, the court is of the opinion that there is sufficient evidence to commit the defendant for trial to the crown court, the court shall commit him for trial. If the court is not of that opinion, it shall discharge the defendant.

Committal proceedings may be conducted by a single examining magistrate.

1.05.02   Forms of Committal

Committal proceedings may take three different forms. These are usually called

Old Style Committal.

'Read' Committal.

Section 6(2) Committal.

1.05.03   Old Style Committal

An old style committal is usually held where the defence is of the opinion that the statements served on him disclose no satisfactory case to answer and the defence wish to test that evidence in cross-examination.

An old style committal (usually a 'Read' committal) must be held if the defendant is unrepresented.

1.05.04   Sometimes, where the only evidence against a defendant is given by witnesses whom either party believe may not attend court, either party may ask for an old style committal to see if the witnesses attend.

If the witnesses attend court, the defence may agree to a section 6(2) committal (see **1.05.14**).

1.05.05   'Read' Committal

A 'Read' committal is technically an old style committal. The procedure is the same as in an old style committal except that the prosecution reads and/or summarises the statements of the witnesses and produces the relevant documentary exhibits (see **1.05.18**).

A 'Read' Committal will usually be held where the defence is of the opinion that the statements served on him disclose no case to answer and it would not be in the defendant's interest to test that evidence in cross-examination.

1.05.06   Section 6(2) Committal

A section 6(2) committal is held where the defence is of the opinion that the statements served on him disclose a case to answer.

1.05.07   Attendance of the Defendant

See **1.02: Attendance of the Parties.**

PRACTICE

1.05.08   Identification of the Defendant

The defendant is usually identified by name, date of birth and/or address.

1.05.09   The Charge

The charge or summons is read to the defendant by the clerk (and/or at **1.05.26**)

Mr (name), **you appear before the magistrates today charged that** (the clerk will read from the charge sheet or summons).

1.05.10   Mode of Trial

Mode of trial (in section 6(2) committals only), may be determined if this has not been determined at a previous hearing.

See **1.03.08(d)-(e)** and **1.04: Mode of Trial.**

The court will not have set time aside to hear an old style committal if mode of trial has not previously been determined.

1.05.11   Discharge of Defendant Before Committal

If, after consideration of the evidence, the prosecution are of the opinion that the statements in their possession do not disclose a case to answer, and the prosecution unsuccessfully apply for a remand in order to obtain better evidence, the defence may ask for the defendant to be permitted to change his election (see **1.04: Mode of Trial**), for example:

In view of your decision, the prosecution are unable to proceed.

Would you consider an application for the defendant to change his election, and, that the charges be dismissed?

If the defendant is discharged, he may be re-charged if better evidence later

becomes available. If the defendant's case is dismissed after a plea of not guilty
he cannot then be re-charged.

1.05.12 Reporting Restrictions

The clerk will usually ask the defence:

Do you want reporting restrictions lifted?

The defence replies:

Yes or **No** (usually **No**).

If the defence want reporting restrictions lifted, the court may require a
reason to be given by the defence, for example:

**This is a case which has attracted speculation in the local press which,
I would submit, is not justified on the evidence you are about to hear.**

1.05.13   If there is more than one defendant and one of them objects to the lifting
of reporting restrictions, the court will hear argument before determining whether
publicity should be given to the proceedings.

If in doubt, the court will usually rule against the lifting of reporting restrictions.

In an old style committal or a 'read' committal, omit **1.05.14-1.05.16**.

SECTION 6(2) PROCEDURE

1.05.14   The clerk asks the defence:

Do you consent to a section 6(2) committal?

The defence will answer: **Yes**.

The clerk will then ask the parties if they are prepared for committal.

The prosecution may reply:

**I tender the original statements and documentary exhibits to the court
together with typed copies** (one typed copy is usually sufficient). **The
statements were served on the defence on** (date).

1.05.15   The court will then determine the witness orders (see **1.05.22**).

The clerk will say to the defence:

Could you tell me what witness orders you require?

The clerk will then read out the names of the witnesses and (depending on the practice of the court) state how many pages comprise that witness's statement and whether he produces any exhibits, for example:

Statement of (name) **consisting of** (-) **pages. He produces** (-) **exhibit(s). Witness order?**

The defence will say:

Full/Conditional order, please.

1.05.16 After determination of witness orders, the clerk may say:

Does the defendant object to any statement, wish to call evidence or make any submissions?

The defence will usually answer: **No.**

In which case, you will shortly be committed by the magistrates to the crown court for trial.

In a section 6(2) committal omit **1.05.17-29.**

THE CASE FOR THE PROSECUTION

1.05.17 Prosecution Opening

The prosecution opening should contain:
(a) A brief outline of the evidence to be called, and/or read or summarised.

(b) A brief description of the issues between the parties.

(c) A brief summary of any relevant law.

1.05.18 Prosecution Evidence

The prosecution may:

(a) Call witnesses in the usual way (see **1.06.17-29** and **14.01.01-24**).

(b) Read or summarise the statements of the witnesses.

(c) Combine (a) and (b).

1.05.19   Where witnesses are called, they are usually cross-examined only on the issues on which either the prosecution rely (to establish an essential ingredient of the offence) or on which the defence are seeking to make a submission.

1.05.20   The evidence of the witnesses is written down or typed by the clerk. The written document is called a deposition.

After each witness has given evidence, the deposition is read to the witness. The witness is then required to sign each page of the deposition and initial any corrections.

1.05.21   The parties should ensure that they ask simple, straightforward questions, the answers to which can easily be recorded. Complicated questions lead to answers that cannot easily be recorded and which are often incomprehensible when read out of context (see **14.01.01-10**).

1.05.22   Witness Orders

After each witness has signed his deposition, the defence will be required to state what witness order they require if the defendant is committed for trial.

Full Witness Order (Fully Bound Witness):

Where the witness' evidence is disputed and the witness is required to attend the trial of the defendant at the crown court for cross-examination.

Conditional Witness Order (Conditionally Bound Witness):

Where the witness' evidence is not disputed and the witness is not required to attend the trial of the defendant at the crown court.

SUBMISSION OF NO CASE TO ANSWER

1.05.23   At the conclusion of the prosecution's case, the defence may submit that there is insufficient evidence on which the defendant can be committed for trial.

The grounds on which a submission of no case to answer may be made and the relevant law should be researched in the common practitioners' handbooks.

1.05.24   In practice, the order of submissions is as follows:

(a) The defence may begin:

I submit that there is no case to answer.

Either:

On the ground that the prosecution has failed to establish (an essential ingredient of the offence).

and/or:

On the ground that the evidence is so weak that no jury properly directed could convict on it.

(b) The defence should identify the evidence to which he refers and direct the court to any relevant law.

(c) Reply by the prosecution on mixed law and fact but not on the quality of the evidence.

(d) Response by the defence dealing with any new points raised by the prosecution or the court but not repeating the submissions in (b).

(e) The magistrates may retire to consider their decision.

1.05.25 Decision

The magistrates announce their decision.

Either:

We find that there is no case to answer. Mr (name)**, you are discharged.**

Or:

We find that there is a case to answer.

If the defendant is discharged, the defence may make an application for a defendant's costs order (see **7.02.22(b)**), for example:

Would you make a defendant's costs order?

1.05.26 Reading the Charge

The charge (or summons) is read to the defendant by the clerk (although this may be omitted if the defendant is represented and the charge has already been read to the defendant, see **1.05.09**).

1.05.27   Caution

In some courts the clerk may ask the defendant, (although there is some doubt as to whether this is the correct procedure):

Is there anything you wish to say in answer to the charge?

The defence will usually answer: **No.**

THE CASE FOR THE DEFENCE

1.05.28   In practice, the defence do not call the defendant in committal proceedings and, only rarely, call evidence in support of the case.

The decision to call evidence should only be made after careful consideration because it will involve disclosing the defendant's defence to the prosecution.

An example of when evidence may be called:

The prosecution case is based exclusively on expert evidence. The defence are able to call an expert who will conclusively refute the prosecution's evidence.

1.05.29   The order of the defence case is as follows:

(a)   Defence opening (if appropriate).

(b)   Defence evidence recorded in deposition:

    (i)   Defendant (if called)

    (ii) Defence witnesses.

(c)   Prosecution closing (if defence opened).

(d)   Defence submission (see **1.05.23-24**).

(e)   Decision (see **1.05.25**).

(f)   Witness orders determined (if not determined at **1.05.22**).

COMMITTAL TO THE CROWN COURT

1.05.30   The examining magistrate will then say (to the defendant):

> **On the charge(s) that has been read out to you** (or on any other offence disclosed by the evidence) **you will be committed to stand your trial before the** (name) **Crown Court at a date and time to be notified to you.**

There may be argument in some (serious) cases as to which crown court the defendant should be committed.

1.05.31   Alibi Warning

The examining magistrate or the clerk to the court will then ask the defence (or the prosecution):

> **Is the alibi warning appropriate?**

The alibi warning should be given in any circumstance where either party believes that alibi evidence may be given at the crown court.

The examining magistrate or clerk may say:

> **At your trial you may not be permitted to give evidence of an alibi unless you have given notice of that alibi to the solicitor for the prosecution now or within seven days. The solicitor for the prosecution is** (name). **Do you wish to give notice of that alibi today?**

It is unusual for the defence to give notice of an alibi at committal proceedings.

1.05.32   Bail

See **4.02: Bail Applications**.

A defendant who is committed for trial must be remanded in custody or on bail. This includes defendants who appear on summons (see **1.04.03**).

Some, but not all, magistrates' courts, consider that committal is a change of circumstance for the purposes of a bail application.

1.05.33   Legal Aid

The defence should apply for legal aid to be extended to the crown court if no 'through order' has been made:

Could legal aid be extended to the crown court? There has been no change in financial circumstances.

SECTION 6: SUMMARY TRIAL

INTRODUCTION

1.06.01 A summary trial is a trial in the magistrates' court of a charge or summons against the defendant.

The court has jurisdiction to conduct a summary trial of either-way offences only where the defendant consents to be tried before the magistrates' court (see **1.04: Mode of Trial**).

1.06.02 Attendance of the Defendant

See **1.02.02-10**.

1.06.03 Guilty Plea by Letter

A defendant may plead guilty by letter where:

(a) The offence is summary only, and for which the maximum sentence is not more than three months' imprisonment.

(b) The summons was accompanied by:

    (i) A notice explaining the guilty plea procedure.

    (ii) A statement of the facts of the offence.

1.06.04 The practice on the hearing of a guilty plea by letter is usually:

(a) The clerk informs the court that the defendant pleads guilty by letter.

(b) The clerk or the prosecution reads the statement of facts.

(c) The clerk reads the letter in mitigation (if any) sent by the defendant.

(d) Sentence.

1.06.05 If the court is considering disqualification and/or imprisonment, the defendant must attend. He will be informed accordingly.

PRACTICE

1.06.06 Identification of the Defendant

The clerk will identify the defendant usually by name, date of birth and/or address, for example:

Are you (name)? **What is your date of birth? And do you live at** (address)?

1.06.07 The Charge or Summons

The charge or summons is read to the defendant by the clerk:

Mr (name), **you appear before the magistrates today charged that** (the clerk will read from the charge sheet or summons).

1.06.08 Mode of trial (in either-way offences only) will then be determined if this was not done at an earlier hearing.

It is unlikely that the court will have set aside time for a summary trial if mode of trial was not determined at an earlier hearing (see **1.03.08(b)-(c)**).

1.06.09 Introduction of the Parties

The prosecution usually introduces the parties to the court:

I appear on behalf of the prosecution. My (learned) friend, Mr (name) **appears on behalf of the defendant.**

1.06.10 Preliminary Applications

The defence will usually have sufficient information to be able to identify the nature of the evidence likely to be called, for example:

(a) A copy of the charge or summons.

(b) Copies of the advance disclosure (in either-way offences, and sometimes, depending on the prosecuting authority, in summary offences).

(c) Copies of any documentary exhibit (see (b)).

1.06.11   Preliminary applications based on these documents may be made before the charge or summons is put to the defendant.

The most common preliminary applications are:

(a) Amendment of the charge or summons.

(b) Conduct and length of the trial.

(c) Separate trials

    (i)   Where the defendant is charged with two or more offences.

    (ii)   Where two or more defendants are charged with different offences arising out of the same facts.

    (iii) Where a juvenile is jointly charged with an adult.

(d) Reporting restrictions, where a juvenile is involved in the proceedings, whether as a defendant or as a witness.

The law on this subject is complex and should be researched in the common practitioners' handbooks.

1.06.12   After any preliminary applications, the clerk may say:

Can the charge now be put to the defendant? or **Can pleas be taken?**

1.06.13   The clerk will then read the charge or summons to the defendant (if this has not been done) and ask the defendant:

Do you plead guilty or not guilty?

If the defendant pleads not guilty and the prosecution offer no evidence (see also **3.04.07**), the defendant is discharged.

The defence may apply for costs (see **1.06.50**).

THE CASE FOR THE PROSECUTION

1.06.14   Order of Presentation

The order of presentation of the case for the prosecution and for each defendant follows the title order of the case in the court list.

1.06.15   Order of Cross-Examination

The order of cross-examination of prosecution witnesses follows the title order of the case in the court list. The prosection may re-examine.

1.06.16   Prosecution Opening

In the Magistrates' Court the prosecution often does not open the case. If the prosecution decides to open the case, the opening should contain:

(a) A brief outline of the facts.

(b) A brief summary of any relevant law (especially if a technical defence is anticipated, see **1.07.02-03**).

The prosecution may conclude the opening:

I now call (name of first witness).

EVIDENCE ON BEHALF OF THE PROSECUTION

1.06.17   Witnesses Attending Court

Witnesses should remain outside court until called to give evidence. The witness should then remain in court until the conclusion of the case or until he is given permission to leave by the court.

The witness is called and identified by the prosecution as follows:

Are you (name)? **What is your address, Mr** (name)?

The usual rules as to the examination, cross-examination and re-examination of witnesses apply (see **14.01.01-24**).

1.06.18   Refreshing the Memory

A witness (usually a police officer) may wish to 'refresh his memory' from a document made at the time (see **14.01.11-15**).

1.06.19   Questions of Admissibility

Questions of admissibility are determined by the magistrates and, in the event of evidence being excluded, the magistrates should not consider that evidence when reaching their decision.

The clerk never determines questions of admissibility in the absence of the magistrates.

1.06.20   Objecting to Evidence

A witness may be giving or about to give evidence to which the defence objects. The defence may interrupt the prosecution and/or witness, as follows:

I object to this evidence.

If the evidence is clearly inadmissible (for example, hearsay), the clerk may direct the prosecution to omit that evidence.

In any other situation and/or where there is likely to be an argument over the admissibility of the evidence, the court will hear the evidence and rule on its admissibility.

1.06.21   Where there is an argument over a question of admissibility, the order of submissions is usually as follows:

(a) Either party (usually the defence) identifies the evidence to which an objection is taken.

(b) The defence gives reasons for the objection and refers to any relevant law.

(c) Reply by the prosecution.

(d) Response by the defence dealing with any new points raised by the prosecution or the court but not repeating the submissions in (b).

(e) Decision by the court.

Although a magistrates' court is entitled to determine the admissibility of evidence in a trial within a trial (*voire dire*) this is very rarely done.

1.06.22 This situation is entirely unsatisfactory and is, in practice, often by-passed. In this case, the defence may refer to the disputed evidence in his closing speech, as follows:

> **The defendant is then alleged to have said** (quote the disputed evidence). **He admits/denies making that statement which, in any event, I would submit is inadmissible for the following reasons** (state reasons) **and I would invite you to exclude it from your consideration of the case.**

This approach has the following advantages:

(a) The disputed evidence is not highlighted.

(b) The prosecution often do not exercise the right to address the court in closing on points of law (see **1.06.44**).

1.06.23   Tendering a Witness

If a witness gives corroborative evidence, the prosecution may tender that witness for cross-examination (see **14.01.23-24**).

1.06.24   Releasing a Witness

If a witness wishes to leave court after having given evidence, the prosecution may say:

> **Unless there is any objection, perhaps this witness** (and/or any subsequent witness) **could be released?**

1.06.25   Witnesses not Attending Court

Where the evidence of a witness is not disputed by the defence, the statement of that witness may be read to the court if a copy of the statement:

(a) Has been served on the defence at least seven days before the hearing, and

(b) The defence, within seven days of service, has not served (either orally or in writing) notice objecting to its being tendered in evidence.

If an objection is raised by the defence at the hearing, an adjournment may be granted with a note as to costs.

1.06.26 The evidence of the witness is usually introduced by the prosecution as follows:

The next witness is (name) **in the form of a section 9 statement, the original** (or a copy) **of which I will hand to the clerk.**

The statement has been served on the defence.

This is the statement of Mr (name) **who is a** (occupation) **of** (address). **He states:**

The prosecution will then read the statement. The clerk and the magistrates will be familiar with the declaration (that the statement is true) which is usually omitted.

1.06.27   Expert Witness

An expert is entitled to give evidence of opinion on any matter in which he has expert knowledge (see **14.01.16-20**).

1.06.28   Admissions

A formal admission of facts is rare in the magistrates' court.

Admissions may be made by either party and must be made in writing, in practice on a standard section 10 (CJA 1967) form, available from the clerk. If no form is available, the admission may be written on a piece of paper and signed by the party making the admission. The admission is then read to the court.

1.06.29   Close of Prosecution Case

When the prosecution has called and/or read all the evidence and any admissions have been made, the case is said to be closed. The usual form of words is:

That is the case for the prosecution or, more simply, **That is the case.**

SUBMISSION OF NO CASE TO ANSWER

1.06.30   The grounds on which a submission of no case to answer may be made and the relevant law should be researched in the common practitioners' handbooks.

1.06.31   In practice, the order of submissions is as follows:

(a)   The defence may begin:

I submit that there is no case to answer on (specify the charge or summons).

(i) **On the ground that the prosecution has failed to establish** (an essential ingredient of the offence).

and/or

(ii) **On the ground that the evidence is so weak that the court could not convict on it.**

The defence must make it clear to the court that a submission of no case to answer is being made in order that it is not confused with a final speech.

(b) The defence should identify the evidence to which he refers and direct the court to any relevant law.

(c) Reply by the prosecution on mixed law and fact but not on the quality of the evidence.

(d) Response by the defence dealing with any new points raised by the prosecution or the court but not repeating the submissions in (b).

(e) The magistrates may retire to consider their decision.

(f) The magistrates announce their decision.

1.06.32   If a submission of no case to answer is upheld in respect of the charge or all the charges against the defendant, the defendant is discharged.

The defence may apply for costs (see **1.06.50**).

THE CASE FOR THE DEFENCE

1.06.33   Order of Presentation

The order of presentation of the case for each defendant follows the title order of the case in the court list.

If the defence is calling witnesses, the witnesses are called after the defendant has given evidence (if the defendant is giving evidence), and before the case of the next defendant, in title order of the case in the court list.

1.06.34 Order of Cross-Examination

The order of cross-examination of a defendant or defence witness follows the title order of the case in the court list except that the prosecution cross-examines last, for example:

The third defendant has given evidence in chief. The order of cross-examination is:

> 1st defendant.
>
> 2nd defendant.
>
> 4th defendant.
>
> Prosecution.

The 3rd defendant may re-examine.

1.06.35 Defence Opening

The defence have the right to open the case. In practice, this right is *never* exercised because the defence would lose the right, without the leave of the court, to close the case.

The defence would not lose the right to close the case if (on a technical defence) the defence were to open:

I now call the defendant to deal with the following point (state point) **and in due course will refer you to** (state the relevant Act or authorities).

This approach enables the clerk to identify the relevant law and to advise the magistrates accordingly.

EVIDENCE ON BEHALF OF THE DEFENCE

1.06.36 Evidence of the Defendant

The defendant must always be called first where the defence are calling other evidence (including evidence of character).

The usual rules as to the examination, cross-examination and re-examination of witnesses apply except the defendant may not be cross-examined as to credit, namely, whether he is likely, by reason of his bad character, to be untruthful (see **1.06.37**).

1.06.37   Evidence of Character

The law on this subject is complex and should be researched in the common practitioners' handbooks.

There is a brief guide in **3.04.69-71**.

If the defendant is of bad character and the defence make imputations on the character of a prosecution witness, the prosecution may only cross-examine the defendant on his bad character with the leave of the court.

The prosecution should give careful consideration to making an application for leave because, if it is refused, the defence may apply for a fresh trial before a differently constituted court.

1.06.38   The only time when the clerk may ask the magistrates to retire and address the parties in court in the absence of the magistrates is to warn an unrepresented defendant that he may be in danger of being cross-examined on his bad character.

1.06.39   Defence Evidence

The evidence on behalf of the defence is subject to the same rules and is presented in the same way as the evidence on behalf of the prosecution (see **1.06.17-28**).

1.06.40   Alibi

An alibi notice is not required in the magistrates' court, although the court may grant a prosecution application for an adjournment if the prosecution are genuinely taken by surprise by alibi evidence.

Alibi witnesses are called in the usual way after the defendant has given evidence.

1.06.41   Close of Defence Case

The usual form of words is:

That is the case for the defence.

1.06.42   Evidence in Rebuttal

In practice, it is rare for the prosecution to call evidence in rebuttal except in road traffic proceedings (see **1.07.12** and **1.07.25**).

The prosecution must apply for leave (see **3.04.77**).

SPEECHES

1.06.43   Defence Closing Speech

The defence may make a closing speech even if the defendant has not given evidence.

The defence closing speech should contain:

(a)   A summary of the evidence which will enable the court to find the defendant not guilty.

(b)   A summary of the relevant law, where the law may be in dispute.

The defence closing speech should not contain:

(c)   A recital of all the evidence.

(d)   A detailed explanation of the burden and standard of proof.

To do this would insult the experience and intelligence of the magistrates.

1.06.44   The prosecution may reply on disputed points of law raised by the defence in his speech.

1.06.45   The defence may respond, with the leave of the court, on any point of law raised, for the first time, by the prosecution or the court but should not repeat his submissions in **1.06.43**.

VERDICT

1.06.46   The magistrates may retire to consider their verdict.

1.06.47   When announcing the verdict, the court may say:

We find you guilty, or,

We find you not guilty.

A verdict of guilty to a lesser offence is not available in the magistrates' court.

1.06.48   If the verdict is guilty, see **4.01: Sentencing.**

1.06.49   If the verdict is not guilty, the defendant is discharged. The defence may apply for costs.

1.06.50   Costs

The defence may make an application for a defendant's costs order (see **7.02.22(c)**), for example:

Would you make a defendant's costs order?

The effect of the order is that costs reasonably incurred by the defendant are paid out of central funds.

There is no general power to reimburse the defendant for loss of income during the proceedings.

1.06.51   Appeal

Appeal against conviction and/or sentence is to the crown court. The notice of appeal must be served on the clerk to the magistrates' court and the prosecution within 21 days.

The hearing of the appeal at the crown court is a re-hearing of the case before the magistrates' court.

See **3.05: Appeal against Conviction.**

See **3.06: Appeal against Sentence.**

For appeal by case stated, see **8.03.41-56** and the common practitioners' handbooks.

SECTION 7: ROAD TRAFFIC

PART 1: INTRODUCTION

1.07.01   Road Traffic offences are heard by the court, either on charge or (more usually) on summons.

Most Road Traffic offences are summary only and the court will not usually conduct **1.04: Mode of Trial** or **1.05: Committal Proceedings**.

1.07.02   If the defendant pleads not guilty, the practice in **1.06: Summary Trial** should be followed.

1.07.03   The following situations are considered separately:

Driving with Excess Alcohol:

1.07.04-13   **Post Offence Consumption**
                    (The 'hip flask' defence)

1.07.14-30   **Special Reasons not to Disqualify**
                    ('laced drinks')

Penalty Points:

1.07.31-46   **Endorsement of Driving Licence**
                    ('totting')

Disqualification:

1.07.47-53   **Suspension of Disqualification**

PART 2: POST-OFFENCE CONSUMPTION OF ALCOHOL

INTRODUCTION

1.07.04   The consumption of alcohol by a defendant after having driven a motor vehicle, but before the requirement to provide a specimen of breath or blood, is known as the 'hip flask' defence.

The defence is not available to a defendant who has failed or refused to provide a specimen.

The law on this subject is complex and should be researched in the common practitioners' handbooks. The following is a brief guide.

1.07.05   The defendant must prove, on the balance of probabilities, that:

(a) He consumed alcohol between driving and providing the specimen.

(b) The proportion of alcohol would not have exceeded the limit at the time of the offence but for the post-offence consumption.

1.07.06   The defence should consult an expert on the issues raised in **1.07.05(b)**.

1.07.07   Notice of Intention to Call an Expert

If the defence intend to call expert evidence, the defence should notify the prosecution of its intention to do so a reasonable time before the hearing.

It is recommended that the defence notifies the prosecution in writing and makes full disclosure of the expert's evidence in the form of a section 9 (CJA 1967) statement.

1.07.08   The Effect of Giving Notice

(a) The failure to give notice will entitle the prosecution to seek an adjournment (usually with costs) to call expert evidence in rebuttal.

(b) The prosecution may accept (or, omit to object to) the section 9 statement of the expert (see **1.06.25**).

PRACTICE

1.07.09   The defendant pleads not guilty.

The practice in **1.06.14-32** is followed.

1.07.10   As part of the defence case (see **1.06.33-41**), the defence will usually call the following evidence:

(a)   The defendant and any other witnesses to prove **1.07.05(a)**.

(b)   An expert to prove **1.07.05(b)**.

The usual rules as to the examination, cross-examination and re-examination of witnesses apply.

1.07.11   The experts to be called by the defence and the prosecution are usually permitted to remain in court, in order that they may listen to and assess the evidence of the parties, for the purposes of giving an expert opinion as to the effect of the alcohol consumed by the defendant (see **14.01.16-20**).

1.07.12   Evidence in Rebuttal

The prosecution may apply for (and is usually granted) leave to call evidence in rebuttal where there is a discrepancy between the opinions of the expert witnesses (see **1.06.42**).

1.07.13 The practice in **1.06.43-51** is then followed.

PART 3: SPECIAL REASONS: 'LACED DRINKS'

INTRODUCTION

1.07.14   A special reason is a reason not to disqualify (and/or endorse the driving licence of) the defendant.
The law on this subject is complex and should be researched in the common practitioners' handbooks. The following is a brief guide.

1.07.15   A special reason must be established by calling evidence.

1.07.16 What is a Special Reason?

To be a special reason, the reason must:

(a) Be a mitigating circumstance.

(b) Not amount to a defence to the charge.

(c) Be special in relation to the offence and not the offender.

(d) Be a matter which the court ought properly to consider in sentencing.

1.07.17 A common example of a special reason not to disqualify on a charge of driving with excess alcohol is 'laced drinks' (where the defendant contends that he had consumed the alcohol unknowingly).

1.07.18 The defence must prove, on the balance of probabilities, that:

(a) The drink was laced.

(b) The defendant did not know or suspect the lacing.

(c) That, if the drink had not been laced, the defendant's alcohol level would have been below the legal limit.

1.07.19 The defence should consult an expert on the issues raised in **1.07.18(c)**.

1.07.20 Notice of Intention to call an Expert

If the defence intend to call expert evidence, the defence should notify the prosecution of its intention to do so a reasonable time before the hearing.

It is recommended that the defence notifies the prosecution in writing and makes full disclosure of the expert's evidence in the form of a section 9 (CJA 1967) statement.

1.07.21 The Effect of Giving Notice

(a) The failure to give notice will entitle the prosecution to seek an adjournment (usually with costs) to call expert evidence in rebuttal.

(b) The prosecution may accept (or, omit to object to) the section 9 statement of the expert (see **1.06.25**).

PRACTICE

1.07.22   The defendant pleads guilty.

Evidence of special reasons is called in sentencing.

See **4.01.06-08**.

1.07.23   The defence will usually call the following evidence:

(a)   The defendant to prove **1.07.18(b)**.

    If the defendant was substantially in excess of the legal limit, the court is unlikely to accept his evidence that he did not know or suspect that the drink was laced.

(b)   The person or persons who laced the defendant's drink or who knew that the drink had been laced, to prove **1.07.18(a)**.

(c)   An expert to prove **1.07.18(c)**.

The usual rules as to the examination, cross-examination and re-examination of witnesses apply.

1.07.24   The experts to be called by the defence and the prosecution are usually permitted to remain in court, in order that they may listen to and assess the evidence of the parties, for the purposes of giving an expert opinion as to the effect of the alcohol consumed by the defendant (see **14.01.16-20**).

1.07.25   Evidence in Rebuttal

The prosecution may apply for (and is usually granted) leave to call evidence in rebuttal where there is a discrepancy between the opinions of the expert witnesses (see **1.06.42**).

1.07.26   When the parties have called and/or read all the evidence, the defence may address the court on the facts.

1.07.27   The magistrates may retire to consider their decision.

1.07.28   The magistrates announce their decision, for example:

We find that there are/are not special reasons not to disqualify.

If the court finds a special reason, the reason must be recorded in the court register.

1.07.29 The defence may address the court in mitigation (see **4.01.29-33**).

As a general rule, the court will be concerned only with the defendant's financial circumstances for the purposes of a fine (except in cases of repeated offending).

1.07.30. The court will then proceed to sentence.

PART 4: ENDORSEMENT OF DRIVING LICENCE

INTRODUCTION

1.07.31 Road traffic offences are either endorsable or non- endorsable offences.

The law on this subject is complex and should be researched in the common practitioners' handbooks. The following is a brief guide.

1.07.32 If the court orders the defendant's driving licence to be endorsed, the details of the conviction and the number of penalty points will be endorsed on the defendant's driving licence.

The particulars of the endorsement and/or disqualification will be notified to the DVLC.

1.07.33 As a general rule, endorsements remain on the driving licence for a period of four years, although, for the purposes of 'totting up' (disqualification by reason of exceeding the maximum number of points), the endorsement will cease to have effect after three years.

PRACTICE

1.07.34 The defendant:

(a) Pleads guilty by post.

(b) Is found guilty on proof of the summons (and service) in his absence.

(c) Is found guilty after a summary trial.

1.07.35   The defendant produces his driving licence, which may be handed to the court by the defence at the beginning of mitigation, for example:

I produce the defendant's driving licence.

1.07.36   The clerk will then address the magistrates, for example:

The defendant produces a full/provisional clean driving licence.

Or

There are (-) relevant convictions, namely (state previous convictions and penalty points endorsed on the driving licence).

Or

1.07.37   If the defendant is liable to 'totting up' and the offence is one which carries a variable number of penalty points the clerk may say (although practice varies);

There are (-) relevant convictions. I will invite the court to decide on the number of penalty points before reading out the details of these convictions.

1.07.38   The defence should not then address the court on the basis that a minimum number of penalty points should be imposed if the only reason for doing so is to avoid the "totting up" provisions.

The defence may address the court on the basis that a minimum number of penalty points should be imposed because the circumstances of the offence are not (comparatively) serious.

1.07.39   The defence may call evidence of special reasons not to endorse (see **1.07.14-16**).

If appropriate, the court will state whether special reasons have been proved, and the reason must be recorded in the court register.

1.07.40   The defence may then address the court in mitigation (see **4.01.29-33**).

As a general rule, the court will be concerned only with the defendant's financial circumstances for the purposes of a fine (except in cases of repeated offending).

1.07.41   The court announces its decision:

For this offence there will be a fine of £(-). And (-) penalty points will be endorsed on the defendant's licence. And costs of £(-).

1.07.42   Where **1.07.37** applies, the clerk may the say:

There are (-) points on the defendant's licence for (state particulars of the offences and penalty points).

That means that the defendant is liable to disqualification.

Mr (name of defence) **do you wish to address the magistrates on disqualification?**

1.07.43   If the defence wish to address the court on disqualification, the defence will usually call evidence of mitigating circumstances, (usually of exceptional hardship), in 'totting up' proceedings.

The defence may seek an adjournment in order to call this evidence.

1.07.44   Mitigating circumstances in 'totting up' proceedings are not:

(a)   The triviality of the offence(s).

(b)   Hardship to the defendant, other than exceptional hardship.

(c)   Any mitigating circumstances which have previously been considered by the court.

As a general rule, a mitigating circumstance is special to the offender and not the offence (see **1.07.16(c)**).

1.07.45   The court announces its decision.

1.07.46   If the court finds that there are mitigating circumstances, the reasons not to disqualify must be entered in the court register (see **1.07.44(c)**).

PART 5: SUSPENSION OF DISQUALIFICATION

INTRODUCTION

1.07.47   If the defendant is disqualified from driving he may appeal to the crown court against either the conviction or the sentence and disqualification.

See **3.05: Appeal Against Conviction**.

See **3.06: Appeal against Sentence**.

An application to suspend disqualification pending appeal may be made to the magistrates' court when the notice of appeal has been lodged with the court clerk.

PRACTICE

1.07.48   The court announces its decision to disqualify the defendant.

1.07.49   The defence may address the court as follows:

Would you consider an application to suspend disqualification on service of the notice of appeal (which I will prepare as soon as possible).

1.07.50   It is considered to be bad practice (and is often counter-productive) to have a pre-prepared Notice of Appeal ready to serve on the clerk when the court has announced its decision.

1.07.51   When the Notice of Appeal has been prepared, the case is recalled. The defence may say:

I tender the notice of appeal to the court.

1.07.52   The defence may then address the court on the reasons to suspend the disqualification, for example:

I rely on the matters I put before the court in mitigation and (for example), **if I am to address the crown court in due course on the defendant's employment, it is essential that the defendant keeps his licence until the appeal is heard.**

1.07.53   The court announces its decision.

SECTION 8: LIQUOR LICENSING

PART 1: INTRODUCTION

1.08.01   An application for a liquor licence is made to the licensing committee of the Magistrates' Court on a special day, the date of which may be obtained from the Court office.

The law on this subject is complex and should be researched in the common practitioners' handbooks.

1.08.02   The practice in the following common situations is considered:

    1.08.03-31:   **Application for a Liquor Licence**

    1.08.32-43:   **Application for a Protection Order** (to an ordinary sitting of the magistrates' court).

PART 2: APPLICATION FOR A LIQUOR LICENCE

INTRODUCTION

1.08.03   An application for a liquor licence (or the transfer or renewal of a liquor licence) is made to the magistrates' court (licensing justices).

The correct preparation of the application is essential.

PREPARATION

1.08.04   Notice of Application

The application is made on a standard form notice which should be signed by the applicant and state:

(a) The applicant's occupation.

(b) The situation of the premises.

(c) The kind of licence for which the application is made (usually describing the liquor to be supplied).

1.08.05   The notice and a prepaid acknowledgement must be served, at least 21 days before the date of the next hearing, on:

(a) The clerk to the licensing justices.

(b) The police.

(c) The fire authority.

(d) The local authority.

1.08.06   The Notice of the application must be displayed on the premises for at least seven days during the 28 days before the hearing.

1.08.07   The Notice of the application must be advertised in a local newspaper between 14-28 days before the hearing.

1.08.08   A map of the area and/or plans of the premises (as appropriate) should be sent to the court. The clerk should be consulted on the requirements of the licensing justices.

1.08.09   Objections

Except in cases of the renewal (but not the transfer) of a liquor licence, when seven days notice of objection must be given, an objector does not have to give prior warning of his objection(s).

Notice of objection (in cases of renewal) is given to:

(a) The clerk to the licensing justices.

(b) The licensee.

In all other cases, the objector(s) may attend the hearing and make his objection(s) without notice.

1.08.10   Attendance of the Applicant

Where an application is made for a new licence or for the transfer of a licence, the applicant should attend.

If he fails to attend, the application may be dismissed.

PRACTICE

1.08.11   The title of the application is read out by the clerk, for example:

An application for a justices' (state type of) **licence in respect of** (title and address of premises).

THE CASE FOR THE APPLICANT

1.08.12   Introduction of the Parties

The advocate representing the applicant may say:

I appear on behalf of the applicant, Mr (name), **who is the** (owner/ manager/other) **of** (title and address of premises).

(If the objector(s) are known and/or represented):

Mr (name), **objects to this application/appears on behalf of Mr** (name), **who objects to this application.**

The applicant attends court today.

1.08.13   Opening

The advocate may briefly open the application. The opening may contain:

(a)   A description of the area, with reference to a map. (See **1.08.17**).

(b)   A description of the premises, with reference to a plan. (See **1.08.18**).

(c)   A description of the character and background of the applicant.

(d)   Any explanation of the kind of licence for which the application is made.

1.08.14   The advocate will usually then produce the formal evidence on behalf of the applicant (see **1.08.15** or **16**), namely:

(a) Proof of service of the written notices of application.

(b) Proof of the display of the notice of application.

(c) Proof of the advertisement of the notice of application.

(d) Any petitions in support of the application.

1.08.15 (or **1.08.16**)   The advocate may say:

> **I understand that the originals of the notices are with the court.**
>
> **Perhaps, your clerk could confirm that they are in order?**

1.08.16   The advocate may say:

> **I tender written acknowledgement of the application from** (the police/ fire authority/local authority) **who do not object to this application.**
>
> **I tender the notice displayed on the** (state part of premises) **between** (state dates).
>
> **I tender copies of page** (-) **of** (name of newspaper) **for** (date).
>
> **I tender a petition signed by** (-) (persons/residents/other) **in support of the application.**

1.08.17   Maps

An ordnance survey map, on the scale of 25 inches to the mile, with the proposed premises in the centre is usually produced to the court (with copies for any objectors), showing the location, in different colours, of (with suggested colour code):

(a) The proposed licensed premises   (Red)

(b) Public houses   (Black)

(c) Off-licences   (Green)

(d) Licensed premises with a special hours certificate   (Yellow)

(e) Any other licensed premises   (Blue)

Colours may be dictated by directions sent out by the court. If not, the advocate should ensure that the plan has a clear colour code index.

The advocate should draw the court's attention to the local need for the licensed premises by using the map. (The advocate should remember that the licensing justices may have better knowledge of the local area than he has).

1.08.18 Plans

An architect's plan of the premises is usually produced to the court (for new or converted premises).

The advocate should draw the court's attention to:

(a) Fire precautions and/or alternative exits from the premises.

(b) Hygiene facilities for the preparation of food and/or washing of glasses and plates.

(c) Toilet facilities.

(d) Car parking (if appropriate).

1.08.19 Evidence on behalf of the Applicant

The applicant is called and identified by name and address.

The applicant may be examined on the following matters:

(a) Proof of display of the notice.

(b) Proof of advertisment of the notice.

(c) Current occupation(s) during the preceding six months.

(d) Good character (or otherwise).

(e) Local need for the licensed premises.

(f) Experience of the licensed trade.

(g) Knowledge of the licensing law. If the applicant is not experienced he may be tested, for example:

What are the Sunday opening hours?

When can you serve children?

1.08.20   Examination in chief may conveniently be concluded as follows:

Finally, have you read the list of persons disqualified from holding a licence?

And are you so disqualified?

The usual rules as to the examination, cross-examination (by objectors) and re-examination of witnesses apply (see **14.01.01-24**).

1.08.21   Witnesses on behalf of the Applicant

Witnesses on behalf of the applicant may be called, for example:

(a)   Witnesses to give evidence of local need (including prospective customers).

(b)   The architect or surveyor who prepared the plan (if required).

(c)   Character witnesses.

1.08.22   Close of the Applicant's Case

When the advocate on behalf of the applicant has called and/or read and/or produced all the evidence, the case is said to be closed. The usual form of words is:

That is the case on behalf of the applicant.

THE CASE FOR THE OBJECTOR(S)

1.08.23   Opening

The objector and/or the advocate on behalf of the objector may briefly outline his reason(s) for objecting to the application:

(a)   That there is no local need (which often means that the objector may lose business or suffer disruption).

(b)   If the police object, usually that the applicant is not a suitable person to hold a licence.

(c)   If the fire or local authority object, usually that the premises are unsuitable.

1.08.24   In the case of an objection to a renewal of a licence, the objector should prove service of the written notice of objection.

If notice of objection has not been served, the court may adjourn the application.

1.08.25   Evidence on behalf of the Objector(s)

The objector is called and identified by name and address.

The objector then states his objection(s).

The usual rules as to the examination, cross-examination and re-examination of witnesses apply (see **14.01.01-24**).

1.08.26   The objector may call evidence in support of his objection(s).

SPEECHES

1.08.27   Order of Speeches

The parties may address the court at the conclusion of the evidence, as follows:

(a)   Objector(s) in such order as is convenient.

(b)   Applicant.

The parties should confine their addresses to those parts of the application which are in issue.

DECISION

1.08.28   The licensing justices may retire to consider their decision.

1.08.29   When announcing the decision, the court may say:

We grant this application, (subject to conditions), or

We refuse this application.

1.08.30   The court has no power to award costs to either party. For example, a successful applicant cannot be granted costs against an objector even though the applicant may have been put to considerable expense.

1.08.31   Appeal

Appeal by either party is to the crown court. The notice of appeal must be served on the clerk to the licensing justices and any other party within 21 days.

The hearing of the appeal at the crown court is a rehearing of the case before the magistrates' court.

See **3.09: Appeal in Licensing Proceedings**.

Only the objector(s) who were heard at the magistrates' court may appeal to the crown court.

PART 3: PROTECTION ORDER

INTRODUCTION

1.08.32   A person may take over licensed premises before he is able to obtain a transfer of the licence from the licensing justices.

He may apply to the magistrates' court for a protection order until the date of the next meeting but one of the licensing justices.

1.08.33   Notice of Application

The application is made on a standard form notice, which should be signed by the applicant and served, at least seven days before the date of the hearing on:

(a)   The clerk to the court.

(b)   The police.

1.08.34   Objections

An objector does not have to give notice of his objection.

PRACTICE

1.08.35   The title of the application is read out by the clerk, for example:

An application for a protection order in respect of (title and address of premises).

1.08.36   Introduction of the Parties

The advocate representing the applicant may say:

I appear on behalf of the applicant, Mr (name)**, who** (state reason for application, for example: is taking over the lease) **of** (state name of premises).

The current licensee attends and consents to this application.

OR

The current licensee has given his consent in writing to this application which, is with/ I tender to, the court.

EVIDENCE ON BEHALF OF THE APPLICANT

1.08.37   The (outgoing) licensee usually attends and is called to give his formal consent to the protection order.

1.08.38   Evidence on behalf of the Applicant

The applicant is called and identified by his name and address.

The applicant is usually examined on the following matters:

(a)   Current occupation(s) during the preceding 6 months.

(b)   Good character or otherwise.

(c)   Experience of the licensed trade.

(d)   Knowledge of the licensing law. (See **1.08.19(g)** and **1.08.20**).

1.08.39   The advocate representing the applicant may then say:

Unless the court has any questions, I apply for a protection order to be made in favour of (name).

He does not make a speech.

1.08.40   The magistrate (or clerk) may then say:

Are there any (police) objections?

1.08.41   An objection to a protection order is rare. It is usually made by the police on the grounds that the applicant is not a fit and proper person. The advocate is advised to check in advance.

1.08.42   If there is no objection, the magistrates may say:

The protection order is granted.

1.08.43   The court has no power to order costs to either party.

SECTION 9: DOMESTIC COURT

INTRODUCTION

1.09.01   The domestic court deals with matters of family law and the care and maintenance of children.

The proceedings are conducted in private (usually only the parties, their legal representatives and the welfare agencies attend).

1.09.02   The hearing of a complaint in the domestic court is similar to, but less formal than, a summary trial before the magistrates' court.

1.09.03   The powers of the court in relation to custody of, and access to, a child and the variation and enforcement of maintenance orders are complex, and should be researched in the common practitioners' handbooks.

1.09.04   A magistrates' court, when hearing domestic proceedings, is composed of not more than three magistrates, including, so far as practicable, both a man and a woman.

1.09.05   The civil standard of proof applies (see **1.01.06**).

1.09.06   Commencement of Proceedings

The standard method of commencing proceedings is by the making of a complaint leading to the issue of a summons out of the court office.

The summons is in standard form and will require the person named therein (the respondent) to appear before the court.

The summons may be served:

(a)   By delivering it to the person to whom it is directed (Personal Service).

(b)   By leaving it at his usual address.

(c)   By posting it to him at his usual address.

Except where personal service has been made, if the respondent fails to appear, evidence will be required to show that the summons has come to his knowledge before the complaint may be proved in his absence.

1.09.07   Preliminary Issues

Where paternity is in dispute (as a preliminary issue), an application for blood tests and/or DNA fingerprinting may be made to the court in writing before the date of the hearing.

1.09.08   Pre-Hearing Welfare Reports

In cases of custody and access, the court or either party may request a pre-hearing welfare report usually where:

(a)   There is concern for the child

(b)   The court is of the opinion that it will not have sufficient information to exercise its powers.

(c)   Either party is seeking conciliation, (see **1.09.09**).

The request has the effect of involving the welfare agencies at an early stage.

A copy of the report should be given to each party a reasonable time before the hearing.

1.09.09   Pre-Hearing Conciliation

In cases of custody and access the court may hold a preliminary hearing to determine whether conciliation is possible (if the facilities for conciliation are available in any area).

1.09.10   Conduct

Practice varies widely as to whether the advocate should stand or sit to address the court. If it is not possible to ascertain the practice of the court in advance, the advocate should stand, although he may later be invited by the court to sit.

Witnesses should stand to take the oath but may later be invited by the court to sit to give evidence.

1.09.11   Evidence

The strict rules of evidence are often not enforced in domestic proceedings.

The parties should note that practice varies widely and a party should be prepared to prove his case in the usual way.

PRACTICE

1.09.12   The practice on the hearing of a complaint in the domestic court is similar to **1.06: Summary Trial.**

1.09.13   Attendance of the Parties

The complainant and the respondent should attend.

If the respondent does not attend, the court may proceed in his absence if it is satisfied that the summons was served.

If the complainant does not attend, the court may dismiss the complaint.

1.09.14   Identification of the Parties

The clerk usually identifies the parties by name and address.

1.09.15 The Complaint

The complaint is read to the respondent by the clerk, for example:

(Name of respondent), **you appear here today to answer a complaint made by** (name of complainant) **that you** (the complaint is then read to the respondent).

The clerk may give any particulars as are appropriate to identify the issues.

The respondent is asked whether he **admits** or **denies** the complaint.

If he admits the complaint, see **1.09.33-34**.

1.09.16 Introduction of the Parties

The advocate on behalf of the complainant usually introduces the parties to the court:

I appear on behalf of the complainant. My (learned) **friend, Mr** (name), **appears on behalf of the respondent.**

THE CASE ON BEHALF OF THE COMPLAINANT

1.09.17 Complainant's Opening

In the domestic court, the advocate on behalf of the complainant usually opens the case.

The opening should contain:

(a) A brief outline of the allegations made in the complaint.

(b) A brief outline of the history of the parties (if appropriate).

(c) A brief summary of any relevant law (if appropriate).

The advocate may conclude the opening:

I now call (name of complainant).

1.09.18 Evidence of the Complainant

The complainant should be called first and will usually give evidence to substantiate the complaint alleged in the summons.

The usual rules as to the examination, cross-examination and re-examination of witnesses apply (see **14.01.01-24**).

1.09.19 Witnesses on behalf of the Complainant

Witnesses should remain outside court until called and leave court after having given evidence. Each witness is identified by name and address (see **14.01.01-24**).

1.09.20 Questions of Admissibility

Questions of admissibility are determined before the magistrates and, in the event of evidence being excluded, the magistrates should not consider that evidence when reaching their decision.

A witness may be giving, or about to give, evidence to which a party objects. The party may interrupt the advocate and/or witness, as follows:

I object to this evidence.

If the evidence is clearly inadmissible (for example, hearsay), the clerk may direct the party calling the evidence to omit that evidence.

1.09.21 Where there is an argument over a question of admissibility, the order of submissions is usually as follows:

(a) The party objecting to the evidence identifies the evidence to which the objection is taken.

(b) The party gives reasons for the objection and refers to any relevant law.

(c) Reply by other party.

(d) Response by the party objecting on any new point.

(e) Decision by the court.

> If the magistrates' retire to consider their decision, the clerk may be invited to accompany them.

(f) Announcement of decision, for example:

We find that this evidence is not admissible (and we will not take it into consideration when reaching our decision).

1.09.22   This situation is entirely unsatisfactory and is, in practice, often by-passed. The party objecting to the evidence may refer in his closing speech to the disputed evidence, for example:

The evidence you heard on this matter, namely (state evidence), **I would suggest is probably inadmissible. I would invite you not to consider it when reaching your decision.**

1.09.23   Documentary Evidence

The parties may be permitted by the court to produce documentary evidence without calling the maker of the document.

The parties are not required to give notice although, where the document is important, failure to give notice may:

(a) Permit the party taken by surprise to apply for an adjournment, and

(b) Require the party producing the document to prove it in the usual way (see **1.09.11**).

1.09.24   Close of Complainant's Case

When the advocate on behalf of the complainant has called all the evidence and/or documentary evidence has been adduced, the case is said to be closed. The usual form of words is:

That is the case on behalf of the complainant.

SUBMISSION OF NO CASE TO ANSWER

1.09.25   After the close of the complainant's case, the advocate on behalf of the respondent may submit that there is no case to answer, although in practice, a submission of no case to answer is very rarely made.

There is authority for the proposition that in the domestic proceedings, the court should hear evidence from both parties before making a decision.

1.09.26   A submission of no case to answer may be made where the advocate on behalf of the complainant has failed to call evidence to support an essential ingredient of the complaint or where an important witness has failed to attend.

The practice on a submission of no case to answer is set out in **1.06.30-32**.

THE CASE ON BEHALF OF THE RESPONDENT

1.09.27   Respondent's Opening

The advocate on behalf of the respondent has the right to open the case. In practice, this right is never exercised because he would lose the right, without the leave of the court, to close the case.

If he opens his case and the advocate on behalf of the complainant subsequently asks for leave to close, the advocate on behalf of the respondent will be given leave to close but his closing address will be heard before that of the complainant (see **1.09.32**).

1.09.28   If the advocate on behalf of the respondent is calling no evidence he may say:

> **I call no evidence of behalf of the respondent and, with your leave, I will now address you in closing.**

1.09.29   Evidence on Behalf of the Respondent

The evidence on behalf of the respondent is subject to the same rules and is presented in the same way as the evidence on behalf of the complainant (see **1.09.17** to **1.09.24**).

1.09.30   Evidence in Rebuttal

The advocate on behalf of the complainant may, with the leave of the court, call evidence in rebuttal.

SPEECHES

1.09.31   If only the advocate on behalf of the complainant has opened the case, the advocate on behalf of the respondent closes the case.

The advocate on behalf of the complainant may, with the leave of the court, address the court on any question of law.

1.09.32   If the advocates on behalf of the complainant and the respondent have both opened their cases, either party may seek the leave of the court to address the court for a second time.

The advocate on behalf of the complainant may say:

I would seek leave to address the court on the matters raised by the respondent in evidence.

The court (or the clerk) may then say to the advocate on behalf of the respondent:

Mr (name) **do you wish to address us before Mr** (name) (for the complainant)?

He may either waive the right to make a closing speech or he may address the court.

DECISION

1.09.33 The Magistrates will usually retire to reach their decision.

1.09.34 The court announces its decision. The parties will then address the court on the disposal of the case.

1.09.35 In any contested hearing, in cases of custody or access or in any case where maintenance is reduced by reason of conduct, the court must record the reason for its decision in writing in the court register before the decision is announced.

The reason for the decision is recorded for the purposes of an appeal by either party.

The reason may be drawn up in consultation with the clerk.

1.09.36 Costs

The court may order either party to pay costs inter partes but, in practice, rarely does so.

1.09.37 Appeal

Appeal is usually to the divisional court of the family division on service of a notice of motion within six weeks of the decision.

CHAPTER 2

Juvenile Court

Section 1:	**Introduction**
Section 2:	**Criminal Trial**
Section 3:	**Care Proceedings**

SECTION 1: INTRODUCTION

2.01.01 Mode of Address

Juvenile Bench:	Sir or Madam to the chairman.
(The bench should include at least one man and one woman)	(Your Worship(s) is sometimes used).

2.01.02 The Hearing

The hearing of any matter in the juvenile court does not take place in open court.

The following persons may be present in court if concerned in the case.

(a) Members and officers of the court.

(b) Probation officers and social services officers.

(c) The parties and their legal representatives.

(d) Persons authorised by the court (for example, law students).

(e) Representatives of the press (although the press may not report any matter which would lead to the identification of the child).

2.01.03   Rights of Audience

Barrister.

Solicitor.

Child in person, or by his parent or guardian.

(Next-friend does not apply in the juvenile court).

2.01.04   Dress

Barristers and solicitors should be respectably dressed.

The child and any other interested party may appear in normal everyday wear.

2.01.05   Burden of Proof

The prosecution and/or applicant has the burden of proving, in any contested matter, the case.

2.01.06   Standard of Proof

| Criminal trial: | Beyond reasonable doubt. |
| Care proceedings | On the balance of probabilities. |

2.01.07   Seating in Court

The proceedings in a juvenile court are held informally, often in an ordinary room. The authors can offer no general guidance on seating in court.

2.01.08   Addressing the Court

Any party addressing the court should do so standing (unless invited by the court to remain seated).

2.01.09 Witnesses

Criminal Trial

Witnesses should remain outside the court until called to give evidence. The witness should then remain in court until the conclusion of the case or until he is given permission to leave by the court.

Care Proceedings

Witnesses should remain outside the court until called to give evidence. The witness should leave court after having given evidence.

2.01.10 Practice

Practice in the juvenile court is informal. The court and/or the parties' representatives are under a duty to explain the proceedings in ordinary language to the parties.

The child and any witness under 17 years old is generally referred to by his first name.

2.01.11 Expressions

Magistrates' Court	*Juvenile Court*
Conviction	Finding of guilt.
Sentence	Order made upon finding of guilt.

SECTION 2: CRIMINAL TRIAL

INTRODUCTION

2.02.01   As a general rule, the practice in a criminal trial in the juvenile court follows the practice in a summary trial in the magistrates' court.

See **1.06: Summary Trial.**

2.02.02 Attendance of the Parties

See 1.02: Attendance of the Parties.

The parents (or guardian) are also under a duty to attend and a summons and/or warrant may be issued to secure their attendance.

PRACTICE

2.02.03 Identification of the Defendant

The clerk will usually identify the defendant by name and/or address, for example:

Are you (name of defendant)? **When were you born? And where do you live?**

After the defendant has been identified, he is then usually referred to by his first name only.

2.02.04 Identification of the Parents (or Guardian)

The clerk will then usually identify the parents or guardians, for example:

(To the child) **And do you appear here today with your parents/mother/father?**

(To the parents) **And are you** (name of parents/ mother/father)?

Do you understand why (name of defendant) is **here today?**

2.02.05 The Charge or Summons

The charge or summons is read to the defendant by the clerk, who will also usually explain to the parties the nature of the allegation in ordinary language.

2.02.06 Preliminary applications may be made in the juvenile court (see **1.06.11**).

2.02.07 The clerk will then ask the defendant:

Do you plead guilty or not guilty to the charge?

2.02.08 If the defendant pleads guilty to the charge or summons, see **2.02.21-29**.

If the defendant pleads not guilty to the charge or summons the prosecution will call evidence to prove the case.

2.02.09   Age of the Defendant

The age of the defendant is important in a criminal trial in the juvenile court because of the doctrine of *doli incapax* (incapable of crime).

(a)   A defendant under the age of 10 years is presumed to be *doli incapax* and (if charged) not guilty of any offence. The presumption is irrebuttable.

(b)   A defendant between the ages of 10-13 years is presumed to be *doli incapax* but the presumption can be rebutted by the prosecution on the proof, beyond reasonable doubt, that the defendant knew what he was doing was wrong.

The presumption becomes weaker (and its rebuttal easier) as the defendant increases in age between 10-13 years.

(c)   A defendant aged between 14-17 years is not presumed to be *doli incapax*.

2.02.10   The prosecution should pay particular attention to **2.02.09(b)**. If the prosecution fails to rebut the presumption of *doli incapax* the defence may make a submission of no case to answer.

ORDER OF PRESENTATION

2.02.11   Prosecution opening: See **1.06.14-16**.

2.02.12   Prosecution evidence: See **1.06.17-29**.

2.02.13   Submission of no case to answer: See **1.06.30-32**.

2.02.14   Defence evidence: See **1.06.33-41**.

2.02.15   Evidence in rebuttal: See **1.06.42** and (if appropriate) **3.04.77**.

2.02.16   Defence closing speech See **1.06.43-45**.

2.02.17   There are few set formulae of words in a criminal trial in the juvenile court because the proceedings are conducted informally and in a conversational manner. The advocate should, however, remember that he is in court and not at a case conference.

FINDING OF GUILT

2.02.18   After all the evidence has been called and any party entitled to address the court has addressed the court, the magistrates may retire to consider their decision.

2.02.19   When announcing the decision, the court may say:

We find you guilty, or

We find you not guilty.

A finding of guilt to a lesser offence is not available in the juvenile court.

2.02.20   If the finding is not guilty, the defendant is discharged.

The defence may make an application for the defendant's costs (see **7.02.01-03 & 20-30**).

DETERMINING THE ORDER ON A FINDING OF GUILT

2.02.21   Previous Findings of Guilt

The court may hear evidence (from the social services or the prosecution) of, or receive any documents setting out, any previous findings of guilt and/or police cautions recorded against the defendant.

The information should be read to the defendant and his parents (or guardian) so that they, or the defendant's representative may explain, admit or deny (as appropriate) any previous matter.

2.02.22   Reports

The court may consider reports from any suitably qualified person, for example:

(a)   Social enquiry report.

(b)   School report.

(c)   Medical and/or psychiatric report.

The magistrates will usually retire to read the reports.

The reports are not usually read aloud, but the substance of any report material to a party should be disclosed in order that the party has the opportunity to contest it.

2.02.23 If any of the reports are not available and the court feels it needs information on a particular matter before making an order, the court may adjourn the case, for example:

> **We feel we need to know more about** (state matter). **We will remand this case for a** (state nature of) **report.**

2.02.24 The defence or the child, his parent or guardian, may address the court in mitigation (see **4.01.29-33**).

2.02.25 Decision

After consideration of the reports and any further representations, the magistrates will usually retire to make their decision.

When the magistrates return to court, the chairman will tell the parties how they are considering dealing with the case and invite representations (although this is often omitted).

If this procedure is followed, the defence should not repeat the representations in **2.02.24**. The defence will usually only address the court if the proposed order has not been recommended in any report.

2.02.26 If the juvenile court is of the opinion that the defendant is in need of care or control which he is unlikely to receive unless the court makes an order, the court may proceed to care proceedings (see **2.03.4A(f)-4B** and **2.03.47-51**).

2.02.27 The court will then announce its decision. The court must explain the nature and effect of any order in ordinary language to the defendant and his parents or guardians.

2.02.28 Costs

See **7.02.09-10 & 20-22(a)&(c)**.

2.02.29 Appeal

Appeal against a finding of guilt (if the defendant pleaded not guilty to the charge) and/or order of the juvenile court is to the crown court. It is a rehearing of the case.

The notice of appeal must be served within 21 days on:

(a) The prosecution.

(b) The clerk to the juvenile court.

2.02.30   A parent or guardian may appeal where the juvenile court has ordered him to pay the fine, compensation or costs ordered against the defendant.

SECTION 3: CARE PROCEEDINGS

INTRODUCTION

2.03.01   The practice on the hearing of care proceedings in the juvenile court differs greatly from court to court.

The following summary is intended only as a general guide, and the advocate should note that parts of the summary are, in practice, omitted by different courts.

2.03.02   Care proceedings are heard in two distinct and separate parts:

(a) The juvenile court will hear evidence to prove one or more of the conditions for making an order in care proceedings specified in **2.03.04A.**

(b) If one or more of the conditions is proved, the juvenile court will consider reports and hear evidence of proposals for the future care and upbringing of the child.

2.03.03   The two parts can be summarised as follows:

(a) Are any of the conditions for making an order proved? **(2.03.04A).**

(b) Should an order be made? **(2.03.04B).**

2.03.04A   Conditions for Making an Order

The juvenile court may make an order for the care of a child if it is satisfied, on the balance of probabilities, that one of following conditions has been proved, namely:

(a)   The child's proper development is being avoidably prevented or neglected or his health is being avoidably impaired or neglected or he is being ill-treated, or

(b)   Another child in the household has been taken into care on the grounds set out in (a) or a person living in that house- hold has been convicted of an offence in relation to a child, or

(c)   He is exposed to moral danger, or

(d)   He is beyond the control of his parents, or

(e)   He is not receiving suitable full-time education, or

(f)   There has been a finding of guilt against him (see **2.02.26**).

AND

2.03.04B   The juvenile court is satisfied that he is in need of care or control which he is unlikely to receive unless the court makes an order.

2.03.05   Commencement of Proceedings

The usual method of commencing proceedings is for the Local Authority to send a standard form notice specifying one or more of the conditions (see **2.03.04A**) to the clerk of the court.

Copies of the notice must be served on the child's parent(s) and any other interested person.

2.03.06   Place of Safety Order

Where the local authority wishes to remove the child into immediate care, it may apply *ex parte* to a magistrate for a place of safety order.

The local authority should provide *prima facie* evidence of one or more of the conditions in **2.03.04A (a)-(f)** and **2.03.04B**. The clerk should be consulted on the form of that evidence.

A place of safety order is usually only made to last until the next sitting of the juvenile court. The local authority will often serve the standard form notice (see **2.03.05**) on the parent(s) when the child is removed to a place of safety.

2.03.07   Parties to Care Proceedings

The parties to care proceedings will usually be:

Applicant:

(a)   Local authority.

Respondent and/or persons opposing the order:

(b)   Child.

(c)   Parent(s) (or guardian).

(d)   Grandparent(s) (with an interest).

(e)   Any other interested person (for example, a relative or friend who has cared for the child).

The court may appoint a guardian *ad litem* if it considers that there is a conflict of interest between the child and any interested party.

2.03.08   Attendance of the Parties

The following persons must attend:

(a)   Local authority.

(b)   Child (subject to certain exceptions).

(c)   Guardian *ad litem* (if appointed).

(d)   Parent(s) (or guardian).

The following persons may attend:

(e)   Any other interested person.

2.03.09   Failure of a Party to Attend

(a)   If any person specified in **2.03.08 (a)-(d)** does not attend, an adjournment is likely to be granted. The court is unlikely to dismiss the application. The court may issue a warrant to secure the attendance of the child and/or parent(s) (or guardian)

(b) If any person specified in **2.03.08 (e)** does not attend, the court may proceed in that person's absence.

PRACTICE

2.03.10   The advocate should note that:

(a)   Practice in care proceedings in the juvenile court varies between different courts.

(b)   Care should be taken to ensure that the proceedings are informal and conducted in ordinary language.

(c)   If the full hearing lasts more than one day, and there have been previous interim care orders, then continuations should be sought each night

2.03.11   Identification of the Parties

The clerk usually identifies the parties by name and/or address, for example:

Are you (name of child)? **When were you born? And where do you live?**

After the child has been identified, he is then usually referred to by his first name only.

2.02.12   The court should usually see the child in care proceedings (if the child is over five years old), although it may not require the child to remain in court for the hearing.

Practice varies and the clerk should be consulted.

2.03.13   The clerk will then usually identify the other parties, for example:

Are you (name of parent(s))? **And you are the** (parents/father/mother) **of** (name of child).

2.03.14   The Notice

The clerk will then usually read the allegation in the notice to the parties, for example:

It is alleged that (child's name) **proper development is being avoidably prevented and neglected and that his health is being avoidably impaired and neglected and that he is being ill-treated.**

2.03.15   The court is under a duty to explain to the parties the nature of the allegation in ordinary language.

The clerk may say, for example:

> **That means** (parent(s) name) **that you have not been properly looking after** (child's name). **And that the Local Authority feel that he would be better looked after in some other way. Do you understand?**

The clerk then explains the nature and order of the proceedings to the parties.

2.03.16   Order of Presentation

The usual order of presentation is:

(a)   Local authority opening.

(b)   Local authority evidence.

(c)   Respondent's opening, but see **2.03.34.**

(d)   Evidence on behalf of the respondent and/or other interested person in order:

    (i)   Child.

    (ii)   Parent(s) (or guardian).

    (iii)   Grandparent(s).

    (iv)   Any other interested person.

(e)   Speeches on behalf of the respondent and/or other interested person.

(f)   Reply by the local authority on a matter of law only.

2.03.17   There are few set formulae of words in care proceedings because the proceedings are conducted informally and in a conversational manner. The advocate should, however, remember that he is in court and not at a case conference.

2.03.18   Introduction of the Parties

The advocate appearing for the local authority may introduce the parties to the court (if this has not already been done):

I represent the Social Services Department of the (local authority). **Mr**

(name) **represents** (first name of child) **and Mr** (name) **represents Mr and Mrs** (name of parents).

2.03.19   The advocate may then state whether the application for the order sought (see **2.03.49**) is opposed. If the order is not opposed or an alternative disposal of the case is sought (see **2.03.36**) the evidence must still be called but may be treated briefly.

2.03.20   Local Authority Opening

The local authority usually opens the case. The opening should contain:

(a)   A brief outline of the family's history.

(b)   A brief outline of the allegation made in the notice.

The local authority may conclude the opening by saying:

I now call (name of first witness).

2.03.21   Evidence on Behalf of the Local Authority

The local authority must establish one of the grounds for making a care order (see **2.03.04A**) by calling evidence.

2.03.22   Social enquiry reports are not admissible at this stage.

2.03.23   The parties may agree the admissibility of documents, records and statements but the court may require the evidence to be given orally in the usual way, unless a document can be admitted under a statutory provision, for example, a medical certificate.

Care should be taken to ensure that even if the parties agree a point, the party seeking the agreement is able to prove it if necessary.

2.03.24   Witnesses on Behalf of the Local Authority

Witnesses should remain outside court until called to give evidence and leave court after having given evidence.

Each witness is identified by name and address and usually also by his relationship to the child.

The usual rules as to the examination, cross-examination and re-examination of witnesses apply (see **14.01.01-24**).

2.03.25   Order of Cross-Examination

The order of cross-examination of a witness called by the local authority will often be determined by the court, but may be as follows:

(a)   Child.

(b)   Guardian *ad litem* (if appropriate).

(c)   Parents in such order as is convenient, if separarely represented (cross-examination only where allegations have been made against them by that witness).

(d)   Grandparents (as at (c)).

The local authority may then re-examine.

The court may ask questions at any time.

2.03.26   Questions of Admissibility

In care proceedings evidence is heard informally and it is unusual for the magistrates to be asked to determine a question of admissibility of evidence.

The clerk will normally direct a party calling evidence that such evidence is inadmissible.

2.03.27   Statements made by children, who are too young to give evidence, to a witness in the case are usually admitted in evidence. The law on this subject is complex and should be researched in the common practitioners' handbooks.

2.03.28   Close of Local Authority's Case

When the local authority has called its evidence and/or any documents have been admitted or admissions made by the parties, the case is said to be closed. The usual form of words is:

That is the case.

2.03.29   Submission of No Case to Answer

In practice, a submission of no case to answer after the close of the applicant's case, is not made in care proceedings.

2.03.30   A submission of no case to answer could be made where the applicant had obviously failed to call evidence to support an essential ingredient of one of the grounds for making a care order (see **2.03.04A**) or where an important witness failed to attend.

THE RESPONDENT'S CASE

2.03.31   The court is under a duty to explain to the parties the nature of the proceedings in ordinary language. The chairman or the clerk may say to the child and/or his parents:

> **You have heard the witnesses say** (for example) **that** (name of parents) **have not been properly looking after** (name of child). **You have a choice. You do not have to answer the allegations. You can give evidence or call witnesses or you can do both. Or you can make a statement before we decide whether the allegations are proved. Do you understand? What do you want to do?**

2.03.32   If the advocate on behalf of the child decides to call evidence he will usually tell the magistrates', for example:

> **I will be calling** (name of child) **and/or** (names of witnesses who may include the child's parents).

2.03.33   If the advocate on behalf of the child is not calling evidence and/or not opposing the application for an order (see **2.03.19**), he should make this clear, for example:

> **I will be calling no evidence on behalf of** (name of child).

2.03.34   Respondent's Opening

The respondent has the right to open the case. In care proceedings this right is never exercised because the respondent would lose the right, without the leave of the court, to close the case. If the court subsequently gives leave to the respondent to close the case, the local authority will be permitted to address the court last.

2.03.35   Evidence of the Child

Whether or not the child gives evidence is a matter for the advocate representing the child. There is no compulsion and some courts will be very reluctant to hear any evidence from young and vulnerable children.

2.03.36   It may sometimes happen, for example, that the child does not wish to live with his parents but to live with a former foster parent or other interested party who is willing to have him. This should be made clear because it will enable the court to consider whether the grounds for making a care order (see **2.03.04A**) have been proved (subject to the evidence of the parent(s)).

2.03.37   The local authority may also be able to give an informal undertaking that if the grounds for making a care order are proved the wishes of the child will be respected (where possible).

2.03.38   Evidence on Behalf of the Child

If there is no conflict of interest between the parents and/or other interested persons and the the child, those persons are usually called to give evidence on behalf of the child.

The cases of the other parties are then dealt with at the same time.

2.03.39   Evidence on behalf of the child is called in the usual way (see **2.03.21** to **2.03.28**).

2.03.40   Evidence of the Guardian *ad litem*

The guardian *ad litem* may, but in practice, does not give evidence at this stage (see **2.03.47**).

2.03.41   Evidence of the Parents/Other interested person·

If a party has not been called to give evidence on behalf of the child, the clerk may say:

> **Is there anything you wish to say to the magistrates about what you have heard?**

The party may then be called to give evidence to rebut any allegation made against him and/or make any other representations to the court.

2.03.42   Where appropriate the parents and/or other interested persons may call evidence in support of their case but care should be taken to ensure that the evidence is relevant (see **2.03.03(a)**).

2.03.43   Speeches

The order of speeches will usually be in the order of presentation of the respondents' cases but may be changed by agreement and/or with the consent of the court.

2.03.44   If the local authority has opened the case, the local authority may reply only on a matter of law raised for the first time by another party with the leave, or by invitation, of the court, for example:

> **Mr** (name of advocate) **has mentioned the case of** (name of case) **on which I have not addressed you. I would be grateful if I could address you in reply.**

2.03.45   If both parties have opened their cases, either party may seek leave to address the court for a second time. In practice, this leave is never refused and the application can be made informally, for example:

> **May I address you now on behalf** of (name of party).

2.03.46   Decision by the Court

The magistrates will usually retire to reach their decision.

The court should indicate, in relation to each condition if more than one is alleged, whether it finds the condition proved or not.

If no condition is proved, the care proceedings are dismissed. No further steps are necessary.

DISPOSAL OF THE CASE

2.03.47   Reports

If one or more condition is proved, the court then proceeds to the Reports Stage. The purpose of reports is to enable the court to determine the disposal of the case (see **2.03.03(b)** and **2.03.04B**).

The court may consider reports from any suitably qualified person, for example:

(a) Guardian *ad litem's* report.

(b) Social Enquiry report.

(c) School report.

(d) Medical and/or psychiatric reports.

The magistrates will usually retire to read the reports.

The reports should not be read aloud, but the substance of any report material to a party should be disclosed in order that the party has the opportunity to contest it.

2.03.48 Each party has the right to call further evidence to supplement or attack the reports (and may ask for an adjournment to do so).

Each party also has the right to make representations as to what kind of order, if any, should be made.

2.03.49 Orders which may be made

(a) Supervision order.

(b) Care order.

(c) Parental recognisances.

(d) Hospital order.

The law on this subject is complex and is constantly changing and should be researched in the common practitioners' handbooks.

2.03.50 Decision

After consideration of the reports and any further representations the magistrates will usually retire to make their decision.

When the magistrates return to court, the chairman may tell the parties how they are considering dealing with the case and invite representations (although this is often omitted).

The parties should not repeat the representations in **2.03.48** and will usually only address the court if the proposed order has not been recommended in any report.

2.03.51 The court will then announce its decision. The court must explain the nature and effect of the order to the parties in ordinary language.

2.03.52 Appeal

Appeal against an order of the juvenile court in care proceedings is to the crown court. It is a rehearing of the case. The notice of appeal must be served within 21 days on:

(a) The local authority.

(b) The clerk to the juvenile court.

CHAPTER 3

Crown Court

SECTION 1: INTRODUCTION

3.01.01   Mode of Address

Mr Justice (name)   My Lord.

His Honour Judge (name),
   sitting as a Judge of the High Court   My Lord.

All Judges sitting at the Central Criminal Court	My Lord.
His Honour Judge (name)	Your Honour.
His Honour Judge (name) sitting as a deputy circuit judge	Your Honour.
Mr Recorder (name)	Your Honour.
Mr Assistant Recorder (name)	Your Honour.

3.01.02   The Hearing

Unless otherwise stated, the hearing of any matter in the crown court takes place in open court.

3.01.03   Rights of Audience

Barristers.

Solicitors (in appeals, including appeal of refusal of bail and committals for sentence where they represented the defendant in the magistrates' court).

Defendant in person.

3.01.04   Dress

Barristers are robed except in chambers.

Solicitors are robed except in chambers.

The most common applications in chambers are:

(a)   Appeal of refusal of bail from the magistrates' court.

(b)   Appeal against orders made in care proceedings by the juvenile court.

Defendants in person should be respectably dressed.

3.01.05   Seating in Court

In court, the defence will usually sit in the rows and/or seats closer to the jury.

3.01.06   Addressing the Court

Any party addressing the court should do so standing.

3.01.07   Burden and Standard of Proof

The burden of proof is on the prosecution.

The standard of proof is 'beyond reasonable doubt' (except **3.08** and **3.09**).

3.01.08   Order of Presentation

The order of presentation and speeches follows the title order of the case.

3.01.09   Witnesses

Witnesses should remain outside court until called to give evidence. The witness should then remain in court until the conclusion of the case or until he is given permission to leave by the court (except **3.08** and **3.09**).

SECTION 2: DIRECTIONS

3.02.01   A case may be listed for directions, which may be shown on the court list as follows:

> For directions
>
> For pre-trial review
>
> For pleas: no witnesses
>
> For pleas and directions

3.02.02   The following matters may be considered by the court (and are usefully considered by the parties when preparing any case for trial):

(a) Pleas and/or alternative pleas. (Pleas are usually taken if the case is listed For Pleas).

(b) Which prosecution witnesses are required by the defence at the trial. In particular, whether any witness can be made conditionally bound or dispensed with altogether.

(c) Whether there are witnesses who may be called by the prosecution where no notice of additional evidence has yet been served.

(d) Admissions by either party which can be agreed and put in writing under section 10, CJA 1967.

(e) Length of trial.

(f) Exhibits and schedules which can be admitted.

(g) Medical condition of the defendant, if appropriate, and any relevant reports where the medical condition may affect the disposal of the case.

(h) (i) Points of law which can be agreed and, if not agreed, a list of authorities and/or written submissions (sometimes called a skeleton argument).

   (ii) Questions of admissibility.

   (iii) Editing of witness statements by agreement.

(i) Disclosure of unused material by the prosecution and/or the names and addresses of witnesses who have made statements.

(j) Alibi evidence and, in particular, whether an alibi notice should be served.

(k) (i) Order of calling witnesses.

   (ii) Order and page numbering of documentary evidence.

(l) Provision of an opening note and/or case summary.

See also **3.04.10.**

3.02.03 The list can be used as a checklist by either party for the preparation of a trial (see **3.04.01**).

PRACTICE

3.02.04 Practice on directions varies greatly. The parties are advised to discuss pleas and directions before the case is called into court in order that the required directions in **3.02.02** can be outlined to the judge (usually by the prosecution) and/or either party can make an application that pleas are not taken where, for example, there are negotiations for alternative pleas.

3.02.05 If the case has been listed for pleas, the clerk will usually put the indictment to the defendant(s) (see **3.04.12**).

The defendant will enter a plea of not guilty (see **3.02.06**) or guilty (see **3.02.07**).

3.02.06   Not Guilty

A date may be fixed for trial or the case may be stood out to be listed in the usual way.

Either party (usually the prosecution) may say:

There will obviously be a trial in this case.

(We have discussed this matter outside court and) The estimated length of the trial is (state time estimate).

The dates to avoid are (state dates when witnesses are not available).

OR

The prosecution will undertake to inform the list office of the dates to avoid within (usually 7 or 14) **days.**

The following directions are agreed (state agreed directions).

The judge may then ask any other party if they require additional directions or the judge may give directions.

3.02.07   Guilty

See **4.01: Sentencing**.

The defence may apply for reports (see **4.01.30(f)**). The case will be stood out for the defendant to be sentenced at a later date.

3.02.08   Where there is more than one defendant

Where there is more than one defendant and one defendant pleads guilty and the other not guilty, the sentence of the defendant who has pleaded guilty will usually be stood out until the conclusion of the trial of the other defendant.

3.02.09   Bail

If the case is stood out, the defence may apply for bail (see **4.02: Bail Applications**).

SECTION 3: SEEING THE JUDGE

INTRODUCTION

3.03.01   An informal discussion may take place between counsel and the judge. It is called seeing the judge.

In any criminal proceedings it is the exception and not the rule for counsel to ask to see the judge.

Seeing the judge may be arranged as follows:

(a)   The party wishing to see the judge should indicate informally to the other party or parties that he wishes to do so.

(b)   The party or parties will ask the clerk if the judge will see them and state briefly the reasons for the request.

3.03.02   It is a matter for the discretion of the judge whether he will see counsel. If the judge agrees to see counsel:

(a)   The judge will not usually see a party in the absence of the other party or parties (except see **3.03.13**).

(b)   The judge will usually ask for a (shorthand) note to be taken.

3.03.03   Different judges take different views as to whether they are prepared to see counsel privately.

Many judges are not prepared to see counsel privately especially in relation to the ultimate disposal of the case (see **3.03.07-3.03.11**).

3.03.04   Counsel should exercise discretion:

(a)   When making the initial approach through the clerk (see **3.03.01**).

(b)   When addressing the judge in his room (see **3.03.09-12**).

(c)   When advising the defendant about what was said in the judge's room. An indication from the judge is not a promise.

3.03.05   Dress

Counsel will usually remain robed in the judge's room. The judge may invite counsel to remove wigs and/or gowns.

3.03.06   Mode of Address

In the judge's room, the judge is addressed as **Judge**. A registrar or assistant registrar may be addressed as **Sir** (although practice varies and most advocates address him as **Judge**).

3.03.07   Conduct

The parties should not sit down unless invited to do so by the judge.

The parties must be careful not to embarrass the judge or compromise the hearing of the case in open court.

3.03.08   Introduction of the Parties

Counsel who has asked to see the judge will usually introduce the other counsel:

Judge, I represent (name of party). **Mr** (name) **represents** (name of party). **It is my request to see you.**

REASONS FOR SEEING THE JUDGE

3.03.09   Pleas

Counsel should not plea bargain. A potential plea may be introduced as follows:

I take the view that if the defendant were to plead to count (-) **that**

would meet the justice of the case, for the following reasons (state reasons), and would avoid the need for a trial (state time saved). Perhaps you could indicate your view.

3.03.10 Points of Law

It would assist me in advising the defendant on his plea if you could indicate your view of the law on (state count and nature of evidence).

3.03.11 Sentence

Counsel should not ask the judge to indicate the actual sentence which he is minded to impose.

A potential disposal of the case may be introduced as follows:

If the defendant were to plead to count (-), he is obviously anxious about the possible sentence. The defendant would be entitled to credit for a plea of guilty and (state briefly best feature(s) of mitigation). Perhaps, you could indicate your view?

The judge may either give a definite indication or he may give no indication or he may simply say:

This is/is not a serious case and I would sentence accordingly.

In this example, it is unlikely that the judge will give any better indication and counsel should not, as a general rule, press the judge to do so.

3.03.12 Mitigation

The defendant will be pleading to (state pleas). There are certain matters that I would not wish to raise in mitigation in open court (state matters) for the following reasons (state reasons, for example, that the defendant is an informer).

3.03.13 Personal Problems of the Counsel

For example: listing problems; illness in the family.

3.03.14 Any other matter

Counsel may raise any other matter which he feels should be raised privately and not in open court.

For example, where it is suspected that there has been an improper communication between the defendant and/or the jury and/or prosecution witnesses.

3.03.15 Leaving the Judge's Room

At the conclusion, counsel who made the request to see the judge will usually say:

Thank you for seeing us, Judge.

SECTION 4: TRIAL ON INDICTMENT

PREPARATION

3.04.01 In preparation, the parties to a trial on indictment should give consideration to the matters listed in **3.02 Directions**, whether or not the case was listed for directions.

INTRODUCTION

3.04.02 Attendance of the Defendant

The defendant will usually be warned by his solicitors of the likely date of his trial when the case is in the warned list (if it has not been fixed).

It is the defendant's duty to keep in contact with his solicitors who should warn him of the date and place of his trial.

The defendant must attend.

If the defendant fails to attend, a bench warrant (with or without bail) may be issued (see **1.02.02-06**).

3.04.03   Identification of the Defendant

When the case is called, the clerk will usually identify the defendant by name, for example:

Are you (full name of defendant)?

If there is an application for an adjournment by either party it may be made after the identification of the defendant whether or not he has surrendered to custody.

3.04.04   In a short trial which has been prepared by all the parties and where the defendant and witnesses attend, **3.04.05-11** may be omitted.

3.04.05   Attendance of Prosecution Witnesses

If any prosecution witness(es) fail to attend court the prosecution may apply:

(a)   For the case to be stood out, if a plea has not been taken (see **3.04.12**).

(b)   For the case to be adjourned, if a plea has been taken.

3.04.06   The defence may oppose the application for the case to be stood out or adjourned:

This case has been fixed for (-) months/This is the (-) time the prosecution have applied to stand out/adjourn this case.

The prosecution may reply.

3.04.07   If the application is refused, the prosecution must decide whether to proceed on the evidence available or to offer no evidence.

If the prosecution decide to offer no evidence and a plea has not been taken the defence should ask for the indictment to be put to the defendant (see **3.04.12**).

The defendant will plead not guilty. The prosecution will then offer no evidence. The defence may apply for costs (see **3.04.96**).

IF THE TRIAL IS EFFECTIVE

3.04.08   Jury 'In' or 'Out'?

If the indictment contains more than one count and the defendant is going to plead guilty to one or more counts, or if there is a preliminary application (see

3.04.10-11), the usual practice is to exclude the jury when the indictment is put to the defendant. The indictment is then amended before it is read to the jury (see **3.04.23**).

The clerk or usher may ask either party (usually the defence), when the case is called but before the judge is brought into court:

Do you want the jury?

3.04.09   Preliminary Applications

The parties to a trial on indictment will usually have (in addition to any other documents):

(a) A copy of the indictment

(b) Copies of the written statements and/or depositions tendered at the magistrates' court

(c) Copies of any documentary exhibits

(d) Copies of any notices of additional evidence.

3.04.10   Preliminary applications based on these documents may be made before the indictment is put to the defendant.

The most common preliminary applications are:

(a) Amendment of the indictment

(b) Severance of counts and/or defendants

(c) Joinder of counts and/or defendants

(d) Quashing the indictment.

(e) Conduct and length of the trial.

(f) A view of the *locus in quo* (see **3.04.55**).

The law on this subject is complex and should be researched in the common practitioners' handbooks.

3.04.11   Either party may introduce a preliminary application. The usual form of words is:

Before the indictment is put, there is a preliminary matter upon which I would seek to address Your Honour.

The judge will then hear submissions (see also **3.04.40-41**).

3.04.12   The Indictment

At the conclusion of any preliminary applications, the indictment is put to the defendant by the clerk, for example:

(Name of defendant) **you are charged on an indictment containing** (number) **counts.**

On the first count you are charged that (the statement and particulars of offence are then read to the defendant).

To that count do you plead guilty or not guilty?

The defendant will plead either guilty or not guilty.

There are alternative pleas which should be researched in the common practitioners' handbooks.

3.04.13   Reporting Restrictions

Either party may apply for an order imposing reporting restrictions, for example:

(a) Juveniles

One of the defendants is a juvenile/a number of the witnesses in this case are juveniles. Would you make an order under the Children and Young Persons Act that the defendant/witnesses not be identified.

The new video link procedure is complex and should be researched in the common practitioners' handbooks.

(b) Second trial

The defendant is to be tried on a second indictment following on from this indictment. Would you make an order under the Contempt of Court Act that this matter not be reported until the conclusion of the second trial.

The defence should not attempt to make an application to impose reporting restrictions for the personal convenience of the defendant.

3.04.14   Questions of Admissibility

After the defendant has pleaded to the indictment, questions of admissibility of evidence may be determined before the jury are sworn:

(a)   Where the prosecution would have no evidence to put before the jury if that evidence were excluded, for example:

Where the only evidence is admissions which it is proposed to challenge in a trial within a trial (see **3.04.42-43**).

(b)   Where the inclusion or exclusion of that evidence would materially affect the prosecution opening.

(c)   Where it is convenient to all the parties to do so.

The usual form of words is

Before the jury are sworn there is a matter of law on which the prosecution/the defence/we would seek Your Honour's direction.

3.04.15   The parties should clarify the position with the judge in open court as a preliminary application because practice varies and some judges require the jury to be sworn and sent away.

3.04.16   Bail During the Trial

If the jury have been excluded, the defence may address the judge on the question of bail during the course of the trial. The usual form of words is:

The defendant has been on unconditional/conditional bail to date. Would Your Honour grant bail during the course of the trial or until further order?

3.04.17   If the jury have not been excluded the defence may address the judge on the question of bail immediately before the next adjournment of the court. The usual form of words is:

Your Honour, I have an application which does not concern the jury.

The judge will either exclude the jury and hear argument or the prosecution will indicate that bail is not opposed by saying, for example:

There is no objection.

THE JURY

3.04.18   At the conclusion of applications the judge may say:

Can we have the jury in now?

3.04.19   The prospective jurors are identified by name and called to the jury box by the clerk. All jurors must take the oath in the presence of each other.

3.04.20   The prosecution may *stand by* any prospective juror, for example, if it appears that the juror is incompetent or unwilling to try the case.

Before the juror is sworn, the prosecution may call out:

Stand by for the Crown.

The prosecution should not use the right to stand by jurors to obtain a pro-prosecution jury.

3.04.21   Challenges by the defence can only be made for cause, namely that the juror is not a proper person to try the case. The cause must be personal to the juror.

Before the juror is sworn, the defence may call out:

Challenge for cause.

The practice on challenging for cause is currently unclear. The following is intended as a guide:

(a)   The cause should not be stated in the presence of the juror and/or jury.

(b)   The jury should be excluded and the matter argued before the judge.

(c)   If necessary, evidence should be called to establish the cause.

3.04.22   In a case where the juror is known, the defence may challenge the juror as follows:

This juror is known to the defendant/me.

3.04.23   When all the jurors have been sworn the clerk will read the indictment to the jury and say:

To this indictment the defendant has pleaded not guilty and it is your

charge to say, having heard the evidence, whether he be guilty or not.

3.04.24   Conduct in the Presence of the Jury

The parties should remember that any contact between the parties and the jury should always be made through the judge.

As a matter of courtesy, any documents or exhibits should only be given to the jury with the leave of the judge.

3.04.25   Introductory Remarks by The Judge

The judge may (either at this stage or immediately before any adjournment of the court):

(a)   Direct the jury not to discuss the case outside court.

(b)   Direct the jury that they are the judges of the facts and that when matters of law arise, they may be asked to leave court (see **3.04.39**).

(c)   Direct the jury on any matter relating to time/practice.

The judge will then indicate that he is ready for the prosecution to open the case, for example:

Yes, Mr (name of prosecution).

THE CASE FOR THE PROSECUTION

3.04.26   Introduction of the Parties

The prosecution will usually introduce the parties to the court, as follows:

May it please Your Honour, members of the jury, I appear on behalf of the prosecution. My learned friend Mr (name) **appears on behalf of the defendant.**

The prosecution then opens the case, see **3.04.31**.

3.04.27   Order of Presentation

The order of presentation and speeches follows the title order in the indictment.

3.04.28   Order of Cross-Examination

The order of cross-examination of prosecution witnesses follows the title order in the indictment. The prosecution may re-examine.

3.04.29   Duties of the Prosecution

The duties of the prosecution have been defined in many ways. The best definition is to say that the prosecution has a duty to be fair.

In particular, the prosecution should disclose to the defence in advance of the trial all unused material (subject to certain exceptions) and any criminal conviction(s) recorded against a prosecution witness.

The prosecution should not seek to win the case at all costs.

3.04.30   Purpose of Opening

The purpose of opening is to assist the jury (and, in a complex case, the judge and any other party) to understand the case (see **14.02.13-15**).

The prosecution may provide the judge and any other party (but not the jury) with an opening note.

3.04.31   Prosecution Opening

The prosecution opening to the jury should contain:

(a)   A brief introduction of the case describing the circumstances of the case in words the jury will understand.

(b)   An explanation of the nature of the charge(s). Copies of the indictment may be handed to the jury (with the leave of the judge).

(c)   An outline of the evidence upon which the prosecution intends to rely.

(d)   An explanation of the burden and standard of proof.

The prosecution should not open matters to the jury which are likely to be the subject of argument over admissibility (see **3.04.40-43**).

3.04.32   The prosecution may conclude the opening by saying:

I have nothing further to say by way of opening the case and I now propose to call the evidence. The first witness is (name of witness).

3.04.33   The following phrase is sometimes used:

And with Your Honour's leave I now propose to call (the first witness).

It is an elegant phrase but, strictly speaking, it is unnecessary because the leave of the judge is not required to call witnesses (except **3.04.43(vi)**).

EVIDENCE ON BEHALF OF THE PROSECUTION

3.04.34   Witnesses Attending Court: Fully Bound Witnesses

Witness should remain outside court until called to give evidence.

The prosecution must ensure the attendance at court of all fully bound witnesses and any witness whose statement is served as a notice of additional evidence (unless dispensed with), whether or not the prosecution intend to rely on the evidence of that witness.

3.04.35   The witness is called and identified by the prosecution as follows:

Are you (name)? **What is your address, Mr** (name)?

The usual rules as to the examination, cross-examination and re-examination of witnesses apply (see **14.01.01-24**).

3.04.36   Refreshing the Memory

A witness (usually a police officer) may wish to 'refresh his memory' from a document made at the time (see **14.01.11-15**).

The judge will usually explain to the jury why a witness is permitted to refresh his memory.

3.04.37   Objecting to Evidence

A witness may be giving or about to give evidence to which the defence objects. The defence may interrupt the prosecution and/or witness as follows:

I object to this evidence.

3.04.38 If the evidence is clearly inadmissible (for example, hearsay), the judge may direct the prosecution, in the presence of the jury, to omit that evidence.

In any other situation and/or where there is likely to be an argument over the admissibility of the evidence the jury should be excluded.

3.04.39 Excluding the Jury

In order to enclude the jury, either party may say:

There is a matter of law on which I would wish to address Your Honour in the absence of the jury.

The judge may then explain:

Members of the jury, I decide all matters of law. You, on the other hand, are the judges of the facts. It follows, therefore, that matters of law do not concern you. Could you go to your room please.

3.04.40 Questions of Admissibility

All matters of law (which include questions of admissibility of evidence) are decided in the absence of the jury.

3.04.41 Where there is an argument over a question of admissibility, the order of submissions is usually as follows:

(a) Either party (usually the defence) identifies the evidence to which an objection is taken.

    (i) If the objection is on a point of law (for example, whether the evidence is hearsay) the argument can be made on the statements and no evidence need be called.

    (ii) If the objection is on mixed fact and law (for example, the circumstances in which an alleged admission was made are disputed) evidence will usually need to be called in a trial within a trial (see **3.04.42-43**).

(b) The defence gives reasons for the objection and refers to any relevant law.

(c) Reply by the prosecution.

(d) Response by the defence dealing with any new points raised by the prosecution or the judge but not repeating the submission(s) in (b).

(e)   Decision by the judge.

(f)   Jury recalled.

3.04.42   Trial within a Trial (*Voire Dire*)

A trial within a trial takes place where evidence is called on the admissibility of a confession or other admission by the defendant. It will usually take place immediately before that evidence is called (or before the jury are sworn, see **3.04.14-15**).

3.04.43   A trial within a trial takes place in the absence of the jury (see **3.04.39**).

After **3.04.41(a)(ii)** substitute the following procedure:

(iii)   The prosecution call witness(es) to prove that:

(a) An alleged confession or other admission was made by the defendant, and

(b) It was made in circumstances that make it admissible (for example, that it was made voluntarily).

(iv)   The defence will cross-examine.

(v)   The prosecution may re-examine.

(vi)   The defence may, **with the leave of the judge**, call the defendant to prove that the alleged confession or other admission was not made in circumstances that make it admissible. The usual form of words is:

With Your Honour's leave, I will now call the defendant.

(vii) The prosecution will cross-examine the defendant.

(viii) The defence may, **with the leave of the judge**, call witnesses (for example a doctor who gives evidence of recent injury to the defendant on release from police custody).

3.04.41(b)-(f) should then be followed.

3.04.44 Tendering a Witness

If a witness gives corroborative evidence, the prosecution may tender that witness for cross-examination (see **14.01.23-24**).

3.04.45   Releasing a Witness

A witness who has given evidence should remain in court until the conclusion of the case or until he is given permission to leave by the judge.

If a witness wishes to leave court after giving evidence, the prosecution may say:

Unless there is any objection, perhaps this witness (and/or any subsequent witness) **could be released?**

3.04.46   Witnesses not Attending Court: Conditionally Bound Witnesses

Conditionally bound witnesses are witnesses upon whose evidence the prosecution rely and whose evidence is not disputed by the defence.

3.04.47   The evidence of a conditionally bound witness is usually introduced by the prosecution as follows:

The next witness is (name of witness) **who is conditionally bound and whose evidence will be read.**

The judge may then say to the jury:

What this means is that the defence do not dispute the evidence of (name of witness). **There is no point in him coming to court and, therefore, his statement will be read to you. But you must treat his evidence in exactly the same way as if he had come to court and given evidence from the witness box.**

3.04.48   In some courts the clerk reads the statement of the witness. However, the generally accepted practice is that the prosecution reads the statement in order that:

(a)   The court is not seen to be playing a part in the prosecution of the defendant.

(b)   Any editing of the statement can be done by agreement between the parties.

The usual rules as to the admissibility of evidence apply.

3.04.49   After the judge has explained the significance of the evidence to the jury, the prosecution continue:

This is the statement of (name of witness) **aged** (the witness' age is often omitted) **of** (address) **who makes the following declaration:**

This statement consisting of (number) **pages, each signed by me, is true to the best of my knowledge and belief and I make it knowing that, if it is tendered in evidence, I shall be liable to prosecution if I have wilfully stated in it anything which I know to be false or do not believe to be true.**

The statement is dated (date).

It is signed by (name of witness) **and the signature is witnessed by** (if at all).

He states: (The statement is then read).

3.04.50 The evidence of subsequent conditionally bound witnesses is usually introduced by the prosecution as follows:

The next witness is (name of witness) **whose evidence will be read. The witness' address is** (address of witness). **He makes the usual declaration. The statement is dated** (date of statement).

He states (the statement is then read).

3.04.51 Expert Witnesses

An expert witness is entitled to give evidence of opinion on any matter in which he has expert knowledge.

The prosecution should establish his qualifications before adducing evidence of opinion (see **14.01.16-20**).

3.04.52 Oral Admissions

An admission need not be in writing in the crown court. The prosecution may be asked to make a simple oral admission, for example, that the defendant is of good character:

I am asked to make an admission that the defendant is of good character, and I do so.

3.04.53 Written Admissions

Admissions in writing are introduced by the prosecution in the following way:

Mr (name of defence) **and I have agreed an admission, the original of which I hand to the court. With Your Honour's leave there are copies available for the jury.**

The judge will then explain the nature of an admission to the jury. The admission is usually then read by the prosecution to the jury.

3.04.54 Schedules, maps, plans, photographs, etc. may be agreed and introduced in the same way.

3.04.55 A View

An application for a view of the *locus in quo* may be made by either party. A view attended by the judge and jury is rare.

A view means exactly what it says. It is not a discussion of the evidence at the *locus in quo*.

3.04.56 Close of Prosecution Case

When the prosecution has called and/or read all the evidence and any admissions have been made, the case is said to be closed.

The usual form of words is:

That is the case for the prosecution/Crown or, more simply, **that is the case.**

SUBMISSION OF NO CASE TO ANSWER

3.04.57 A submission of no case to answer is made in the absence of the jury (see **3.04.39**).

The grounds on which a submission of no case to answer may be made and the relevant law should be researched in the common practitioners' handbooks.

3.04.58 In practice, the order of submissions is as follows:

(a) The defence may begin:

I submit that there is no case to answer (on count (-) of the indictment).

    (i) **On the ground that the prosecution has failed to establish** (an essential ingredient of the offence)

and/or

    (ii) **On the ground that the evidence is so weak that no reasonable jury, properly directed, could convict on it.**

(b) The defence should identify the evidence to which he refers and direct the judge to any relevant law.

(c) Reply by the prosecution.

(d) Response by the defence dealing with any new points raised by the prosecution or the judge but not repeating the submissions in (b).

(e) Decision by the court.

(f) Jury recalled.

3.04.59 If a submission of no case to answer is upheld in relation to one or more but not all the counts on the indictment, the judge will usually direct the jury to find the defendant not guilty of those counts when the jury are recalled.

If the submission is upheld in respect of all the counts on the indictment, the judge will direct the jury to find the defendant not guilty of all the counts on the indictment when the jury are recalled.

The defendant is then discharged. The defence may apply for costs (see **3.04.96**).

THE CASE FOR THE DEFENCE

3.04.60 Order of Presentation

The order of presentation and speeches follows the title order in the indictment.

If a defendant is giving evidence and calling witnesses, the witnesses are called after the defendant has given evidence and before the case of the next defendant in title order in the indictment.

3.04.61   Order of Cross-examination

The order of cross-examination of a defendant or defence witness follows the title order in the indictment except that the prosecution cross-examine last, for example:

The third defendant (or a witness on behalf of the third defendant) has given evidence in chief. The order of cross- examination is:

1st defendant.

2nd defendant.

4th defendant.

Prosecution.

The 3rd defendant may re-examine.

3.04.62   When can the defence open?

In practice the defence do not usually make an opening speech unless:

(a) The defence consider the jury might have difficulty understanding the defence case.

(b) The defence consider that emphasis should be given to the defence evidence (or any part of it).

3.04.63   The defence may make an opening speech where:

(a) The defendant is giving evidence and the defence are proposing to call other evidence on the facts.

(b) The defendant is not giving evidence but the defence are proposing to call other evidence on the facts.

The defence may **not** make an opening speech where:

(c) No evidence is being called on behalf of the defendant, although the defence may address the court as follows:

Mr (name of defendant) **exercises his right not to give evidence.**

(d) The defendant only is giving evidence and the defence are not proposing to call other evidence on the facts.

(e) The defence is calling character evidence only.

3.04.64 Duties of the Defence

The defence should present the defendant's case 'fearlessly'. The defence does not have the same duty to be fair as the prosecution, although the defence must never mislead the court, for example:

(a) The defence need not draw the prosecution's attention to a technical flaw in its case.

(b) The defence need not disclose the previous convictions of the defendant or a defence witness (although the defence must not present them as persons of good character).

(c) The defence need not disclose in advance the names of defence witnesses.

3.04.65 However, the advocate on behalf of the defendant should withdraw from the case if the defendant substantially changes his instructions and/or asks the advocate to make up a defence.

The advocate may say to the judge:

As a result of certain instructions, I am professionally embarrassed. I would seek your leave to withdraw from the case.

3.04.66 Defence Opening Speech

The defence opening may contain the following:

(a) An outline of the evidence upon which the defence intends to rely (including evidence of alibi). The defence should not open the evidence in the same detail as the prosecution.

(b) A criticism of the prosecution evidence.

(c) An explanation of the burden and standard of proof.

The defence may conclude the opening by saying:

I have nothing further to say by way of opening the case and I now propose to call the defendant. Mr (name) **could you come into the witness box.**

3.04.67   Evidence of the Defendant

The defendant must always be called first where the defence are calling other evidence (including evidence of character).

As a matter of practice, special care should be taken to allow the defendant to 'tell his own story'.

3.04.68   The usual rules as to the examination, cross-examination and re-examination of witnesses apply (see **14.01.01-24**), except the defendant may not be cross-examined as to credit, namely, whether he is likely, by reason of his bad character, to be untruthful (see **3.04.69-71**):

3.04.69   Evidence of Character

The law on this subject is complex and should be researched in the common practitioners' handbooks.

The following is intended as a brief guide.

If the defendant is of good character:

(a)   The defence will usually prove the defendant's good character in cross-examination of an appropriate prosecution witness, for example:

Is it correct that the defendant is of good character?

And that there are no convictions recorded against him?

(b)   The defence may call the defendant to give evidence of his good character.

(c)   The defence may call witnesses of the defendant's good character whether or not the defendant himself gives evidence. In practice, the prosecution does not cross-examine the witness on the defendant's character but may do so.

3.04.70   If the defendant is of bad character:

(a)   The defence may make imputations on the character of a prosecution witness in cross-examination but the defendant may be at risk of being cross-examined about his bad character if he gives evidence.

The prosecution may only cross-examine the defendant on his bad character with the leave of the judge.

(b)   The defence may choose not to call the defendant in which case the prosecution cannot introduce evidence of his bad character.

(c) The defence may not call witnesses of the defendant's good character if, where (a) applies, the defendant does not give evidence.

(d) The defence may call evidence of the defendant's good character if, as a general rule, evidence of the defendant's bad character is also adduced: ('Part in, all in').

3.04.71 Role of Co-Defendants

Where there is more than one defendant and one defendant gives evidence against a co-defendant in the same proceedings (for example, a 'cut throat defence'), the co-defendant may cross-examine that defendant on his bad character (usually with the leave of the judge, although this is not strictly necessary).

3.04.72 Defence Evidence

The evidence on behalf of the defence is subject to the same rules and is presented in the same way as the evidence on behalf of the prosecution (see **3.04.34-55**).

3.04.73 Alibi Evidence

Evidence of alibi may not be called unless an alibi notice has been served by the defence on the prosecution.

The notice should be served within seven days after the end of committal proceedings (see **1.05.31**). In practice, evidence of alibi may be called if the notice is served a reasonable time before the trial (see **3.02.02(j)**).

3.04.74 An alibi notice need not be detailed, but must contain the relevant information, for example:

R v (name of defendant) (Name of) **Crown Court, Indictment Number:**

To the solicitor for the prosecution:

On (the date and time of the offence) **the defendant was at** (state place) **in company with:**

(Name. Date of birth. Address).

3.04.75 Alibi witnesses are called, in the usual way, after the defendant has given evidence.

3.04.76 Close of Defence Case

The usual form of words is:

That is the case for the defence.

3.04.77 Evidence in Rebuttal

In practice, it is rare for the prosecution to call evidence in rebuttal. The prosecution must apply for leave.

It is more likely that either party will make an application (usually in the absence of the jury) for leave to recall a witness where:

(a) Either party examined that witness inadequately, for example:

There is an important matter which I omitted to put to (name of witness) **namely** (state question). **I understand that the witness is at court/has been made available. And I would seek Your Honour's leave to ask the witness that question.**

(b) The defence failed to examine a prosecution witness on a relevant matter. The prosecution may say:

In his evidence the defendant said (state evidence). **That matter was not put to** (name of witness). **That witness is at court/has been made available. And I would seek Your Honour's leave to recall that witness in order that** (name of defence) **should properly challenge his evidence.**

3.04.78 Legal Argument

Before speeches either party or the judge may:

(a) Seek clarification of relevant matters of law.

Or, the defence may, in rare circumstances:

(b) Renew a submission of no case to answer.

(c) Seek leave of the judge for special verdict(s).

SPEECHES

3.04.79   Prosecution Closing Speech

The prosecution closing speech may contain:

(a) A summary of the main points of the evidence (including the evidence of the defendant and any defence witnesses) tending to show that the defendant is guilty of the offence charged.

(b) An explanation of the burden and standard of proof.

3.04.80   The prosecution may choose not to make a closing speech where:

(a) The defence called no evidence.

(b) The defence called evidence but the case lasted only a short time.

For example:

Members of the jury, although I am entitled to address you in closing, there is little I can add to what I said in opening/this has been a short case, and I do not propose to address you again.

3.04.81   Defence Closing Speech

The defence may make a closing speech even if the defendant has not given evidence.

The defence closing speech may contain:

(a) A summary of the defence case.

(b) A summary of the weaknesses in the prosecution case.

(c) A summary of the allegations made in cross-examination of the prosecution witnesses.

(d) An explanation of the burden and standard of proof.

The defence closing speech should not contain:

(e) Any reference to the likely sentence if the defendant is convicted.

(f) Any reference to the defendant's instructions which are not in evidence.

(g) Any attack on the prosecution's witnesses which was not made in cross-examination.

(h) A politically motivated attack on the prosecuting authorities.

3.04.82 The defence closing speech is usually less formal than the prosecution closing speech. For this reason, the defence advocate should feel comfortable with his style. Although this will come with experience, a good rule is to ''be natural''.

If the advocate is not normally accustomed to illustrating his day to day conversation with anecdotes or jokes, he should not do so in his speech to the jury (see **14.02.22-29**).

SUMMING UP

3.04.83 Checklist

The judge's summing up should contain:

(a) Functions of the judge and jury.

(b) Burden and standard of proof.

(c) The ingredients of the offence(s) charged.

(d) Separate consideration of defendants and/or counts.

(e) The effect of good or bad character.

(f) Other directions as appropriate to the case (for example: identification, corroboration).

(g) A summary of the evidence for the prosecution.

(h) A summary of the evidence for the defence.

The defence should make a note of the judge's summing up for the purpose of advising on appeal.

3.04.84   Conclusion of Summing Up

The judge will usually conclude his summing up with a direction to the jury to reach a unanimous verdict.

The judge will then indicate to the jury bailiff that he is ready for the jury to retire.

3.04.85   Correcting Errors in the Judge's Summing Up

An advocate should exercise care before correcting an error in the judge's summing up. If necessary, it should be done before the jury bailiff takes the jury oath.

Despite the authorities to the contrary, a correction may be made by either party. It should only be made where the judge has made an important error either in law or in fact, for example:

> **Your Honour omitted to summarise to the jury the evidence of the defendant. Perhaps that is a matter which Your Honour would wish to consider.**

3.04.86   A correction should not be made on a contentious matter in the presence of the jury.

If in doubt, the jury should be excluded, for example:

> **Before the jury bailiff is sworn, there is a matter on which I would wish to address Your Honour in the absence of the jury.**

3.04.87   Retirement of the Jury

After the jury bailiff has taken the jury oath, the jury will retire to consider their verdicts.

The jury may take with them:

(a) Any exhibits (or copy exhibits)

(b) Any notes made during the trial.

If the jury take longer than a court day to consider their verdicts, they must be confined overnight (usually in a local hotel) and will return to court the next day to continue their deliberations.

As long as the jury are considering their verdicts, they must have no contact with anyone outside their number.

3.04.88 Questions from the Jury

A question from the jury is usually written down and handed to the judge (who will hand it to the parties) for consideration.

The judge will usually canvass the parties in open court (in the absence of the jury) for an agreed answer.

When the jury return to court, the judge will answer the question but the jury may not:

(a) Hear further evidence.

(b) Hear submissions from either party.

3.04.89 Verdicts

The jury must return verdicts on each count and in respect of each defendant unless the Judge has discharged them from giving a verdict (see **3.04.59**) (or where there are alternative counts on the indictment).

The verdict will be guilty or not guilty.

3.04.90 A special verdict may be returned where, by agreement between the parties and the judge after legal argument (see **3.04.78**), the jury have been asked to consider it.

3.04.91 Majority Direction

The judge may give a majority direction after at least 2 hours 10 minutes.

The judge will usually ask both parties in the absence of the jury:

> **I propose to give a majority direction. Do either of you have anything to say about that?**

Either party may object.

3.04.92 The majority varies according to the size of the jury:

Number of jurors	Size of the majority
12	11-1 or 10-2
11	10-1
10	9-1
9	9

3.04.93 If the majority direction has been given, the size of the majority will only be stated where the defendant is found guilty.

3.04.94 If the defendant is found guilty:

See **4.01: Sentencing**.

3.04.95 If the defendant is found not guilty, the defence will usually say:

Could the defendant be discharged?

3.04.96   Costs

If the defendant is found not guilty the defence may make an application for the defendant's costs (see **7.02.20-30**), for example:

Would Your Honour make a defendant's costs order?

The effect of the order is that costs reasonably incurred by the defendant are paid out of central funds.

There is no general power to reimburse the defendant for loss of income during the trial.

3.04.97   Appeal

Appeal against conviction and/or sentence is to the court of appeal.

The notice of application for leave to appeal either conviction or sentence and the grounds of appeal must be served on the crown court within 28 days.

If sentence is delayed, it may be necessary to serve the appropriate notice and grounds of appeal against conviction before the final disposal of the case.

See **8.02: Court of Appeal (Criminal Division)**.

SECTION 5: APPEAL TO THE CROWN COURT AGAINST CONVICTION

INTRODUCTION

3.05.01   An appeal to the crown court against conviction is heard by a judge and usually two magistrates.

It is a rehearing of the case heard before the magistrates' court (or juvenile court).

An appeal against conviction can only be made where the appellant pleaded not guilty at the magistrates' court (or juvenile court).

If an appellant pleaded guilty at the magistrates' court (or juvenile court), for example, as a result of misunderstanding the nature of the charge, he must apply to the crown court for leave to appeal.

The following sections should be used as a guide:

1.06: Summary Trial.

2.02: Criminal Trial in the Juvenile Court.

3.05.02   Either party may call witnesses who were not called at the magistrates' court (or juvenile court) or not call witnesses who were called at the magistrates' court (or juvenile court).

3.05.03   Attendance of the Appellant

The appellant must attend. If he fails to do so, his appeal is usually dismissed unless he has been involuntarily detained.

It is the appellant's application and therefore there is no power to issue a warrant to secure his attendance.

3.05.04 Identification of the Appellant

The clerk may say:

This is an appeal against conviction by (name). **Are you** (name)?

3.05.05 Introduction of the Parties

The respondent opens the case:

I appear on behalf of the respondent in this case. My (learned) **friend, Mr** (name) **appears on behalf of the appellant.**

3.05.06 Respondent's Opening

The respondent may then say:

The appellant was convicted before the (name) **Magistrates' Court** (juvenile court) **on** (date) **of** (state briefly the nature of the offence). **He now appeals against that conviction by a notice of appeal dated** (date) **on the ground(s) that** (state briefly the nature of the ground(s), or) **he is not guilty of the offence.**

3.05.07 Although the crown court will have a copy of the notice of appeal, the judge and magistrates will not usually know the sentence or order imposed by the magistrates' court (or juvenile court).

It is not considered good practice to state, in opening, the the sentence imposed.

3.05.08 The respondent's opening should contain:

(a) A brief outline of the facts.

(b) a brief summary of any relevant law (usually where there is a technical defence).

3.05.09 The respondent may conclude the opening:

I now call (name of first witness).

3.05.10 Practice

1.06.17-49 (and **2.02.9-26**) apply with the amendment of the names of the parties.

Magistrates' court (juvenile court)	Crown court
Prosecution	Respondent
Defence	Appellant

3.05.11 Decision

The judge announces the decision of the court (either with or without a short judgment):

This appeal is allowed

OR

This appeal is dismissed.

Care should be taken to ensure that the appellant understands the decision. It often happens that an appellant, hearing the word 'dismissed', believes that the charge against him has been dismissed.

3.05.12 Sentence

If the appeal is dismissed, sentence is 'at large' even if the sentence has not been appealed (see **4.01: Sentencing**).

This means that the sentence can be reviewed and, in some cases, increased provided that any sentence imposed by the crown court could have been imposed by the magistrates' court (or juvenile court).

3.05.13 Guidelines on Review

The judge may say to the respondent:

Could you tell us what sentence was passed by the magistrates' court (or juvenile court)?

After having heard the details of any sentence or order passed by the magistrates' court (or juvenile court), the Judge may say to the appellant:

Do you wish to address us on sentence?

If sentence was not appealed, the appellant may say:

Sentence was not appealed.

3.05.14   The judge may say:

But sentence is at large.

This may mean that the court is considering reviewing the sentence (and may indicate to the appellant any proposed sentence). A short plea in mitigation should be made (see **4.01.29-33**).

3.05.15   The judge may say:

But this court has power to increase the sentence.

This may mean that the court is considering increasing the sentence and a full plea in mitigation may be made (see **4.01.29- 33**).

3.05.16   Costs

(a)   If the appeal is allowed, the court may make a defendants' costs order (see **7.02.24(a)**).

(b)   If the appeal is dismissed, the court may order the appellant to pay the respondent's costs (see **7.02.09(c)**).

SECTION 6: APPEAL TO THE CROWN COURT AGAINST SENTENCE

INTRODUCTION

3.06.01   An appeal against sentence is a rehearing of Sentencing before the magistrates' court (or juvenile court).

The following sections should be used as a guide:

4.01: Sentencing.

2.02.21-27: Determining the Order on a Finding of Guilt.

The appeal is heard by a judge and usually two magistrates.

3.06.02 Attendance of the Appellant

The appellant must attend. If he does not do so, his appeal will usually be dismissed unless he has been involuntarily detained.

It is the appellant's application and therefore there is no power to issue a warrant to secure his attendance.

3.06.03 Identification of the Appellant

The clerk may say:

This is an appeal against sentence by (name). **Are you** (name)?

3.06.04 Introduction of the Parties

The respondent opens the case:

I appear on behalf of the respondent in this case. My (learned) **friend Mr** (name) **appears on behalf of the appellant.**

3.06.05 Respondent's Opening

The respondent may then say:

The appellant was convicted/pleaded guilty before the (name) **Magistrates' Court** (Juvenile Court) **on** (date) **of** (state briefly the nature of the offence) **and received a sentence of** (state sentence).

He now appeals against that sentence by a notice of appeal dated (date) **on the grounds that** (state briefly the nature of the grounds).

3.06.06 The practice in **4.01.04-34** and/or **2.02.21-27** is then followed.

3.06.07 Costs

(a) If the appeal is allowed, the court may make a defendant's costs order (see **7.02.24(b)**).

(b) If the appeal is dismissed, the court may order the appellant to pay the respondent's costs (see **7.02.09(c)**).

SECTION 7: COMMITTAL FOR SENTENCE

INTRODUCTION

3.07.01   If the magistrates' court is of the opinion that: **greater punishment should be inflicted on the defendant than it has power to impose** (see **1.04.17**), it may commit the defendant to the crown court for sentence.

3.07.02   **A** committal to the crown court for sentence is heard by a judge and usually two magistrates.

3.07.03   Attendance of the Defendant

The defendant is usually committed in custody.

If the defendant is not committed in custody, he must attend. If he does not attend, a warrant may be issued to secure his attendance (see **1.02.02-06**).

3.07.04   Identification of the Defendant

The clerk may say:

Are you (name)?

On (date) **were you convicted/did you plead guilty, before the** (name) **Magistrates' Court of** (state offence)?

And were you committed from that court to this for sentence?

3.07.05   The practice in **4.01.03-34** is then followed.

3.07.06   Costs

The court may order the defendant to pay the prosecution's costs (see **7.02.09(a)**).

SECTION 8: APPEAL TO THE CROWN COURT IN CARE PROCEEDINGS

INTRODUCTION

3.08.01   An appeal to the crown court in care proceedings is a re-hearing of care proceedings in the juvenile court. The appeal is heard in chambers.

The following section should be used as a guide:

2.03: Care Proceedings.

3.08.02   The appeal is heard by a judge and usually two magistrates, who must be members of the juvenile panel.

The members of the court must include a man and a woman.

3.08.03   Either party may call witnesses who were not called at the juvenile court or not call witnesses who were called at the juvenile court.

3.08.04   Attendance of the Parties

If a party appealing the order (other than the child) does not attend, the appeal may be dismissed.

3.08.05   Identification of the Parties

The clerk may say:

This is an appeal of a care order made to the (name) **local authority in respect of** (name of child) **by** (name of appellant).

Are you (name of child)?

Are you (name of parent(s))?

And are you the (father/mother) **of** (name of child)?

And are you (or, name of appellant) **appealing the care order?**

3.08.06   Introduction of the Parties

The advocate appearing on behalf of the local authority may introduce the parties to the court (if this has not already been done).

3.08.07   The practice in **2.03.20-51** is then followed.

SECTION 9: APPEAL TO THE CROWN COURT IN LICENSING PROCEEDINGS

INTRODUCTION

3.09.01   An appeal to the crown court in licensing proceedings is a re-hearing of the application for a liquor licence in the magistrates' court. The appeal is heard in open court.

The following section should be used as a guide:

1.08.03-31: Application for a Liquor Licence.

3.09.02   The applicant or objector may appeal to the crown court (although an objector who did not object to the application at the magistrates court may not appeal to the crown court).

3.09.03   The appeal is heard by a judge and usually four magistrates, two of whom must be magistrates in the petty sessional area in which the case originated.

3.09.04   Either party may call witnesses who were not called at the magistrates' court or not call witnesses who were called at the magistrates' court.

3.09.05   Attendance of the Parties

If a party appealing the order does not attend, the appeal will usually be dismissed.

3.09.06   Identification of the Parties

The clerk may say:

This is an appeal of a refusal/grant of a (state type of) **licence in respect of** (title and address of premises) **by** (state name of appellant).

3.09.07   Introduction of the Parties

The advocate appearing on behalf of the applicant will usually introduce the parties to the court. The parties will usually include a barrister appearing on behalf of the licensing justices.

3.09.08   The practice in **1.08.03-30** is then followed except service/display/advertisement of the notice of application need not be proved (see **1.08.15-16**).

3.09.09   Costs

The crown court has power to award costs to the successful party.

The parties should be ready to state their costs to the court in the event of a successful appeal.

CHAPTER 4

Sentencing and Bail

Section 1:   Sentencing

Section 2:   Bail Applications

SECTION 1: SENTENCING

INTRODUCTION

4.01.01   This section is intended for use in any court having the jurisdiction to consider and/or review sentence.

It will follow on from:

Magistrates' court:	Summary trial (see **1.06**)
Juvenile court:	Criminal trial (see **2.02**)
Crown court:	Trial (see **3.04**)
Crown court:	Appeal against conviction (see **3.05**)
Crown court:	Appeal against sentence (see **3.06**)
Crown court:	Committal for sentence (see **3.07**)

Court of Appeal: Appeal against sentence (see **8.02**)

Court martial: Plea or trial (see **12.03**)

4.01.02   This section is designed to illustrate the practice in these courts. It is impossible to describe the powers of the courts.

Powers of sentencing should be researched in the common practitioners' handbooks.

THE CASE FOR THE PROSECUTION

4.01.03   Introduction of the Parties

If this has not already been done, the prosecution will usually introduce the parties.

4.01.04   Prosecution Opening

The prosecution should open the facts of the case in as much detail as is thought necessary depending upon the court and/or the nature of the offence.

The prosecution will not usually open the facts where the defendant is sentenced by the same court which convicted him after a trial.

4.01.05   The prosecution opening should contain:

(a) An outline of the facts of the offence. Where the facts are disputed, see **4.01.06-08.**

(b) Particulars of any injury or loss (as appropriate).

(c) Reference to any aggravating or mitigating feature of the offence.

(d) A summary of any explanation made by the defendant.

For the duties of the prosecution, see **3.04.29.**

4.01.06   Calling Evidence of the Facts: A Newton Hearing

It sometimes happens that there is a substantial dispute by the defence of the facts of the case.

Where possible this should be resolved by agreement between the parties. If it cannot be resolved by agreement, the defence may address the court as follows:

Having heard the prosecution opening, I will be addressing you on the basis that (state main point(s) of dispute between the parties).

I would invite you to sentence on that basis.

The court will then indicate whether it will sentence the defendant on his version of the facts or whether the prosecution should call evidence of the facts.

4.01.07 Calling evidence in sentencing to establish the facts of the offence is called a *Newton Hearing*.

The usual standard of proof in criminal proceedings applies.

4.01.08 The practice in a Newton Hearing is usually as follows:

(a) The prosecution will usually open the main points of dispute between the parties to assist the court in understanding the issues.

(b) The prosecution will call witness(es) to give evidence on the issues in dispute.

(c) The defence will usually cross-examine.

(d) The defence will usually call the defendant and/or witness(es) on his behalf to give evidence (except where the prosecution case has been discredited by cross-examination).

(e) The prosecution may cross-examine the defendant, and/or witnesses, if called.

(f) The defence may address the court on the facts.

g) Decision by the court.

The court should express its view on the facts before hearing mitigation, for example:

We are minded to sentence on the basis that (state basis, for example: **We accept the evidence of the victim**).

If **4.01.06-08** do not apply, after the prosecution has opened the facts of the case:

4.01.09 Magistrates' court: The prosecution will usually give details of any previous convictions, breaches of court orders (see **4.01.17**), and offences to be taken into consideration (see **4.01.19**).

Omit **4.01.10-20** and **4.01.26-28**.

4.01.10   Crown court: The prosecution will usually call evidence of the defendant's antecedent history and previous convictions, as follows:

4.01.11   The prosecution will call the officer in the case (or the court antecedents' officer) who is sworn.

The officer will then identify himself.

4.01.12   The prosecution may say:

> **Do you produce antecedents relating to the defendant** (name) **dated** (date of preparation of the antecedents' form). **Does Your Honour have a copy?**

4.01.13   Was the defendant born on (date) **and is now aged** (age)?

4.01.14   And are there (state number) **findings of guilt** (juvenile convictions) **and** (state number) **previous convictions recorded against him?**

4.01.15   In a case where there are a substantial number of previous convictions the prosecution will usually ask the judge:

> **Where does Your Honour wish me to start?**

4.01.16   The prosecution will then usually read the details of the defendant's previous convictions and the sentences passed on him to the officer in the case, for example:

> **On** (date) **was the defendant convicted of** (offence) **for which he was** (fined/ sentenced to (-) months' imprisonment)?

Omit **4.01.17** and **4.01.18** if there is no breach of any court order.

BREACH OF COURT ORDER

4.01.17   If the defendant is in breach of any court order (suspended prison sentence, probation, conditional discharge), it may be dealt with at this stage for example:

The prosecution may say:

> **And was the defendant sentenced to** (-) **months imprisonment suspended for** (-) **years?**

And is he therefore in breach of that sentence?

Could that be put?

4.01.18   The clerk will say:

(Name of defendant). **Is it correct that on** (date) **at** (state name of) **court for an offence of** (specify), **you were sentenced to** (-) **months imprisonment suspended for** (-) **years?**

And do you accept that the offence for which you will be sentenced today was committed during the operational period of that sentence?

And that this court can now deal with you for that offence?

Omit **4.01.19** & **4.01.20** if there are no offences to be taken into consideration.

OFFENCES TAKEN INTO CONSIDERATION

4.01.19.   The prosecution may say:

The defendant is asking for (state number of) **offences to be taken into consideration. There/here is the form signed by the defendant.**

Could those matters be put to the defendant?

4.01.20   The clerk will say:

(Name of defendant). **Have you read and signed this form? Does it contain details of** (state number) **offences committed by you? Do you wish the court to take these offences into consideration when dealing with you for the offence to which you have pleaded guilty/the offence of which you have been convicted?**

4.01.21   The prosecution may then give details of the defendant's antecedent history to the court (which may include the defendant's accommodation, job, education, financial circumstances and any other relevant matter).

The prosecution may ask the officer in the case, for example:

Does the defendant live at (address) **with his** (details of family)? **And, does he have mortgage repayments of** (state amount).

COMPENSATION

4.01.22   The details of an application for compensation will usually be given by the prosecution, for example:

> **Compensation is sought by** (name) **in the sum of** (amount) **on** (state the charge or count). **The claim is made up as follows** (state how the amount is calculated).

Evidence may be called to substantiate the claim for compensation where there is a dispute between the parties.

In a case where it is unlikely that the defendant will be able to pay compensation (for example where imprisonment is likely) it is often sufficient for the prosecution to say:

> **There is an application for compensation of** (amount).

COSTS

4.01.23   The prosecution may say:

> **There is an application for costs of** (amount) **made up as follows** (state how the amount is calculated).

> See **7.02.09-15**.

FORFEITURE, DISPOSAL OR DESTRUCTION OR OTHER ORDER

4.01.24   The prosecution may say:

> **There is an application for the forfeiture/disposal/destruction of** (state nature of goods).

4.01.25   The prosecution should then mention any other matters relevant to the sentencing of the defendant and/or further disposal of the case at this stage (for example, an order under the Drug Trafficking Offences Act).

4.01.26   Crown Court only: In conclusion, the prosecution will usually say to the officer:

> **Could you stay there? There may be further questions** (from the defence or court).

4.01.27   The defence may cross-examine the officer in order to elicit from him any matter which is favourable to the defendant, and/or to rebut any aggravating feature of the offence.

The defence may conclude cross-examination by saying:

Thank you. I have no further questions.

4.01.28   After any re-examination of the officer, the prosecution will usually say:

That is the case (for the prosecution).

THE CASE FOR THE DEFENCE: PLEA IN MITIGATION

4.01.29   There is no set formula for a plea in mitigation. However, the defence may wish to address the court in relation to the following matters (and any mitigating factors arising out of the defendant's background, see **4.01.30**):

(a)   Mitigating factors arising out of the offence.

(b)   Plea of guilty (if appropriate).

(c)   Co-operation with police.

(d)   Contrition and/or voluntary restitution.

(e)   Previous convictions.

(f)   Alternative sentences available to the court.

4.01.30   Mitigating factors arising out of the defendant's:

(a)   Background.

(b)   Employment.

(c)   Financial circumstances.

(d)   Education.

(e)   Medical or psychiatric condition.

(f)   Social enquiry, medical, psychiatric or other reports.

4.01.31   Evidence of Character

The defence may call character evidence to substantiate any of the matters in **4.01.29-30**.

Character evidence is more persuasive to the court than an address by the defence based on his client's instructions.

4.01.32   Documents

The defence may produce documents to substantiate the matters in **4.01.30**, for example:

(a)   Character references.

(b)   Job references.

(c)   Offers of employment.

(d)   Offers of accommodation.

4.01.33   The defence may conclude:

> **Unless I can assist the court further, there are no other matters upon which I would wish to address the court.**

4.01.34   Sentence

The court will then proceed to sentence.

4.01.35   Appeal

After sentence, the defence should see the defendant and advise him of any right of appeal (see **8.02.06**).

The defence should be realistic in his advice.

SECTION 2: BAIL APPLICATIONS

INTRODUCTION

4.02.01   This section is intended for use in any court having the jurisdiction to consider bail.

In some courts (for example, a busy magistrates' court), the decision to withhold bail is announced as follows:

Bail is refused. Schedule 1, paragraph 2(c) applies.

For this reason, the paragraph numbers in the Bail Act, 1976, have been followed where possible.

4.02.02   The court must consider the question of bail at each hearing and may either grant bail or withhold bail without application by either party.

EXCEPTIONS TO RIGHT TO BAIL

4.02.03   Imprisonable Offences

A defendant appearing before the court should be granted bail except where the court is satisfied that there are substantial grounds for believing that if released on bail, the defendant would (under Bail Act 1976, Schedule 1, Part I):

Paragraph 2(a)   Fail to answer bail.

Paragraph 2(b)   Commit an offence whilst on bail.

Paragraph 2(c)   Interfere with witnesses or obstruct the course of justice.

Bail may also be refused in the particular circumstances listed in Bail Act 1976, Schedule 1, Part I:

Paragraph 3   For the defendant's protection.

Paragraph 4	Defendant serving a custodial sentence.
Paragraph 5	Insufficient information on defendant.
Paragraph 6	Defendant arrested for actual or probable breach of bail or conditions in current proceedings.
Paragraph 7	Bail impractical in order to prepare report on defendant.

4.02.04   Non Imprisonable Offences

A defendant appearing before the court should be granted bail except where the court is satisfied that (under Bail Act 1976, Schedule 1, Part II):

Paragraph 2	The defendant has previously failed to answer bail and would fail again.
Paragraph 3	The defendant needs protection.
Paragraph 4	The defendant is serving a custodial sentence.
Paragraph 5	The defendant has been arrested for actual or possible breach of bail or bail conditions in the current proceedings.

4.02.05   Reasons for Finding Exceptions to Right to Bail

When considering a bail application the court should have regard to the following:

(a) The nature and seriousness of the offence (and the probable method of dealing with the defendant).

(b) The strength of the evidence against the defendant.

(c) The likelihood of further offences.

(d) The defendant's previous failure to comply with bail (or conditions).

(e) The defendant's lack of fixed address.

(f) The defendant's character and antecedents.

(g) The defendant's associations and community ties.

(h) The likelihood of the defendant

    (i)   Interfering with witnesses,

    (ii) Interfering with property,

    (iii) Assisting others not yet charged,

    (iv) Being injured by others.

(i) Bail enquiries incomplete due to lack of time.

(j) Any other matter which appears to be relevant.

PRACTICE

4.02.06 The court will grant the application by either side for a remand or adjournment. The court should postpone consideration of a new date if a bail application is to be made, for example:

We grant the application for a remand. What is the position as to bail?

4.02.07 The prosecution may say:

The prosecution object to bail on the grounds that (state exceptions to right to bail).

OR

The prosecution ask for bail with conditions (state exceptions to right to bail).

4.02.08 The prosecution will usually briefly describe the circumstances of the offence and give reasons for the application, for example:

The prosecution believe that the defendant would, if released on bail, fail to answer bail. The defendant has (-) previous convictions for absconding (state dates and circumstances). **It is also believed that the address he gave the police is temporary accommodation.**

See also example in **4.02.14**.

4.02.09 In the crown court the prosecution will usually call an investigating (or other) officer to give the objections (exceptions to right to bail) from the witness box (either on oath or otherwise). The defence may cross-examine the officer.

In the magistrates' court, an officer does not usually attend.

4.02.10   Bail Application

The defence may then address the court, giving reasons why the defendant should be released on bail, and may call evidence relevant to the proceedings.

There is no set formula for a bail application. The defence should consider each objection (exception to right to bail) and should address the court or call evidence to rebut any reason for finding exceptions to the right to bail.

4.02.11   When making a bail application, the defence may offer bail conditions (conditional bail).

The suggested bail conditions must be relevant to the reasons for finding exceptions to the right to bail.

4.02.12   Method

The defence should approach the application as follows:

(a)   Why are the prosecution objecting to bail? (see **4.02.05**).

(b)   How can the objection(s) be answered?

(c)   What bail conditions can be offered? (see **4.02.13**).

4.02.13   Bail Conditions which may be Offered

(a)   The provision of a surety (imprisonable offences only).

(b)   The provision of a security (where the defendant is unlikely to remain in the UK only).

(c)   A condition of residence.

(d)   A condition to remain at a place of residence during certain times (curfew).

(e)   A condition to report to a police station.

(f)   A condition to surrender passport and/or not to apply for any travel documents.

(g) A condition not to go within a certain distance of a named location.

(h) A condition not to contact or approach any named individual (usually a prosecution witness) or co-defendant either directly or indirectly.

(i) A condition to co-operate in the preparation of medical/psychiatric/social enquiry reports.

(j) Any other appropriate condition.

4.02.14   See example in **4.02.08** and Method in **4.02.12**.

(a) The prosecution are objecting to bail under Schedule 1, Part II, paragraph 2(a).

(b) The objection can be answered if the defence is able to offer bail conditions which make it unlikely that the defendant will fail to answer bail.

(c) The bail conditions which may be considered are: **4.02.13: (a) (c) (e) (f)**.

4.02.15   It would not be a sufficient answer to the reasons for finding exceptions to the right to bail in **4.02.08** for the defence to ask the court, for example, to consider a condition that the defendant not go within a certain distance of a named location.

   The imposition of such a condition would not answer the objection that the defendant would fail to answer bail.

4.02.16   When making a bail application, the defence may call evidence of, or address the court on, the defendant's:

(a) Residence (and proof thereof).

(b) Home circumstances.

(c) Financial circumstances (see legal aid application).

(d) Job (or job prospects).

(e) Previous convictions.

(f) Any other special circumstances, for example, medical condition.

4.02.17   The defence may conclude:

> **Unless I can assist the court further, there are no other matters upon which I would wish to address You/Your Honour/the court.**

4.02.18   The court will then announce its decision:

Bail is refused for the following reasons (state reasons). (Omit **4.02.20-23**).

OR

The court is prepared to grant bail with conditions. (Omit **4.02.20-22**).

OR

The court is considering bail with a surety of (state amount) **and/or conditions.**

OR

The court grants unconditional bail. (Omit **4.02.20-22** and **4.02.24-27**).

4.02.19   If bail is refused, where custody time limits apply, the defendant may not be remanded in custody for longer than a specified time.

The prosecution should check whether a custody time limit applies and if necessary apply for an extension of time.

If the defendant is charged with murder or attempted murder, manslaughter, rape or attempted rape the court will give reasons for granting bail:

The court is prepared to grant bail. The reasons for granting bail are (state reasons).

SURETIES

4.02.20   If the court grants bail with a surety, the surety will usually be taken by the court. The defence may make an application for the surety to be taken (later) at a police station, or (in the magistrates' court) by a court clerk.

If the surety is taken at a police station, the defendant will not be released until the court has been informed accordingly.

4.02.21   If the surety is taken by the court:

(a)   The surety will be called by the defence to the witness box, sworn and identified by name and address.

(b) The defence may say:

Mr (name) **do you agree to stand surety for the attendance of the defendant at this court** (or, name of court) **on** (date of adjourned hearing) **in the sum of** (state amount)?

The following matters should be considered:

(i)   The relationship of the surety to the defendant.

(ii) The proximity of his home address.

(iii) Whether the surety regularly associates with the defendant.

(c) The defence may say:

Do you understand what is meant by standing as a surety: that if the defendant fails to attend court you could lose all or part of that sum and if you do not have it, you could go to prison?

How can you raise that sum?

The surety will reply (usually giving evidence of money in a bank account or equity in a house).

The surety is acceptable to the prosecution. Is the court satisfied that Mr (name) **is a suitable surety for the attendance of the defendant at court?**

The defence is advised to provide the full name, address and date of birth of the proposed surety to the prosecution before the bail application in order that the prosecution can check those details and any previous convictions.

(d) The court will then announce its decision.

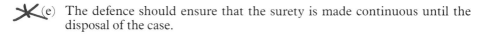
(e) The defence should ensure that the surety is made continuous until the disposal of the case.

4.02.22   If the deposit of a security is required, the defendant will not be released until the deposit (in cash or banker's draft) is with the court.

4.02.23 Pronouncement of Bail

The court should explain bail and/or conditions of bail to the defendant:

You are released on unconditional/conditional bail with the following conditions (state conditions). **If you fail to attend court on** (date) **you will have committed an offence which is punishable by a fine and/or imprisonment. Do you understand?**

Magistrates' Court only:

4.02.24 The defendant will be permitted to make two bail applications at the first two hearings only. Subsequent bail applications cannot be made unless there has been a significant change of circumstance, except on committal to the crown court, although practice varies (see **1.05.32**).

4.02.25 If bail is refused the court should issue a full argument certificate under the Bail Act 1976 (s5(4) & (5)).

The defence may ask for a full argument certificate in order to:

(a) Appeal the decision to the crown court.

(b) Avoid repeated requests by the defendant for further bail applications (see **4.02.24**).

4.02.26 Remand in Absence of Defendant

If the defendant is remanded in custody and the period of remand is longer than the defendant's right (in practice) to weekly production before the court, the court may say to the defence:

Does the defendant object to being remanded in his absence until (date of hearing)?

If it is anticipated that the defendant will be remanded in custody, the defence should have taken instructions on his remand in absence beforehand.

4.02.27 Variation of Bail Conditions

Bail conditions may be varied upon application to the court by either party (usually the defence) where there is a change of circumstance, for example:

This case is listed at the request of (name of party) **for an application to change bail conditions. The application is/is not opposed. The application is for** (state bail conditions sought).

APPEAL OF BAIL

4.02.28   Appeal of Bail From the Magistrates' Court

Where the magistrates' court has refused bail or granted bail with conditions (usually sureties) which the defendant cannot meet, the defence may appeal to the crown court (see **4.02.30-31**) or to a judge in chambers of the High Court (see **4.02.32-33**).

4.02.29   The usual practice is to apply for bail to the crown court and, if unsuccessful, then to apply to a judge in chambers of the High Court.

4.02.30   Crown Court

The application is made on notice on a standard form which must be supported by the full argument certificate to the crown court and to the prosecution at least 24 hours before the hearing.

4.02.31   The appeal is a rehearing of the application before the magistrates' court.

The appeal is heard in chambers (either in court or in the judge's room) and is a more informal hearing than the application to the magistrates' court. The defence should avoid open-court style of advocacy.

The parties are not robed.

4.02.32   Judge in Chambers

The application is made on summons supported by affidavit (giving reasons for the application), copies of which must be served on the prosecution, in practice, 24 hours before the hearing.

4.02.33   The application is heard on affidavit evidence. (see **14.01.25-26**).

The application is heard in chambers (see **4.02.31**). The parties are not robed.

4.02.34   If bail is refused by the crown court or by a judge in chambers, the defence may make a subsequent application to the magistrates' court if there has been a change of circumstance.

APPEAL OF BAIL FROM THE CROWN COURT

4.02.35 An appeal of a bail decision of the crown court is extremely rare. In practice, the defence cannot appeal a bail decision of the crown court before conviction.

The defence may make an application for bail after conviction.

4.02.36 Where the defendant has been convicted, the defence may apply to a single judge of the Court of Appeal for bail on service of the notice and grounds of appeal (see **8.02.10**).

CHAPTER 5

High Court

SECTION 1: INTRODUCTION

5.01.01 Divisions of the High Court

There are three divisions of the High Court. The distribution of the work between the three divisions is complex and should be researched in the common practitioners' handbooks. The following is intended as a brief guide:

Queen's Bench Division	Contract.
	Tort.
	Defamation.
	The Divisional Court of the Queen's Bench Division exercises supervisory jurisdiction over courts of lower jurisdiction and tribunals.
Chancery Division	Trusts.
	Companies.
	Land.
	Administration of Estates.
	Insolvency.
	Intellectual property.
	Contentious probate.
Family Division	Divorce.
	Guardianship.
	Custody of, access to and maintenance of children.
	The Divisional Court of the Family Division will hear appeals from the Domestic Court.

5.01.02 The work of the divisions overlaps and the commencement of proceedings in the wrong division is rarely fatal to the claim.

5.01.03 The essential purpose of the divisions is to enable some specialisation as to subject matter.

As a general rule, the differences in practice between the divisions are mainly procedural. The differences are noted (where appropriate) in the following sections.

5.01.04 The High Court sits at the Royal Courts of Justice (RCJ) in London and at district registries in other major towns in England and Wales.

5.01.05   Each division operates on two levels:

Masters and registrars.

Judges.

MASTERS AND REGISTRARS

5.01.06   In practice, a master, registrar or district registrar exercises all such powers as may be exercised by a judge in chambers, subject to certain specified exceptions.

5.01.07   Mode of Address

Master	Master (both sexes).
Registrar	Sir/Madam.

5.01.08   Right of Audience

Barristers.

Solicitors

Experienced solicitors' clerks.

Litigants in person.

5.01.09   Dress

Barristers and solicitors are not robed.

All parties should be respectably dressed.

5.01.10   Seating

The parties usually stand before a QBD Master for all hearings in chambers.

At the invitation of the master, the parties may be seated on private room appointments (see **5.02.24**). The parties usually sit before a chancery master.

In private room appointments, solicitors (or their clerks) attending counsel should sit along side them in order to:

(a) Take a note.

(b) Produce any necessary papers.

(c) Give instructions.

5.01.11 Conduct

If a person is addressing the master or registrar, see **5.01.10**.

The hearing is usually less formal than in open court. The parties are encouraged to be brief and not to exceed the duration of the appointment.

The advocate who prepares his case in advance, who has his papers in order and available and presents his case clearly will build up for himself and his future clients a fund of goodwill with the masters who, next time round, will give him credit and assistance.

5.01.12 Admission of the Public

Members of the public are almost always excluded except when the hearing is in open court, for example, for assessment of damages, trials of interpleaders and trials by consent of the parties.

JUDGES

5.01.13 A judge will hear the trial of the action and some interlocutory applications.

5.01.14 Mode of Address

Description of judge	Status of judge
The Honourable, Mr Justice (name)	High Court judge
His Honour Judge (name)	Circuit judge sitting as a High Court judge or official referee
Mr Recorder (name)	Recorder sitting as a deputy High Court judge

In practice, all Judges sitting in the High Court are referred to as My Lord/Lady (except official referees who are referred to as Your Honour).

5.01.15   Right of Audience

Barristers.

Solicitors (in some uncontested applications).

Litigants in person.

5.01.16   Dress

Open court	Barristers and solicitors are robed.
In chambers	All parties should be respectably dressed.

5.01.17   Seating

The advocates will sit in the rows and/or benches facing the judge.

Queen's Counsel sit 'within the bar of the court' (which is a small gate in most courts at the RCJ), junior counsel sit outside it. Solicitors attending Queen's Counsel sit at a table in front of the Queen's Counsel, but sit behind junior counsel when only a junior is instructed.

The plaintiff will usually sit in the rows and/or seats on the left hand side of the court facing the bench.

5.01.18   Conduct

In open court and in chambers (in the court room), any person addressing the judge should do so standing.

In chambers (in the judge's room), any person addressing the judge will usually do so seated.

5.01.19   Admission of the Public

When the judge is sitting in open court, members of the public are usually admitted.

5.01.20 When the judge is sitting in chambers (in the court room), members of the public are usually excluded. If a party wishes to have other persons in court with him, for example, family or friends, that party should seek the leave of the judge or registrar.

5.01.21 When the judge is sitting in chambers (in the judge's room), members of the public are almost always excluded.

GENERAL PRACTICE

5.01.22 Witnesses

If the judge is sitting in open court, witnesses will usually be present in court throughout the proceedings and/or the day, or part of the day, on which the witness gives evidence.

If the judge is sitting in chambers (in the judge's room), witnesses will very rarely be present in the room.

If the judge is sitting in chambers (in the court room), practice varies although witnesses will not usually be present in the court room.

A witness should always take the oath standing. The solicitor should always check beforehand in what manner the witness wishes to be sworn (and inform the usher accordingly).

5.01.23 Standard of Proof

The civil standard of proof, 'on the balance of probabilities' applies (except in committal proceedings, see also **6.08.01**).

5.01.24 Relationship to Practice in the County Court

As a general rule a plaintiff in an action in contract or tort, will be able to choose whether to bring proceedings in the High Court or the county court if the value of the claim is below the current financial limit(s).

An action in the High Court is likely to be more expensive than an action in the county court.

5.01.25 The High Court is more appropriate where complex questions of law are involved.

5.01.26   The county court is more appropriate where the plaintiff requires a speedy resolution of the proceedings.

However, many London and some provincial solicitors use the High Court for claims where the county court limits would otherwise apply due to:

(a)   The greater experience of masters in resolving interlocutory applications.

(b)   The more effective methods of execution available.

(c)   The ease of process, for example, a party can issue and serve a writ the same day out of the central office, whereas in the county court they must rely on the court staff to do so (see **5.01.27**).

5.01.27   Service of Proceedings

As a general rule, proceedings in the High Court are served by one party on the other and are not served by the court.

SECTION 2:
INTERLOCUTORY APPLICATIONS
(METHOD)

PART 1: INTRODUCTION

5.02.01   An interlocutory application is any application made between the issue of proceedings and the final determination of the action, or part of the action, at trial.

5.02.02   Types of Interlocutory Applications

Interlocutory applications may be made *ex parte* or by summons or motion on notice.

5.02.03 Ex Parte Applications

An *ex parte* application is made by a party without giving notice to the other party or parties to the action.

The following applications are usually made *ex parte:*

(a) An application of an administrative nature which does not directly affect the existing parties, for example, leave to issue a third party notice, service of writ of possession of vacant premises.

(b) An application in relation to any matter before the service of the originating process, for example, service out of jurisdiction.

(c) An urgent application where proper notice is not possible, for example, an urgent injunction application, *habeus corpus.*

(d) An application where proper notice is not desirable, for example, for a Mareva or Anton Piller order.

(e) Certain applications to enforce judgments, for example, garnishee orders nisi or charging orders nisi.

5.02.04 Applications by Summons or Motion on Notice

An application by summons or motion is made by a party on notice to the other party or parties to an action.

The following applications are usually made on notice:

(a) Interlocutory injunctions.

(b) Summary judgment (Order 14).

(c) Directions.

5.02.05 Affidavit

An interlocutory application is almost always made on affidavit.

The affidavit may be made by the applicant or any authorised person, for example, the solicitor having the day to day conduct of the action.

The affidavit should contain:

(a) The name, address and status of the deponent.

(b) The purpose of the affidavit, for example:

I make this affidavit in support of my/the plaintiff's/the defendant's application for (state relief sought).

(c) The matters upon which the applicant relies in support of the application.

As a general rule the affidavit should contain only matters which are within the deponent's own knowledge and belief, although an affidavit may also contain hearsay.

Where information is derived from hearsay (usually apart from information derived from a party's own solicitor) its source should be stated, for example:

I am informed by (name) **and verily believe that:**

The grounds and sources of any belief should be stated.

5.02.06   A party should:

(a) Note, in the top right hand corner of the first page of the affidavit, the name of the party, the name of the deponent, the number of the affidavit and the date, for example:

Pl. A.Smith. 2nd. 4.9.89.

(b) Initial all alterations.

(c) State the full address at which the affidavit was sworn.

(d) Paginate exhibits containing correspondence.

A party should not

(e) Bind exhibits into the body of the affidavit.

(f) Place the jurat on a separate page to the body of the affidavit.

5.02.07   Affidavit in Reply

In an application by summons or motion on notice, where the party responding to the application wishes to rely on an affidavit in reply, the affidavit should be served a reasonable time before the hearing.

Where the affidavit is served either immediately before or at the hearing, and the applicant has no opportunity to answer it, the applicant may apply for an adjournment with costs against the other party.

PART 2: QUEEN'S BENCH DIVISION

5.02.08   Introduction

In the Queen's Bench Division, all interlocutory applications are heard by the master, although any application may be heard by a judge in chambers if the leave of a master has first been obtained.

5.02.09   As a general rule, applications of an administrative nature are made to the master.

Certain applications, such as for Mareva or Anton Piller relief have to be made to the judge as they carry a penalty involving the liberty of the individual.

5.02.10   Right of Audience

Barristers although:

(a) A certificate for counsel is unlikely to be granted in ex parte applications and applications by summons on notice in the solicitors' (10.30, 11.00 and 11.30) list.

(b) A hearing may be adjourned with costs if a party instructs counsel without notifying the other party or parties in advance.

Solicitors.

Experienced solicitors' clerks.

Litigants in person.

5.02.11   Dress

Barristers and solicitors are not robed.

All parties should be respectably dressed.

5.02.12   Mode of Address

Master   Master (both sexes).

Judge   My Lord/My Lady.

5.02.13   Conduct

On an *ex parte* application or a short application in solicitors' or counsel's list the master will be seated. The parties will remain standing to address him.

Practice on an interlocutory application varies greatly. As a general rule, the application will be dealt with briefly. The advocate should take care to draw to the attention of the master the most important points of the application.

The party making the application should always ensure that his opponent has an equal share of the time allotted for the hearing.

MASTERS

EX PARTE APPLICATIONS

5.02.14   Preparation

An *ex parte* application is usually made by lodging the affidavit in support of the application with the Masters' Secretary's Department.

An *ex parte* application (usually in an urgent matter) can also be made to the practice master of the day at the RCJ. The practice master is listed in the Cause List and a board appears on his door.

5.02.15   Some matters can be dealt with by post but, as this takes longer, a party will usually attend in person.

PRACTICE

5.02.16   The party should attend at the master's room.

If there are any other persons waiting, the party should join the queue. If there are no other persons waiting, the party should knock on the door and enter the room. If the master is busy the party should leave the room and wait.

5.02.17 If the master is ready, the party should go to the master's desk. The party may then say

Master, this is my application for (state nature of application).

5.02.18 The party should hand to the master:

(a) The original of the writ and any appropriate pleading (or draft pleading), if required by the master. (The party should always have these documents ready).

(b) Any affidavit in support of the application (if not already filed). If filed at an earlier hearing, the party must bespeak (apply for) the affidavit from the registry.

(c) The draft order.

5.02.19 The party may then refer the master to any relevant pleading (or draft pleading) and the affidavit (in such detail as required).

The master may indicate that he wishes to read the documents. He may then ask some questions to clarify matters.

The master will hear either party before making the order, if present.

5.02.20 The Order

The master will endorse a minute of his order on the summons, affidavit or draft order.

The master's minute of order will be written in shorthand which the solicitor will have to interpret when he draws the full order, for example:

J	Judgment
O2	Unconditional leave to defend
O3/O4	Conditional leave to defend
Pl	Plaintiff
Df	Defendant
Pl c	Plaintiff's costs
S/c	Scale costs
ciae	Costs in any event

cic	Costs in cause
CON/A	Charging order nisi/absolute
GON/A	Garnishee order nisi/absolute
on a/s	On affidavit of service
TTRIA	Time to run in August

5.02.21 Appeal

Appeal from the refusal of a master to make an order lies to a judge in chambers.

The notice of appeal must be issued usually within five days of the order appealed against.

APPLICATIONS BY SUMMONS ON NOTICE

5.02.22 An application by summons on notice is made by issuing the summons out of the Masters' Secretary's Department. The clerk will allocate an 'assigned Master' and all subsequent summonses must be issued before the same master unless he releases it.

The party should always use the original summons and not a copy.

5.02.23 Notice Required

The length of the notice required varies according to the nature of the application.

An application will usually require at least three clear working days' notice. The following are common examples:

Summary judgment (Order 14)   10 days

Summons for directions   14 days

5.02.24 Types of Hearing

There are three types of hearing:

Solicitors' List (for applications not exceeding 10 minutes)

Summonses in the QBD are usually listed in the solicitors' list (usually at 10.30 11.00 and 11.30). See **5.02.10(a)**.

Counsel's List (for applications not exceeding 20 minutes)

If a party taking out a summons intends to instruct counsel at the hearing, this should be stated on the summons. The summons will be listed in counsel's list (usually at 12.00).

Private Room Appointments

If it is anticipated that the hearing will take longer than 20 minutes, the parties should apply to the master's secretary, on a standard form, for the application to be taken out of the list and heard as a private room appointment.

PRACTICE IN CHAMBERS

5.02.25   Solicitors' or Counsel's List

The parties should check in with the usher for the appropriate room. The party whose summons it is should give the original summons to the usher.

If the case is listed in the solicitors' list, the usher will allow all the parties in a particular list to go and sit at the back of the room. The parties should not talk.

If the case is listed in counsel's list the parties will wait outside the master's room until the case is called.

5.02.26   When the master calls the case on, the parties should stand at the master's desk. The party making the application should hand to the master:

(a)   Any pleadings (if appropriate).

(b)   The affidavit(s).

The practice in **5.02.29-37** is then followed except that the parties should always remember to be brief.

When the master has made his order, he will keep the affidavits but will hand back the summons on which he will have written his minute of order.

PRACTICE IN A MASTER'S PRIVATE ROOM

5.02.27   It is prudent for the parties to attend the masters' corridor early as much can be negotiated before going before the master.

5.02.28 The parties enter the room and sit down. The party making the application should then hand to the master:

(a) The summons.

(b) Any affidavit in support of the application (if not already filed) (see **5.02.18**).

The party should have available any exhibits and copy correspondence (if appropriate) for the master.

5.02.29 The party making the application will usually introduce the parties:

Master, I appear on behalf of (name of party). **My name is** (name). **My** (learned) **friend, Mr** (name), **appears on behalf of** (name of party).

The party making the application should give the master a note of the names of counsel.

This is my application for (state nature of application).

This is an agreed application/The application is opposed.

5.02.30 The party making the application will then:

(a) Outline the nature of the application.

(b) Explain the facts giving rise to the application.

(c) Direct the master to any relevant pleading (or draft pleading) and/or document.

(d) Direct the master to any affidavit or part thereof.

(e) Direct the master to any relevant law. (A list of authorities should be provided to the Masters' Messengers room before 10.00 on the day of the hearing).

(f) State the power of the master to give the order (if appropriate).

5.02.31 Agreed Application

On an agreed application, the party making the application may omit **5.02.30(a)-(f)**.

The party may briefly outline the application (with reference to the affidavit) and conclude by asking for the order by consent.

5.02.32 Opposed Application

On an opposed application, the party should address the master on any of 5.02.30(a)-(f) (with reference to the affidavit) in such detail as required.

5.02.33 The Case for the Party Opposing the Application

The party opposing the application may then present his case in the same way (see **05.02.30 and 32**).

If the party is relying on an affidavit in reply, see **5.02.07**.

5.02.34 The party opposing the application may:

(a) Outline the reasons for opposing the application.

(b) Direct the master to any relevant pleading (or draft pleading) and/or document.

  In an application for summary judgment the defendant may have a draft defence.

(c) Direct the master to any affidavit or any part thereof.

(d) Direct the master to any relevant law.

5.02.35 The master may invite either party to address him for a second time on the merits of the application although practice varies.

5.02.36 Order

The master may grant or refuse the application and/or give further directions (see **5.04: Directions**).

The master will endorse a minute of his order on the summons (see **5.02.20**).

Counsel should always remember to ask for a Certificate for Counsel (see **7.01.21-26**).

5.02.37 Appeal

Appeal from the refusal of a master to make an order lies to a judge in chambers.

The notice of appeal must be issued usually within five days of the order appealed against.

JUDGE IN CHAMBERS

EX PARTE APPLICATIONS

5.02.38 Documents

A party making an *ex parte* application to a judge in chambers should have the following documents:

(a) Writ.

(b) Any pleading (or draft pleading).

(c) Affidavit in support (see **5.02.05-06**).

(d) Draft minute of order.

The documents should be in proper form, although in urgent cases an unsworn affidavit may be accepted.

5.02.39 Listing an *Ex Parte* Application

An *ex parte* application may be listed for hearing before a judge in chambers at 10.00 on any weekday by a party delivering the relevant documents to the chief clerk to the judge in chambers by 3.00 on the preceding day.

5.02.40 Urgent Applications

An appointment in an application of exceptional urgency may be made by telephoning the clerk to the judge in chambers.

An application may also be made by a party attending with the relevant documents at Room 98, RCJ, (off the waiting area known as the Bear Garden).

The party should attend before 9.50 for an appointment in the judge in chambers' 10.00 list, and before 1.50 for an appointment in the 2.00 list.

The party should wait outside Room 98. The usher will come out and ask if there are any *ex parte* applications. The usher will ask the party to complete a form and to hand to him the completed form and any documentation.

PRACTICE

5.02.41   See **05.02.18-20**. The usher will take the parties to the judge.

5.02.42   Appeal

Appeal is (usually with leave) to the Court of Appeal (see **8.01.04**).

APPLICATIONS BY SUMMONS (ON NOTICE)

5.02.43   An application by summons on notice is made by issuing the summons out of the Central Office.

A fixed date may be given or the application may be listed to go into the warned list at a future date.

A date will usually be given for a Room 98 appointment which can either be used or vacated by agreement between the parties.

5.02.44   Documents

A party making an application by summons on notice should prepare a bundle containing the following documents:

(a)   The notice of application or appeal (see **5.02.37**).

(b)   The pleadings (as appropriate).

(c)   The originals of any affidavits which, if filed at an earlier hearing should be bespoken from the registry (see **5.02.18(b)**), (together with any exhibits on which the party is intending to rely).

(d)   Any relevant order made in the action.

5.02.45   The Bundle

The bundle should be agreed and copies made available to the other party or parties to the application.

On a fixed date appointment the bundle should be filed at least five days before the hearing.

In any other application, the bundle should be filed at least 48 hours after the case has entered the warned list or notification has been given of the date of the hearing.

PRACTICE

5.02.46   See **05.02.27-36**.

5.02.47   Appeal

Appeal is (usually with leave) to the Court of Appeal, see **8.01.04**.

PART 3: CHANCERY DIVISION

INTRODUCTION

5.02.48   In the Chancery Division, interlocutory applications are usually heard by the master in chambers.

Most of the matters dealt with by a judge in chambers in the other divisions are dealt with in court on motion.

5.02.49   Apart from some statutory exceptions (and any application which is referred to the judge by the master), an interlocutory application is usually only made to a judge where the order sought is for:

(a)   A Mareva injunction.

(b)   An Anton Piller order.

(c) An injunction restraining a threatened wrong or to preserve the *status quo* until trial.

(d) A declaration of right.

MASTER

5.02.50 Right of Audience, Dress, Mode of Address, Conduct

See **5.02.10-13**.

EX PARTE APPLICATIONS

5.02.51 The Chancery Master

Chancery masters are available at 2.15 each day to hear short *ex parte* applications without appointment.

An *ex parte* application is usually made on affidavit without a summons by attending before the master. The court file should be bespoken (see **5.02.18(b)** and **55**) before noon on the day of the application.

Certain applications may be made simply by leaving the affidavit with the master's clerk, for example:

(a) Application for leave to serve process outside the jurisdiction.

(b) Application for substituted service.

(c) Application for charging or garnishee order.

PRACTICE

5.02.52 See **5.02.16-20**.

5.02.53 Appeal

See **5.02.37**.

APPLICATIONS BY SUMMONS (ON NOTICE)

5.02.54 Preparation

The summons is issued out of Chancery Chambers in London (or out of the District Registry).

The length of notice required varies according to the nature of the application (see **5.02.23**).

The summons will bear a date and time. If the summons gives a time estimate for the application which the respondent considers is unrealistic, an application should be made for another appointment.

PRACTICE

5.02.55 See **5.02.27-36**.
The court file will be before the master at the hearing and should contain all filed documents. The party should have copies of the documents available in case documents lodged recently for filing have not actually been placed upon the court file.

5.02.56 Appeal

See **5.02.37**.

JUDGE

5.02.57 **Right of Audience**

Barristers.

Litigants in person.

5.02.58 **Dress**

Barristers are robed.

Litigants in person should be respectably dressed.

5.02.59 Mode of Address

Judge: My Lord/My Lady.

5.02.60 Conduct

The hearing is in open court. A party addressing the court should do so standing. The party should be brief and to the point.

5.02.61 Introduction

As a general rule, interlocutory applications to a judge of the Chancery Division are made by motion.

A court is set aside each day for the hearing of motions (although other judges may assist).

Ex parte applications on motion may be heard at any time on application to the judge's clerk. Applications on motion on notice are listed before the judge. Both are heard in open court in the absence of any special reason to the contrary (for example, Anton Piller orders).

5.02.62 The Court

The court sits at 10.30 each morning. The clerk will usually be present in court before 10.30 and should be given any additional documents or affidavits.

A party should inform the clerk before the hearing starts if he has an urgent application (if this has not been done beforehand).

PRACTICE

5.02.63 It is up to the advocate to make sure he is in court at the right time. The ushers do not usually call the parties into court.

If a party is not ready, a motion is likely to be struck out.

EX PARTE MOTIONS AND APPLICATIONS BY MOTION ON NOTICE

5.02.64   The usual practice is to distinguish between effective and ineffective motions.

An effective motion is one which is either *ex parte* (so that the evidence has to be read) or inter partes and opposed.

5.02.65   The list is called first time round and a party is expected to tell the judge simply whether the case is effective or ineffective, and, if effective, to give a time estimate.

The party making the application may say:

This is my application for (state nature of application, see **5.02.49**).

The (name of party) **is represented by** (name).

The application is ineffective.

OR

The application is effective.

I would say (state time estimate, for example, half an hour to an hour).

5.02.66   Ineffective Applications

The judge will usually take all ineffective applications before dealing with the effectives unless an application is exceptionally urgent.

The judge may say:

I will take all ineffective matters first.

The party making the application may say:

We are agreed that the case is ineffective (state reason). **And would therefore ask that the case be stood out for** (-) **days.**

5.02.67   Effective Applications

The court will not entertain an opposed application on a motion day if it is likely to last for more than two hours. When the evidence is complete, the party making the application may say:

Would you stand over the motion to come on as a motion by order on a day to be fixed (not before the (-) day of (-)) with a time estimate of (state time estimate).

This may be done before the evidence is complete when the words **not before the** (-) **day of** (-) will be included in order to enable it to be completed.

Directions may be given at this stage (see **5.04**).

5.02.68   Applications in Camera

It is usual on an application for an Anton Piller order, and sometimes on a Mareva, to ask the court to sit *in camera*.

The party making the application may say:

This is an application for (state nature of application). **If the public are admitted, irreparable damage may be caused. I therefore ask that the court sit** *in camera*.

5.02.69   Agreements

On an *ex parte* application or on an application which is *inter partes* and the parties are agreed on the order, the parties are advised to provide the judge with a draft of the order he is being asked to make (which may be signed by the parties). This will save time.

The agreement is then handed to the judge.

The parties should take care to use correct English usage as Chancery judges often pick up poor grammar and/or syntax.

5.02.70   Hearing a Motion

A motion is heard on affidavit evidence. It is rare that the court will hear oral evidence.

The party moving opens the case

The practice in **5.02.29-36** is then followed save that the parties stand to address the court.

5.02.71 Appeal

See **5.02.42**.

PART 4: FAMILY DIVISION

5.02.72 Introduction

The Family Division deals primarily with matters relating to:

(a) Divorce or judicial separation (see **5.08.01-19**).

(b) Applications for ancillary relief (see **5.08.20-55**).

(c) Applications for custody of and access to children (see **5.08.56-76**).

5.02.73 In London most family matters are dealt with in the Divorce Registry which has the equivalent status to the county court. Outside London, most matters are dealt with by the county court.

Almost all applications in the Family Division are in chambers (see **5.08.09**).

THE REGISTRAR

5.02.74 In the Family Division the business undertaken by a master in the QBD and Chancery Division is undertaken by the registrar.

5.02.75 Right of Audience, Dress, Mode of Address

See **5.02.10** and **5.08.16-19**.

5.02.76 Conduct

A registrar will usually adopt a less formal and more flexible approach than a master of the QBD because of the nature of the business of the Family Division.

EX PARTE APPLICATIONS

5.02.77 An *ex parte* application to the registrar may be made, for example, to restrain a party from disposing of, or dealing with, matrimonial assets; or, to dispense with service of a petition on a respondent.

5.02.78 Preparation

An *ex parte* application may be made by attending before the registrar of the day at the RCJ (Divorce Registry) or at a county court having family jurisdiction.

It is also usually possible to arrange an appointment at short notice by telephone.

5.02.79 Documentation

The applicant should have:

(a) An affidavit (or draft affidavit) in support of the application.

And, where time permits:

(b) The Notice of Application.

(c) A draft order for signing.

PRACTICE

5.02.80 See **5.02.16-20**, except the order is drawn up by the court.

5.02.81 Appeal

See **5.02.21**.

APPLICATIONS ON NOTICE

5.02.82 The following applications are on notice:

(a) Applications for ancillary (financial) relief (see **5.08.20-55**).

(b) Applications for custody of and access to children (see **5.08.56-76**).

(c)   Directions (see **5.08.29-30** and **69-72**).

5.02.83   Appeal

See **5.02.37**.

JUDGE IN CHAMBERS

EX PARTE APPLICATIONS

5.02.84   The most common *ex parte* applications relate to the custody of children and the personal safety of any party or any children.

5.02.85   Preparation

An *ex parte* application may be made by attending before a judge at the RCJ with the jurisdiction to hear both High Court and county court matters.

It is also possible to arrange an appointment at short notice by telephone to ascertain when a judge will be available.

5.02.86   Documents

The applicant should have:

(a)   An affidavit (or draft affidavit) in support of the application.

And, where time permits:

(b)   The petition.

(c)   The summons (or draft) summons.

(d)   A draft note of order.

Where proceedings have not been commenced, the party should be ready and willing to undertake to commence proceedings (or to swear and/or file any documents required).

PRACTICE

5.02.87 See **5.02.18-20**.

If the hearing is in the court room, the parties will stand to address the judge.

APPLICATIONS BY SUMMONS (ON NOTICE)

5.02.88 See **5.08.16-76**.

5.02.89 Appeal

Appeal is, usually with leave, to the Court of Appeal within 28 days (see **8.01.04** and **8.01.08**).

SECTION 3: SUMMARY JUDGMENT (ORDER 14)

INTRODUCTION

5.03.01 Proceedings may be commenced by:

(a) Writ.

(b) Originating summons.

(c) Originating motion.

(d) Petition.

5.03.02 In an action commenced by writ, the defendant will be served with a form of Acknowledgement of Service.

5.03.03 The defendant must return the Acknowledgement of Service within 14 days to the court office where the writ was issued.

5.03.04 If the defendant fails to return the Acknowledgement of Service or returns the Acknowledgement of Service but fails to serve a defence, the plaintiff may apply for judgment to be given against the defendant in default.

5.03.05 Judgment in Default

The plaintiff should apply on the appropriate form to the Court office out of which the writ was issued.

In some cases, the plaintiff must apply by summons before a master/registrar for leave. The law on this subject is complex and should be researched in the common practitioners' handbooks.

5.03.06 If the defendant has not returned the Acknowledgement of Service, the plaintiff must prove service of the writ (usually by affidavit).

5.03.07 If the defendant has returned the Acknowledgement of Service but has failed to serve a defence, the plaintiff may apply, without leave, for judgment in default.

5.03.08 Setting Aside a Judgment in Default

The defendant should issue an *inter partes* summons returnable before a master/registrar supported by affidavit.

If the judgment has been entered irregularly (for example, it has been entered too soon or where the writ was never received by the defendant), the judgment will be set aside, as of right.

Costs will usually be the defendant's in any event (see **7.01.10-11**).

5.03.09 If the judgment has been entered regularly, the defendant must show that there is a triable issue and explain any failure to return the Acknowledgement of Service or serve a defence.

Costs will usually be the plaintiff's in any event (see **7.01.10-11**).

5.03.10 Judgment entered in default may be set aside on such terms as the court thinks fit.

5.03.11 Notice of Intention to Defend

If the defendant gives notice that he intends to defend and the plaintiff considers there is no real defence to the claim, the plaintiff may apply for summary judgment

(Order 14 proceedings).

5.03.12   A defendant may apply for summary judgment where there is no real defence to his counter claim.

5.03.13   Summary judgment is not available in any case which includes a claim by the plaintiff for libel, slander, malicious prosecution, false imprisonment or a claim based on an allegation of fraud or admiralty actions *in rem*.

5.03.14   The purpose of making an application for summary judgment is to enable the plaintiff to obtain the relief he claims without a full trial of the action in a case where the defendant has no real defence. The plaintiff will therefore avoid the necessary procedural steps before the full trial and attendant costs.

5.03.15   Making the Application

The plaintiff should issue an *inter partes* summons for summary judgment on the claim returnable before the master or district registrar in the High Court or the registrar in the county court.

5.03.16   The summons must be supported by an affidavit which should:

(a) Verify the facts set out in the Statement of Claim and give such additional information (as appropriate).

(b) State that the plaintiff believes there is no real defence to the claim (or part of it).

5.03.17   The summons and affidavit in support must be served by the plaintiff on the defendant at least 10 days (High Court) or seven days (county court) before the date fixed for the hearing.

If the plaintiff serves an affidavit in support without making reference to the details of the claim, he should serve his affidavit in sufficient time to enable

(a) The defendant to respond, and

(b) The plaintiff to serve an affidavit in reply.

If a party fails to give sufficient time to the other party to prepare an affidavit, the master will often allow an adjournment (with costs against that party).

5.03.18   In a case where the plaintiff believes that the defendant will not attend the hearing, the plaintiff should prepare an affidavit of service.

5.03.19   Opposing the Application

The application can be made either before service of the defence or after service of the defence where no real defence is disclosed.

In either case the defendant must show that there is a triable issue.

5.03.20   The defendant should serve an affidavit and/or proposed pleading on the plaintiff not less than three days (High Court) before the date fixed for the hearing.

There is no time limit in the county court. The defendant should serve an affidavit and/or proposed pleading on the plaintiff a reasonable time before the date fixed for the hearing. If he fails to do so there is usually an order for costs thrown away.

5.03.21   If it is alleged that there is a sufficient defence disclosed on the pleadings, the affidavit should detail all matters that show there is a triable issue.

5.03.22   If the application is made on the basis that the defence is insufficient, the defence may prepare a full(er) defence setting out the issues more clearly. It is prudent to support this by affidavit but not always essential.

PRACTICE

5.03.23   The practice is similar to the practice on an interlocutory application.

THE PLAINTIFF'S CASE

5.03.24   The plaintiff (or the party making the application) will usually introduce the parties to the master/registrar.

5.03.25   The plaintiff may then say:

This is an application for summary judgment (pursuant to Order 14). The writ and the statement of claim have been served and a defence has been filed.

(A defence will often not have been filed as service of the Order 14 summons extends time for service of the defence till after the hearing).

The Writ alleges (state nature of claim).

The defence filed alleges (state nature of defence).

The plaintiff's affidavit dated (date) **sworn by** (name) **states that he verily believes that there is no** (real) **defence to the claim.**
(State content of affidavit and/or read any relevant paragraph).

5.03.26   The plaintiff may then direct the master/registrar to:

(a) Any other documents.

(b) Any relevant law.

5.03.27   The plaintiff may then say:

In the circumstances, it is the plaintiff's case that there is no real defence or triable issue.

THE DEFENDANT'S CASE

5.03.28   If the defendant has served an affidavit in reply, the defendant will usually refer the master/registrar to the affidavit and defence (if served) in the same way as the plaintiff.

5.03.29   The defendant has to show only that there is a triable issue and should not enter into a lengthy argument on the merits of the case.

After having referred the master/registrar to the affidavit and defence (if served) the defendant may say:

It can be seen that there is a clear dispute of fact which, should be resolved by the hearing of evidence at trial.

SUBMISSIONS

5.03.30   The parties may then be invited by the master/registrar to address him on the merits of the application.

The order of submissions varies. The master/registrar may indicate to either party that he does not require that party to address him (see **5.06.85**).

5.03.31   In submissions, a party will usually:

(a) Draw the court's attention to any relevant law in that party's favour; and/or

(b) Distinguish any relevant law that is not in that party's favour;

(c) Sum up the basic parts of his case on the facts.

5.03.32 A Triable Issue

Different masters/registrars take different views as to the level of dispute needed to show a triable issue.

As a general rule, if the defendant can show a real dispute as to the facts relevant to liability, a trial will be ordered (in particular, if there is an allegation of misrepresentation or misbehaviour).

5.03.33 The best test of whether any defence is genuine is to see if contemporary documents/conversations/complaints support it.

Where a defence is raised for the first time in the defendant's affidavit, and there was an opportunity to raise it earlier but it was not so raised, the master is far less likely to accept it.

The master will then either give judgment or order the payment of the sum claimed into court (or part of it) as a condition of giving leave to defend.

5.03.34 The subject is complex and should be researched in the common practitioners' handbooks.

5.03.35 Powers of the Court

The most common orders (see **5.02.20**) are:

(a) Judgment for the whole or part of the plaintiff's claim (if the plaintiff's claim is for an unliquidated sum, with damages to be assessed).

(b) Order with (unconditional) leave to defend (O2).

(c) Order with (conditional) leave to defend on Payment into court of part or all of the claim (O3/4).

Other orders may be made by the master/registrar. These should be researched in the common practitioners' handbooks.

5.03.36 Costs

The usual orders for costs are:

     · **5.03.35(a):**   Plaintiff's costs or costs to be taxed.

5.03.35(b) or (c):   Costs in cause, if payment is made or unconditional leave to defend is given.

The master/registrar may always dismiss an application for summary judgment with defence costs if it was obvious that there was a defence.

5.03.37 Interest

A party should always work out the interest (and, if possible, agree it with the other side) before the hearing.

5.03.38 Appeal

Either party may appeal to a judge in chambers against the order made by the master/registrar.

The time limit for the service of the notice of appeal is five days.

SECTION 4: DIRECTIONS

INTRODUCTION

5.04.01   Directions may be given at any stage after the commencement of proceedings for the purpose of permitting or compelling any party to carry out the necessary procedural steps in an action, for example: serve a third party notice, file and serve lists of documents, serve experts reports, answer a request for further and better particulars, etc. (see **5.04.09**).

5.04.02   Directions may be given at an interlocutory hearing or on the hearing of a Summons for Directions.

5.04.03   A Summons for Directions is usually issued by the plaintiff after the close of pleadings.

The parties should give general consideration to the pleadings and the evidence required at the trial (and to any particular matter listed in **5.04.09**).

5.04.04   In the county court, the notice to the parties of the date fixed for the Pre-Trial Review (PTR) states that the hearing will be informal and in private. Its purpose is to:

(a)   Make sure that all the parties and the court understand what the case is about.

(b)   See if there is any possibility of settling the dispute and, if not, decide how it is going to be heard and how long the hearing will last.

(c)   Decide what documents or other evidence is needed from both sides.

5.04.05   Practice

In the High Court, the hearing of a Summons for Directions will be before the master or registrar.

In the county court, the hearing of a Pre-Trial Review will be before the registrar.

5.04.06   Mode of Address

High Court:

Master:	Master (both sexes).
Registrar:	Sir/Madam.

County court:

Registrar:	Sir/Madam.

5.04.07   Dress

Advocates are not robed. Advocates (and any party attending) should be respectably dressed.

5.04.08   Conduct

In the High Court, the hearing is in chambers. All parties stand.

In the county court, the hearing is usually in the registrar's room (or it may be in the court room). The parties are usually seated.

If it is not clear from the arrangement of the seats, a party should stand until invited to sit.

5.04.09   Directions

The parties should give consideration to the directions listed on the standard High Court form for a Summons for Directions:

(a) Consolidation of the action with others.

(b) Trial by an official referee (registrar in the county court, by arbitration).

(c) Transfer of the proceedings to the High Court or to the county court.

(d) Amendments to pleading(s).

(e) Applications for further and better particulars of any pleading(s).

(f) Discovery and inspection of documents.

(g) Exchange of experts' reports (see **5.06.59**).

(h) Exchange of witnesses' proofs (see **5.06.11**).

(i) Interrogatories.

(j) Evidence to be taken by deposition/examiner or on commission.

(k) Place of trial.

(l) Mode of trial (judge alone or judge and jury) (see **5.06.34**).

(m) Category of case (in descending order of importance): A, B or C (usually 'B').

(n) Estimate of length of trial.

(o) Date for setting down.

PRACTICE

5.04.10   Obtaining the Order

In most cases directions are agreed before the hearing and the plaintiff only will attend the hearing to obtain the order by consent.

The pleadings must be made available for the master to read and should be lodged when the summons is issued.

If directions are not agreed before the hearing, the parties should attempt to agree the order outside court.

5.04.11   After the case has been called, the plaintiff will usually introduce the application to the master/registrar as follows:

> **Master/Sir, this is the hearing of the Summons for Directions/Pre-Trial Review of this case. This case is** (describe nature of case). **We are agreed as to most directions but** (name of party) **does not agree** (state nature of application).

The parties may then argue the application.

5.04.12   If the order is agreed, the party (usually the plaintiff) may say:

> **Master/Sir, we are agreed as to directions in this case.**
>
> **They are contained in a letter dated** (date)/ **We have put the agreed directions in writing.**
>
> **We would ask you to make a consent order.**

The party may (if the directions are not in writing) dictate the directions to the master/registrar.

5.04.13   If the parties cannot agree, the application may be argued on the pleadings, for example:

> **A request for further and better particulars of the defence dated** (dated) **was served on the defendant on** (date). **To date, no reply has been given.**

A copy of the request should be handed to the court.

> **The following matters are requested** (state the matters requested in such detail as required).
>
> **It is the plaintiff's contention that he is entitled to the information requested** (state reasons).

The defendant may reply on both law and fact.

5.04.14   Where either party is seeking amendments to pleadings, further particulars or interrogatories, the party should ensure that the Master initials the pleadings which he orders or approves.

5.04.15   Directions given at an Interlocutory Hearing

At an interlocutory hearing it may be necessary for directions to be given to carry out immediate necessary procedural steps.

The party or parties should be ready to ask for the directions required (usually to expedite the hearing of the case), for example:

I ask for the following directions:

That the plaintiff be ordered to amend the Statement of Claim within seven days.

That the defence be filed within 14 days thereafter.

Reply, if so advised, 14 days thereafter.

Mutual discovery by lists, 14 days thereafter.

Inspection, seven days thereafter.

And that the case be set down, seven days thereafter, category (-), with a time estimate of (state time estimate).

5.04.16   Costs

Costs on an agreed hearing will normally be in the cause (see **7.01.08-09**).

Costs on a contested hearing (or where the order was substantially agreed but attendance was caused by a party not agreeing one or more items) are likely to be awarded to the successful party.

Costs when directions are given at any other hearing (see **5.04.15**) are not normally dealt with as a separate issue.

5.04.17   Family Proceedings

In proceedings other than family proceedings, a Summons for Directions or a Pre-Trial Review is often dealt with by post, by agreement, and the parties (if represented) do not usually attend.

This is not usually the case in family matters.

In divorce, ancillary relief and children matters, the court attempts to conciliate as much as possible for the benefit of the parties. In these cases it is preferable if the parties attend on such hearings in order to reach agreement, if possible, and/or to narrow the issues in dispute (see **5.08.29-30** and **5.08.69-72**).

SECTION 5: DISCOVERY

INTRODUCTION

5.05.01 The parties to any action will usually have documents and correspondence which have a bearing on the issues. These documents are disclosed to the other parties on discovery.

5.05.02 Discovery may be made in the High Court and county court and in some tribunals (for example **9.01.17**).

See also **5.08.28** for ancillary relief proceedings.

5.05.03 Purpose of Discovery

The purpose of discovery is to enable a party to an action to know what documents are in the possession of the other party.

5.05.04 Documents Which Must be Disclosed

As a general rule, every document in the possession of a party which has a bearing on the case must be disclosed.

This does not entitle the other party to inspect (or take copies of) every document but each document must be identified in sufficient detail to enable that party to know the nature of the document and whether that party is entitled to inspect the document.

5.05.05 Obtaining Discovery

In actions begun by writ in the High Court there are provisions for automatic discovery after the close of pleadings.

Where automatic discovery is not made, a party may make an application for discovery at an interlocutory application or at the hearing of a Summons for Directions or Pre-Trial Review.

5.05.06   Order for Discovery

The court may order (usually on an interlocutory application) any party to make and serve on any other party a list of documents, for example:

Discovery by lists within (-) days.

Inspection (-) days thereafter.

5.05.07   Lists

A party making discovery must serve a list of relevant documents (usually by post) on the other parties within the period ordered.

The list must be in the prescribed form and is divided into schedules as follows:

Schedule 1
Documents relevant to the issue which the party has in his possession, custody or power at the time he serves the list:

Part I:
And which that party does not object to produce to the other parties.

Part II
And which that party objects (on the grounds of privilege) to produce to the other parties. These documents are usually described in general terms.

Schedule 2
Documents relevant to the issue which the party has had (but no longer has) in his possession, custody or power, setting out where they are now and when they left his possession.

5.05.08   Verification of the List

In the High Court (but not usually in the county court) a party may be ordered to verify the list of documents by affidavit deposing to the accuracy of the list.

5.05.09   Specific Discovery

If a party believes that a party serving a list of documents has not disclosed a document, he may request in writing for that document to be disclosed.

If that document is not disclosed or the other party states that the document is not relevant, the party may make an application to the master for specific discovery (see **5.02.25-37**).

The application should be supported by an affidavit.

5.05.10 Inspection

Inspection usually takes place within seven days of the delivery of the list.

A party who has served a list of documents should allow the other party to inspect the documents listed in Schedule 1, Part I although, in practice, the other party will usually ask for copies of the documents. The party asking will be expected to pay for these copies.

5.05.11 Effect of Discovery

The general rules are as follows:

If a document has been discovered, it may be used in the course of the proceedings by any party to the action (subject to admissibility).

If a document has not been discovered, the High Court (but not necessarily the county court, see **6.03.17**) is unlikely to permit any party to use that document in the course of the proceedings and may grant an adjournment (with costs) to a party prejudiced by late defective discovery.

5.05.12 Discovery in the County Court

Discovery and inspection may be made:

(a) By agreement, or

(b) By order of the registrar (usually in a Pre-Trial Review).

5.05.13 Where discovery is made, the rule in **5.05.11** applies except that the rule is generally less strictly enforced in the county court than in the High Court.

SECTION 6: TRIAL

INTRODUCTION

5.06.01   The trial of an action in the High Court represents, in practice, the final determination of the issues between the parties which commenced with the issue of proceedings.

5.06.02   Issue of Proceedings

Proceedings may be commenced by:

(a) Writ.

(b) Originating summons.

(c) Originating motion.

(d) Petition.

5.06.03   Any application made between the issue of proceedings and the final determination of the action, or part of the action, at trial is called an interlocutory application.

See **5.02: Interlocutory Applications.**

5.06.04   The conduct of the trial of an action may be determined on a Summons for Directions (if appropriate).

See **5.04: Directions.**

The purpose of a Summons for Directions is to determine any interlocutory applications which have not been the subject of separate applications.

In preparation, the parties to the trial of an action should give consideration to the matters listed in the form for the Summons for Directions (see **5.04.09**).

PREPARATION FOR TRIAL

5.06.05   A party presenting a case should give consideration to the following:

(a) Formal documents (usually in the possession of the court) for example, pleadings and orders of the court.

(b) Evidential documents (not usually in the possession of the court, for example, correspondence between the parties) which tend to prove the facts alleged in the pleadings.

(c) Law.

FORMAL DOCUMENTS

5.06.06   The party preparing the bundle for a case may find it useful to assemble the formal documents in chronological order (see **5.06.16**).

5.06.07   Action Commenced by Writ and Statement of Claim in the High Court or by Summons and Particulars of Claim in the County Court

The parties to an action commenced by writ/summons are required to serve pleadings.

The parties will have the following pleadings:

(a) Statement/particulars of claim, by the plaintiff, setting out the facts relied on in support of his claim and the relief sought.

(b) Defence, by the defendant, answering the facts relied on by the plaintiff and setting out any new facts on which the defence relies.

The parties may also have the following pleadings:

(c) Counterclaim, by defence.

(d) Reply (to defence), by plaintiff.

(e) Defence to counterclaim, by plaintiff.

(f) Reply to defence to counterclaim, by defence.

(g) Third party notice, by defence.

(h) Defence to third party notice, by third party.

The pleadings may also be clarified by

(i) Request for further and better particulars of (any pleading), by either party.

(j) Further and better particulars of (any pleading), by either party.

5.06.08 Action Commenced by Originating Summons or Petition

The parties will have the following documents:

(a) Originating summons, by the plaintiff, setting out the relief sought.

(b) Affidavit(s) in support of the originating summons, by the plaintiff, setting out the facts relied on in support of the relief sought.

The parties may also have the following documents:

(c) Affidavit(s) in reply, by defence.

(d) Other affidavits, by or for either party.

5.06.09 In an action commenced by originating summons it may be ordered on directions that the originating summons be treated as a statement of claim, for example, where there is a substantial dispute on the facts requiring pleadings.

5.06.10 Orders

The parties should have copies of any interlocutory orders made before trial, for example:

(a) Order for service of any pleading and/or particulars (see **5.02**).

(b) Order on application for summary judgment (see **5.03**).

(c) Directions (see **5.04**).

(d) Order for discovery (see **5.05**).

EVIDENTIAL DOCUMENTS

5.06.11 The party preparing the case should assemble the evidential documents in advance of the trial in chronological order in a bundle (see **5.06.16**).

At this stage, the parties should also give consideration to exchanging proofs of evidence, where this might save time at the trial of the action, even if this has not been ordered on directions (see **5.04.09(h)**).

5.06.12   Documents Between the Parties Created Before the Cause of Action

For example:

(a) Pre-contract enquiries/representations.

(b) Contracts.

(c) Title deeds.

(d) Advertising material.

5.06.13   Documents Between the Parties Created After the Cause of Action

For example:

(a) Correspondence (including the letter before action).

(b) Invoices.

5.06.14   Agreed Documents

For example:

(a) Reports.

(b) Schedules.

(c) Photographs.

(d) Plans.

5.06.15   Privileged Documents

Privileged documents may only be put in a bundle by agreement between the parties.

For example:

(a) Without prejudice correspondence between the parties.

(b) Correspondence with a party's own lawyers.

(c) Medical records or experts' reports that have not been disclosed and upon which a party does not wish to rely.

5.06.16 Presentation of Documents in a Bundle

The bundle of documents is usually prepared by the plaintiff. The bundle may be divided into sections for ease of reference. The sections may follow the paragraph numbers in **5.06.06-15**.

The documents in the bundle must be:

(a) Firmly secured together.

(b) Arranged in chronological order, beginning with the earliest.

(c) Paged consecutively at centre bottom.

(d) Fully and easily legible. If not, a typed copy should also be included.

The bundle should also have an index.

5.06.17   In the absence of any order on directions or agreement to the contrary, copies of the bundle should be served on all parties to the action and the court.

A copy or copies of the bundle should be made available for witnesses and, in particular, where a document (for example, a plan) is likely to be marked by witness(es), extra copies should be made available.

If a bundle has not been served in advance, the party taken by surprise may apply for an adjournment.

5.06.18   Where there is likely to be an argument in relation to the admissibility of a document tending to establish any fact alleged in the pleadings, that document is usually included in the bundle and 'argued out' (except where the judge is hearing the case with a jury).

For example:

(a) A letter alleged to have been sent but not received.

(b) A receipt which is said to be a forgery.

5.06.19   If a document is excluded from the bundle at the request of a party, its admissibility can be argued at any stage or, if appropriate, in a preliminary application at the trial (see **5.06.42**).

LAW

5.06.20   A party intending to raise a matter of law should serve a list of authorities on all the parties and the court at least 24 hours before the hearing.

5.06.21   If it has not been possible to follow the rule in **5.06.20**, the party should serve sufficient (photo)copies of the authorities on all the parties and the court at the hearing.

In the county court, even where the rule in **5.06.20** has been followed, the advocate is advised to take sufficient (photo)copies of the authorities to court wherever possible because many county courts and parties have limited access to legal works at short notice.

A party taken by surprise may ask for an adjournment.

5.06.22   In a case where the legal argument is likely to be complex, a party may serve an outline submission in writing (skeleton argument) on all the parties and the court in advance of the hearing (see also **8.01.31-33**).

5.06.23   Reference to Cases

A party referring to a case should do so as follows:

Donoghue v Stevenson 1932 AC 562:

The case of Donoghue and Stevenson, which is reported in the Appeal Cases for 1932 at page 562.

Price v Strange 1977 3 WLR 943:

The case of Price and Strange, which is reported in the third volume (or, volume 3) **of the Weekly Law Reports for 1977 at page 943.**

ORDER OF PRESENTATION AND SPEECHES

5.06.24 Order of Presentation of Case

The plaintiff will usually present his case to the court first except where all of the burden of proving the case falls on another party, for example:

(a) Where the plaintiff's claim has been struck out on an interlocutory application and there is a counterclaim.

(b) Where the plaintiff's claim is agreed and there is a dispute over contribution between the defendant and other parties.

The party who is to open the case may say:

Due to the fact that the plaintiff's claim was struck out/is agreed, the burden of proof in this case falls on the defendant. Therefore I propose to open the case, subject to (the court's) **agreement.**

5.06.25 Speeches

See **Plaintiff's Opening (5.06.43-46).**

See **Defendant's Opening (5.06.78-80).**

See **Defendant's Closing (5.06.84).**

See **Plaintiff's Closing (5.06.84).**

See **Response (5.06.86).**

In the absence of any ruling by the court and/or agreement between the parties, the order of presentation and speeches is as follows:

5.06.26 Where the plaintiff and the defendant both call evidence:

Plaintiff opens.

Plaintiff's evidence.

Defendant opens.

Defendant's evidence.

Defendant closes.

Plaintiff closes.

Defendant's response (if permitted).

5.06.27   Where the plaintiff calls evidence and the defendant calls no evidence:

Plaintiff opens.

Plaintiff's evidence.

Plaintiff closes.

Defendant closes.

Plaintiff's response (if permitted).

5.06.28   Where there are two or more defendants and/or parties:

The plaintiff calls evidence and the defendants and/or parties call no evidence:

Plaintiff opens.

Plaintiff's evidence.

Plaintiff closes.

Defendants and/or parties close in order of title.

Plaintiff's response (if permitted).

5.06.29   Where there are two or more defendants and/or parties:

The plaintiff and the defendants and/or parties all call evidence:

Plaintiff opens.

Plaintiff's evidence.

1st defendant opens.

1st defendant's evidence.

Continue in order of title.

Defendants and/or other parties close in order of title.

Plaintiff's close.

Defendants and/or other parties response (if permitted, in such order as determined by the court).

5.06.30 Where there are two or more defendants and/or parties:

The plaintiff calls evidence and one or more, but not all, of the defendants and/or parties call evidence:

Plaintiff opens.

Plaintiff's evidence.

Defendant and/or party calling evidence opens.

Defendant and/or party calls evidence.

Continue in order of title.

Defendant and/or party calling evidence close in the order that they presented their cases.

Plaintiff's close.

Defendant and/or party not calling evidence close in order of title.

Response by any party (if permitted, in such order as determined by the court).

PRACTICE

5.06.31   Open Court

The trial of an action is held in open court before a single judge of the High Court.

If the public are excluded and the court is sitting '*in camera*', the conduct of the trial and mode of address are the same as in open court. The advocates are usually robed.

5.06.32   Calling the Case

The associate will stand and read out the name of the case.

The parties should be present in court ready for the case to be called. If the parties are not present:

In the Queen's Bench Division, the case will usually be called outside court.

In the Chancery Division, the case may not be called outside court and the action may be struck out.

5.06.33   Presence of Parties and/or Witnesses in Court

The parties and/or witnesses will usually be present in court throughout the proceedings and/or the day or part of the day on which the party and/or witness gives evidence.

A party may make an application to exclude a witness where, for example, there is an allegation of misconduct by that witness.

5.06.34   Jury Trials

A trial of an action is usually heard by a judge sitting alone although it may be heard with a judge and jury.

In practice, a trial may be heard with a jury in the following circumstances:

(a)   Defamation.

(b)   Actions (against the police) for malicious prosecution or false imprisonment.

(c)   Actions where there is an allegation of fraud.

Application for a jury trial should be made on directions.

5.06.35   If the judge is sitting with a jury, the jury will be called to the jury box and sworn (see **3.04.19-25**).

5.06.36   Introduction of the Parties.

The plaintiff usually introduces the parties to the court:

In this action I appear for the plaintiff.

My learned friend, Mr (name), **appears for the** (name of defendant/party).

OR

Mr (name) **appears in person.**

Where a party appears in person, the judge may ask if the unrepresented party is present and is content not to be represented.

5.06.37 Attendance of the Parties

A party not giving material evidence in his case need not attend but must appear by his legal representative.

A party giving material evidence in his case should attend. If he does not attend or appear by his legal representative, the court may proceed with the trial or adjourn the case, as appropriate.

5.06.38 If a defendant or party does not attend, the plaintiff may say:

The (name of party) **does not appear and is not represented today. I am instructed that a notice giving this date was sent to all parties on** (date). **I would, therefore, seek to prove my case in the absence of** (name of party).

Unless the judge indicates that it is unnecessary, the plaintiff will then call evidence (see **5.06.40**).

5.06.39 If the plaintiff does not attend and the defendant has not served a counterclaim, the defendant may say:

The plaintiff does not appear and is not represented today. I would therefore seek to have the claim dismissed for want of prosecution. And for costs.

If there is a counterclaim, the defendant may also say:

I would seek to prove the counterclaim in the absence of the plaintiff.

The defendant will then call evidence on the counterclaim (see **5.06.40**).

5.06.40 A party seeking to prove his case in the absence of another party should call evidence only from witnesses limited to the matters essential to prove his case against that party.

The evidence may be treated briefly and the advocate should note with care any indication from the Judge to shorten the case.

5.06.41   Where the parties attend, after **5.06.36** there may be preliminary applications or the plaintiff may open the case (see **5.06.43**).

5.06.42   Preliminary Applications

Preliminary applications may include:

(a)   Amendments to pleadings.

(b)   Argument as to admissibility of evidence.

(c)   Holding a split trial.

(d)   Holding a view.

(e)   Administrative matters, for example, timing.

(f)   Where the judge is hearing the case with a jury, questions of the admissibility of evidence may be determined before the plaintiff opens (see **3.04.14-15**).

(g)   See also **5.04.09: Directions.**

THE CASE ON BEHALF OF THE PLAINTIFF

5.06.43   Plaintiff's Opening

The plaintiff will usually open the case. The opening should be carefully prepared (see **14.02.03-06**).

The opening is important because it enables the plaintiff to 'set the scene' and to predispose the court in the plaintiff's favour by:

(a)   Directing the judge's attention to the better points in the plaintiff's case.

(b)   Explaining, in a manner favourable to the plaintiff, any contentious points in the defendant's case as disclosed in the pleadings.

5.06.44   The plaintiff's opening should contain:

(a) An explanation of the nature of the case, for example:

This is an action for (state nature of relief sought) **for** (state cause of action).

(b) A summary of the relevant pleadings, with reference to the plaintiff's case, for example:

The (state cause of action) **is set out in paragraph(s)** (-) **of the Statement of Claim as follows** (state terms). **The defendant contends in paragraph(s)** (-) **of the defence that** (state nature of defence). **Your Lordship may be assisted on** (state issue) **if I were to draw your attention to the document at page** (-) **in the bundle.**

(c) A summary of the points of agreement and/or dispute between the parties.

(d) An outline of the evidence upon which the plaintiff intends to rely and/or whether it is live evidence or in documentary form.

(e) An outline of the contents of the bundle of documents (in such detail as necessary) describing the documents upon which the plaintiff relies and any documents which may be the subject of argument.

(f) A summary of the relevant law upon which the plaintiff relies (if not agreed).

5.06.45 The judge may clarify any matters raised in the opening with the parties, for example:

Mr (name of defendant and/or party) **do you accept the law as put forward by Mr** (name) **for the plaintiff?**

5.06.46 The plaintiff may conclude the opening by saying:

Unless I can assist Your Lordship further, I now propose to call the evidence. And I call the plaintiff in this action.

EVIDENCE ON BEHALF OF THE PLAINTIFF

5.06.47 The plaintiff and/or any witness on behalf of the plaintiff is called and identified as follows:

Are you (name)? **What is your address?**

A witness may be asked to describe his relationship to the plaintiff and/or the action.

The usual rules as to the examination, cross-examination and re-examination of witnesses apply (see **14.01.01-24**).

5.06.48   Refreshing the Memory

A witness may wish to 'refresh his memory' from a document made at the time (see **14.01.11-15**).

5.06.49   Producing Documents

A witness may produce any document (see **14.01.21-22**) which has been disclosed by the parties before trial (see **5.05.11**).

A party is not entitled, without leave, to rely on any document which has not been disclosed. A party taken by surprise may object, for example:

I object. This document has not been disclosed and I would invite (the judge) **not to consider it.**

Any argument will follow the order of submissions in **5.06.52**.

5.06.50   Order of Cross-Examination

The order of cross-examination of the plaintiff's witnesses, where there is more than one defendant and/or party, is in order of title. The plaintiff may re-examine.

5.06.51   Releasing a Witness

If a witness wishes to leave court after giving evidence, the plaintiff may say:

Unless there is any objection, perhaps this witness (and any subsequent witness) **could be released.**

5.06.52   Questions of Admissibility

Questions of admissibility of evidence are complex and should be researched in the common practitioners' handbooks.

Where there is an argument about admissibility, the order of submissions is usually as follows:

(a) Either party (usually the defendant) identifies the evidence to which an objection is taken

(i) If the objection can be considered without hearing/reading the disputed evidence, the party may make his objection without reference to the disputed evidence.

(ii) If the objection cannot be considered without hearing/reading the disputed evidence, the defendant should draw the judge's attention to the disputed evidence.

(b) The defendant then gives reasons for the objection and refers to any relevant law.

(c) Reply by the plaintiff.

(d) Response by the defendant, with the leave of the judge (see **5.06.86**), dealing with any points of law raised by the plaintiff or the judge, but not repeating the submissions in (b).

(e) Decision by the judge. Where (a)(ii) applies and the judge rules against the party intending to call the disputed evidence, the judge will usually state in the summing up that he has not taken that evidence into account.

5.06.53   Where the judge is hearing the case with a jury, questions of admissibility are decided in the absence of the jury (see **3.04.39**).

5.06.54   Affidavit Evidence

A witness who has given evidence on affidavit (for example, in interlocutory proceedings before trial) may be called and examined in the usual way.

A party wishing to rely on affidavit evidence which has not been served in interlocutory proceedings should serve the affidavit and exhibits on the parties and the court a reasonable time before the hearing.

5.06.55   As a general rule, an affidavit to be used at trial should not contain hearsay evidence; for example, an affidavit served in interlocutory proceedings will often contain the words:

I am informed and verily believe that:

What the witness is informed is hearsay.

5.06.56   A party will not usually be permitted to rely upon an affidavit (in the absence of agreement) unless the witness attends court to be cross-examined on it.

5.06.57   The witness giving affidavit evidence is sworn and identified. The practice in **14.01.25-30** may then be followed.

5.06.58   Expert Evidence

An expert witness is entitled to give evidence of opinion on any matter in which that witness has expert knowledge. The practice in **14.01.16-20** may then be followed.

5.06.59   The report of an expert should be disclosed to all parties following directions (see **5.04.09(g)**).

If agreed, the report will usually be part of the bundle (see **5.06.11** and **5.06.14(a)**) and may be opened by any party or it may be referred to at an appropriate time during the evidence.

If not agreed, the expert must attend court to be cross-examined on the report.

5.06.60   Evidence Under the Civil Evidence Acts

The Civil Evidence Acts enable a party to introduce hearsay evidence contained in statements or documents; for example, maps, photographs, plans, computer records.

The relevant law should be researched in the common practitioners' handbooks.

The following (**5.06.61-65**) represents a brief guide to the practice under the Civil Evidence Acts.

5.06.61   The party seeking to introduce hearsay evidence under the Civil Evidence Acts must serve a notice on all other parties (in practice) a reasonable time before the trial.

The notice will usually contain particulars of:

(a) The person by whom a statement or document was made and to whom it was made.

(b) The circumstances in which the statement or document was made.

(c) Particulars of the statement or a copy of the document.

(d) The reason(s) that the statement or document is admissible under the Civil Evidence Acts (see **5.06.62**).

5.06.62   A statement or document may be admissible under the Civil Evidence Acts where the person who made the statement or document is:

(a) Dead.

(b) Beyond the seas.

(c) Unfit to attend the trial.

(d) Unidentifiable.

(e) Untraceable.

(f) Unlikely to be able to remember

5.06.63   A party may serve a counternotice requiring the party serving notice to call the maker of the statement or document where the reason(s) given in **5.06.61(d)** and **5.06.62** is not substantiated.

If a counternotice is not served, the party may introduce the evidence described in **5.06.61(c)** at the trial.

5.06.64   The party introducing the evidence may say:

The evidence of the next witness has been served by notice under the Civil Evidence Act on (date). **The relevant document is at page** (-) **of the bundle.**

The notice states (state reason in **5.06.61(d)** and refer the court to any supporting evidence).

5.06.65   If a counter-notice has been served, the party may then say:

A counter-notice was served on (date). **And we would therefore seek your ruling on whether this evidence can be adduced.**

The argument will follow the order of submissions in **5.06.52**.

5.06.66   Oral Admissions

An oral admission may be made at the hearing by agreement between the parties, for example:

I have been asked to admit that (state admission).

And I make that admission.

5.06.67   Written Admissions

A written admission (including any admission made in the Pleadings) is usually made before the hearing. The party seeking the admission may serve a Notice to Admit Facts.

The failure by a party on whom the Notice to Admit Facts has been served to serve a counter-notice usually within seven days (or any extended time) is deemed to be an admission of the fact alleged.

5.06.68   At the trial, the party must prove service of the notice, for example:

On (date) **the plaintiff's solicitors served a notice on the defendant to admit that** (state nature of admission).

The defendant was asked to serve any counter notice within 14 days and has not done so. A copy of the notice is to be found at page (-) **of the bundle.**

5.06.69   Agreements

The parties to an action may make any agreement which the court is satisfied is a lawful agreement. Where a party making an agreement is under a disability (for example, a child), the court must also be satisfied that it is a reasonable agreement.

An agreement may be made at any stage and, if necessary, put in writing for the judge.

5.06.70   A View

If a view is considered appropriate, an application should be made by any party either at directions or as a preliminary issue (see **5.06.42**) or it may be made at any convenient time.

A view may be made either before, during or after the evidence is heard.

5.06.71   On a view, the parties may point out, for example; objects, site lines, landmarks and obstructions to the judge, but should not discuss them.

5.06.72   Close of the Plaintiff's Case

When the plaintiff and/or the party calling evidence (see **5.06.24**) has called and/or read all the evidence and any admission and/or agreement has been made, the case is said to be closed.

The usual form of words is:

That is the case for the plaintiff.

SUBMISSION OF NO CASE TO ANSWER

5.06.73 The grounds on which a submission of no case to answer may be made and the relevant law should be researched in the common practitioners' handbooks.

In practice, a submission is very rarely made because the court will usually 'put the defendant to his election'. This means that the court will only hear the submission of no case to answer if the defendant elects not to call evidence in support of his case.

The practice should be clarified with the judge, for example:

I am considering a submission of no case to answer. I would be grateful if Your Lordship would indicate whether, if I make a submission and it is not upheld, I would be permitted to call evidence on behalf of the defendant.

The judge may indicate that the defendant will be 'put to his election' for example:

No, Mr (name)**, the usual rule must apply.**

5.06.74 In practice, if a submission of no case to answer is made, the order of submissions is as follows:

(a) The defendant may begin:

I submit that there is no case to answer on the ground that the plaintiff has failed in law to establish any case against the defendant for the following reasons (state reasons).

(b) The defendant should identify the evidence to which he refers and direct the judge to any relevant law.

(c) Reply by the plaintiff.

(d) Response by the defendant, with the leave of the judge.

(e) Decision by the judge.

In practice, if there is more than one defendant and/or party, the judge will not hear a submission of no case to answer.

For the procedure in a case where the judge is hearing the case with a jury, see **3.04.57-59.**

THE CASE FOR THE DEFENDANT AND/OR OTHER PARTY

5.06.75 Preparation

See **5.06.5-23.**

5.06.76 Presentation

See **5.06.24-30.**

5.06.77 Calling No Evidence

Where a defendant and/or party is not calling evidence, he should state this in clear terms:

I call no evidence on behalf of (name of defendant and/or party).

5.06.78 Defendant's Opening

The defendant has the right to open the case if he is calling evidence (see **14.02.03-06**).

5.06.79 The defendant's opening may contain:

(a) A summary of the defendant's pleadings (usually where the defendant's pleadings were not opened by the plaintiff).

(b) Where there is a counterclaim, an explanation of the nature of the counterclaim if it has not become clear from cross-examination.

(c) A criticism of the plaintiff's case (usually where it has been discredited by cross- examination).

(d) An outline of the documents in the bundle on which the defendant relies.

(e) A summary of the relevant law on which the defendant relies (if not agreed).

5.06.80   The defendant may conclude the opening by saying:

Unless I can assist Your Lordship further, I now propose to call the evidence. And I call (name of defendant or party or witness).

5.06.81   Evidence on Behalf of the Defendant and/or Parties

The evidence on behalf of the defendant and/or parties is subject to the same rules and is presented in the same way as the evidence on behalf of the plaintiff (see **5.06.47-72**).

5.06.82   A submission of no case to answer by the plaintiff on a defendant's counterclaim may be, but in practice is very rarely, made.

SPEECHES

5.06.83   For the order of speeches, see **5.06.26-30**.

5.06.84   Content of Closing Speeches

See **14.02.07-12**.

In closing, a party will usually:

(a) Sum up the basic points of his case in so far as those points will assist the judge to give judgment for him.

(b) Compare the evidence of the parties and the character and motives of the witnesses (if relevant).

(c) Refer the court to any relevant law (see **5.06.20-23**).

5.06.85   The judge will listen to the speeches of the parties in turn but may interrupt to indicate agreement or otherwise on any point, for example:

I need not trouble you on that point, but I would like to hear you on (state issue).

The party addressing the judge should address the judge on that issue before continuing his speech.

If the judge has reached a decision by the end of all the speeches, apart from the plaintiff's and, if that decision is in the plaintiff's favour, he may say:

I need not trouble you Mr (name of plaintiff).

5.06.86   Response

A party may respond, on a matter of law only, with the leave, or by invitation, of the judge, for example:

My learned friend has referred to the case of (name of case) **on which I have not addressed you. I would be grateful if I could address you on that point.**

OR the judge may say:

What do you say about (state issues raised by other party in closing)**, Mr** (name)**?**

JUDGMENT

5.06.87   The judge may:

(a)   Deliver a full judgment.

(b)   Deliver a short judgment with reasons to follow.

(c)   Reserve judgment (usually to another day).

5.06.88   The judgment will usually contain:

(a)   A description of the parties.

(b)   A summary of the nature of the case.

(c)   A summary of the issues.

(d)   A summary of the evidence.

(e)   A description of the manner in which the judge intends to approach the relevant evidence.

(f)   A summary of the legal argument and his ruling thereon.

(g)   A determination of the facts, with reference to any documentary evidence (if appropriate).

The parties should take a full note of the judgment in order that it can be considered before an appeal is lodged.

5.06.89   Judgment Order

The judgment order may follow the judge's determination of the facts.

If the judge has not announced the judgment order at the conclusion of his judgment, the successful party may say:

I ask for judgment for the (state name of party) **for/on** (state nature of relief sought) **in the sum of** (state sum).

And that the (name of unsuccessful party's) (relief sought) **be dismissed.**

And, for interest on (state sum) **at the rate of** (-) **per cent per annum from** (appropriate date) **to today.**

And, for costs (see **7.01:Costs**).

5.06.90   Interest

The total interest due should have been calculated by each party in advance.

5.06.91   Interest is only obtainable where it has been claimed in the pleadings:

(a)   If the case relates to an agreement in which a rate of interest is specified, then that rate will normally apply:

The plaintiff's claim includes a claim for interest which is set at (-) **% per annum in clause** (-) **of the contract and I would submit that this is the appropriate rate.**

(b)   In other cases, the rate will be such as may be approved by the judge:

Interest is claimed at the rate of (-) **%. That has been the prevailing rate throughout most of the time these proceedings have been in existence.**

And I would submit that interest at (-) **% would be the appropriate rate.**

(c) Interest on general damages for pain and suffering in personal injury cases
     is awarded at a lower rate.

The law on this subject is complex and should be researched in the common
practitioners' handbooks.

5.06.92   Costs

It is not unusual for there to be an argument on the question of costs, in
particular, where there have been a number of interlocutory applications (see
7.01.03-20 & 27).

5.06.93   Appeal

Appeal from a judgment of the High Court is to the Court of Appeal (Civil
Division). The Notice of Appeal must be served on the parties and the court
within 28 days.

Any party contesting the appeal must serve a Respondent's Notice within 21
days thereafter (see **8.01: Court of Appeal (Civil Division)**).

SECTION 7: THE COMPANIES COURT

WINDING UP A COMPANY

5.07.01   There is no separate court which deals with matters arising from the
operation of a company, although where a matter is within the jurisdiction of the
companies registrar in the Chancery Division it is often said to be in the Companies
Court.

5.07.02   As a general rule, the practice will follow the practice described in the
preceding sections of this chapter.

The practice on an uncontested winding up of a company is distinct. The
following is a brief guide.

PREPARATION

5.07.03   A person who wishes to obtain satisfaction of a debt owed by a company may apply to 'wind up' that company.

5.07.04   In order for a creditor to petition to wind up a company, the company must be indebted to that person for a sum in excess of the current financial limit.

5.07.05   The petitioner is usually described as either:

A trade creditor (see **5.07.06**), or

A judgment creditor (see **5.07.07**).

5.07.06   A trade creditor is a person who is owed money by the company; it does not necessarily have to be a trade debt in the normal sense of the word 'trade'.

5.07.07   A judgment creditor is a person who has an unsatisfied judgment outstanding against the company and whose attempts to enforce that judgment in other ways have failed.

5.07.08   The Statutory Demand

Before a petition is presented and filed it is usual for there to be a statutory demand. This is a formal written demand for the sum due.

A statutory demand sets out the amount of the debt, the way it arises and full particulars of how it is calculated. It also sets out the purpose and effect of the document and how to comply with it. It is signed by the creditor or a person authorised to sign on his behalf.

Whether or not a statutory demand has been served, it is necessary that the company's debt should be undisputed. The Companies Court is not the proper forum for trying disputed debts.

If an alleged creditor threatens to present a winding up petition based upon a disputed debt, the company may seek an injunction to restrain presentation of the petition. In such a case, the process is instituted by originating motion in the Companies Court (see **5.02.49(c)** and **5.02.57-71**).

If it is too late, the company may apply to restrain advertisement of the petition. An ordinary notice of motion in the petition may then be used.

5.07.09   The Petition

The petition must contain full details of the debt and any statutory demand. Three copies of the petition must be filed with an affidavit (which must be filed not later than seven days after the petition) verifying the facts contained in the petition.

The petition and affidavit are filed in the office of the Registrar. A date and time for the hearing will be fixed.

5.07.10   The Affidavit Verifying the Petition

The affidavit must be made by the petitioner or an officer or servant of the petitioner or other authorised person (usually the petitioner's solicitor). If the deponent is not the petitioner, that person should state his capacity and authority.

5.07.11   Service

The petition must be served on the company at the company's registered office:

(a)   On a person known to be a director, officer or employee of the company, or

(b)   On a person acknowledging himself to be a person named in (a), or

(c)   By leaving the petition at the company's registered office.

(a) or (b) are recommended.

5.07.12   Affidavit of Service

An affidavit of service of the petition (setting out the manner of service) must be made.

5.07.13   Advertisement

The petition must be advertised, usually in the London Gazette. It should appear not less than seven days before the hearing and not less than seven days after service.

The court can give leave for an alternative publication for the advertisement.

The advertisement should contain:

(a)   All information required for any interested party to identify the company and the petitioner(s).

(b) The date of the hearing.

(c) The name of the petitioner's solicitor (if appropriate).

(d) A statement that any party wishing to appear at the hearing must give notice.

5.07.14 Certificate of Compliance

At least five days before the hearing the petitioner or his solicitor must serve on the court a certificate of compliance with the rules as to service and advertisement.

The certificate of compliance must show:

(a) The date of presentation of the petition.

(b) The date fixed for the hearing.

(c) The date of service of the petition.

(d) The date of publication of the advertisement (with a copy of the advertisement).

5.07.15 List of Supporting/Opposing Creditors

By the day of the hearing the party or his solicitor should serve on the court a list of all creditors who have given notice that they support or oppose the petition. This is the 'list' in **5.07.29** and **5.07.32**. If no one has given notice, the list is described as negative.

5.07.16 Time Limit

The Insolvency Rules set out the time limits applied in **5.07.08-15**.

In some limited circumstances (for example, where the advertisement was published a day late) leave can be given by the court, at the hearing, to dispense with that formality but only if there is no possibility of an injustice being occasioned to any interested party.

PRACTICE

5.07.17 Introduction

All unopposed petitions are listed before the registrar of the Companies Court on Wednesdays. The hearing is in open court.

A party addressing the court should do so standing. The party should be brief and to the point.

5.07.18 Mode of Address

The registrar is addressed as **Sir**.

5.07.19 Right of Audience

Barristers.

Solicitors.

Petitioners in person.

5.07.20 Dress

Barristers and solicitors should be robed.

Petitioners in person should be dressed respectably.

5.07.21   The cases are listed in the Daily Cause List in half hour groups at 10.30, 11.00, 11.30, etc.

5.07.22   The court room will probably be very full throughout the day (see **5.07.27**) and it is up to the advocate to make sure he is in court at the right time.

5.07.23   The ushers do not take the names of the parties or call the cases.

5.07.24   If there are any other interested parties (for example, the company or any supporting or opposing creditor) the petitioner's advocate should take the names of their advocates.

5.07.25   The advocate may call out the name of the case outside court or ask in court if attending before 10.30.

The parties may then negotiate or discuss any compromise of the petition.

5.07.26   If there are any queries as to the state of the court file these will be very difficult, if not impossible, to deal with once the court has started. The associate or his assistant is normally in court early and may be consulted.

THE HEARING

5.07.27   The registrar enters and all stand.

Once the registrar sits, those who can find a seat sit down. It is very likely that there will be insufficient seating, so some advocates may have to stand in the side aisles.

5.07.28   The cases will be called on in the order shown on the Daily Cause List.

The case is called by the associate by number and name. If nobody responds to the call it will be repeated. If there is still no response the petition will be dismissed.

The advocate for the petitioner, on hearing the case called, should stand to address the court.

5.07.29   In a straightforward case, the advocate may say:

This is a trade creditor's petition in the sum of £15,525 odd (Note: Figures are rounded to omit pence and called 'odd') **(pursuant to a statutory demand).**

The debtor company is not/is represented by my learned friend Mr (name). **(I believe that) The list** (of supporting creditors) **is negative (or, there is** (-) **supporting creditor represented by** (name)**). (As far as I am aware) The documents are in order** (all relevant documents have been served within the time limits and comply with the rules).

I therefore ask for the usual compulsory order. See **5.07.30.**

The advocate may use the phrases **I believe** and **as far as I am aware** if he has not had the opportunity to check the relevant documents.

5.07.30   The Usual Compulsory Order

Order that:

(a)   The company be wound up, and

(b)   The company pay the petitioner's costs (see **7.01.03**).

5.07.31   **5.07.32-44** apply in a less straightforward case.

5.07.32   The List is Not Negative

The advocate may say:

The (opposing) **creditor does not appear and is not represented (so far as I am aware). In the circumstances, I ask for the usual compulsory order.**

5.07.33 Late Advertisement

The advocate may say:

The documents are in order save that the advertisement was published a day late.

If the company does not appear:

Would you waive that defect.

If the company appears:

The company is represented today. I would be grateful if you would waive that defect and dispense with the need to readvertise.

5.07.34 The Affidavit of Service is Defective

The advocate may say:

Might I have seven days (to file a fresh affidavit).

5.07.35 Payment of the Debt

If the debt has been paid (or arrangements have been made accordingly) before the hearing, the petition may be dismissed.

When the petition is called the advocate may say:

Payment has been made/Suitable arrangements for payment have been made. Accordingly, would you dismiss the petition with/without costs.

5.07.36 Adjournments in the List

It sometimes happens that an offer of settlement is made at the door of the court and negotiations are still taking place when the petition is called on.

The petitioner may say (after introducing the parties):

We are talking. May it be mentioned next time around/at a convenient moment.

Or, simply

Next time around, please.

See **5.07.37-39**.

5.07.37   Next Time Around

When the list (or a group of cases in the list) has been finished, the associate will usually read out the names of the cases not dealt with first time around. These cases may then be dealt with in the same way as they could have been, first time around.

5.07.38   A Convenient Moment

Unless there is a gap caused by a half hour group of cases finishing before the next group starts, a 'convenient moment' will usually be at the end of the list.

5.07.39   How to get a Case Mentioned

(a)   Pass a note to the associate who may fit the case in at a convenient moment.

(b)   When there is a natural break in the proceedings, the advocate may say:

May I mention case (-).

This case is now agreed/to be stood out.

5.07.40   Adjournments to Another Day

If the parties (are negotiating and) agree to ask for an adjournment, either party may apply for the case to be stood out.

A case will be stood out for seven days or a multiple of weeks.

Either party may say:

(We are talking and) I would apply to stand the case out for two weeks.

5.07.41   Substitution

Substitution may occur:

(a) Where the petitioner has been paid his debt but a supporting creditor has not.

(b) Where the petitioner has failed to prosecute the petition.

5.07.42 A supporting creditor may attend and seek to be substituted as the petitioner. The court has a general discretion to permit substitution and may give an order on such terms as it thinks just.

5.07.43   Opposed Petitions

A company opposing the petition must serve an affidavit not less than seven days before the hearing. The company will normally be represented at the hearing.

The petition will usually be taken out of the registrar's list and put into the judge's list which is heard on Mondays.

If the petition is in the registrar's list and there is opposition, there may be argument but if the argument is longer than a few minutes, the petition will be stood out to the judge's list.

5.07.44   Hearing of an Opposed Petition

The hearing of an opposed petition will follow the general practice in **5.02.57-70** and **5.06: Trial**.

SECTION 8: FAMILY

PART 1: INTRODUCTION

5.08.01 Proceedings for divorce and judicial separation are commenced by petition.

A petition is issued out of:

(a) The Divorce Registry in London.

(b) Any county court, which is designated to accept divorce business.

5.08.02   The jurisdiction of the High Court and the county court overlap to a large extent.

This section is a brief guide to High Court practice. As a general rule, there are no significant differences between practice in the High Court and the county court.

5.08.03   The Petition

The Petition will contain:

(a) The names of the parties.

(b) The addresses of the parties (and the address at which they last lived).

(c) The date of the marriage.

(d) The names and dates of birth of any children of the parties.

(e) The particulars upon which the petitioner relies.

5.08.04   The Petition will also contain a *prayer*, claiming the following relief:

For the petitioner only:

(a) A decree of divorce.

(b) A decree of judicial separation.

For the petitioner and/or children:

(c) A property adjustment order.

(d) A periodical payments order.

(e) A lump sum order.

(f) A secured periodical payments order.

(g) Any order relating to the children of the marriage.

(h) Costs.

5.08.05   Special Procedure

Where a divorce is not contested it can proceed by way of Special Procedure in which most matters, except those relating to children, are dealt with by post.

5.08.06   Defended Petitions

If the respondent to a petition files an answer, the petition is treated as defended.

A defended petition is rare.

5.08.07   A defended petition may be heard by:

(a)   A judge of the Family Division.

(b)   A county court judge, sitting as a judge of the High Court.

(c)   A county court judge in a county court designated as a divorce trial court.

5.08.08   For the trial of a defended petition, see **5.06: Trial**.

PRACTICE

5.08.09   As a general rule, all divorce/family matters are heard in chambers, except:

(a)   Trials of petitions.

(b)   Applications for committal for breach of an order or undertaking.

Proceedings in Open Court before a Judge of the High Court

5.08.10   Right of Audience

Barristers.

Parties in person.

5.08.11   Dress

Barristers are robed.

Parties in person should be respectably dressed.

5.08.12 Mode of Address

Judge: My Lord/My Lady.

Proceedings in Open Court before a Judge of the County Court

5.08.13 Right of Audience

Barristers.

Solicitors.

Parties in person.

5.08.14 Dress

Barristers and solicitors are robed.

Parties in person should be respectably dressed.

5.08.15 Mode of Address

Judge: Your Honour.

Proceedings in chambers before:

(a) **A judge of the High Court**

(b) **A judge of the county court**

(c) **A registrar of the High Court or county court**

5.08.16 Right of Audience

Barristers.

Solicitors.

Experienced solicitors' clerks.

Parties in person.

5.08.17 Dress

Barristers and solicitors are not robed.

All parties should be respectably dressed.

5.08.18 Mode of Address

High Court judge:	My Lord/My Lady.
County court judge:	Your Honour.
Registrar:	Sir/Madam.

5.08.19 Conduct in 5.08.10 – 5.08.18

Although the system of resolving disputes between the parties is adversarial, the parties should (and are actively encouraged to) settle disputes by compromise (see also, **5.08.70**).

PART 2: ANCILLARY RELIEF APPLICATIONS

INTRODUCTION

5.08.20   Ancillary relief is financial relief which is ancillary to the matrimonial proceedings.

Ancillary relief includes the payment of maintenance, the payment of a lump sum and property transfer orders.

5.08.21   As a general rule, the courts will enforce a party's obligations to the children of the marriage.

In all other cases, the principles upon which the court will exercise its powers to make an order for ancillary relief and the orders which are available are complex and should be researched in the common practitioners' handbooks.

5.08.22 Application for Ancillary Relief

The application should be made in the petition (see **5.08.04**) or it can be made at any other time, with the leave of the court, except where the party making the application has remarried.

5.08.23 The application is made on a standard form which is filed with the registrar of the court.

The party making the application should file:

(a) The notice of application (in duplicate).

(b) An affidavit in support of the application.

5.08.24 A copy of the notice of application and affidavit in support should be served on the respondent(s) within four days of filing.

Where any order may affect another person, for example, a mortgagee, the application should also be served on him.

5.08.25 Affidavit

The affidavit in support is usually made by the applicant (petitioner) (see **5.02.05-06**).

The affidavit should contain

(a) The name, address and status of the deponent.

(b) The purpose of the affidavit, for example:

I make this affidavit in support of my application for (state relief sought).

(c) The matters upon which the applicant relies in support of the application.

(d) The details of any property (including any mortgage), if the application relates to land.

The affidavit should not contain:

(e) Unnecessary reference to the behaviour of the respondent, except where the applicant is claiming that such behaviour should be taken into account.

5.08.26 Affidavit in Reply

The respondent to the application must serve an affidavit in reply. The affidavit should be served within 14 days of receipt of the notice of application and affidavit in support (see **5.02.07**). For the content of the affidavit, see **5.08.25**.

5.08.27 Disclosure of Financial Matters

Both parties are under a duty to make full disclosure of all financial matters.

5.08.28 Rule 77(4) Questionnaires

In an application for ancillary relief, a Rule 77(4) Questionnaire is a mixture of a Request for Further and Better Particulars, Discovery and Interrogatories combined.

It may be in the form of a letter, setting out the information requested in numbered paragraphs.

If a party fails to reply, adequately or at all, the court may make such directions as are necessary.

5.08.29 Directions

A party may apply by summons on notice for directions (see **5.04**) or discovery (see **5.05**), or directions may be given at the hearing of an interlocutory application, for example, an application for maintenance pending suit (see **5.08.31**).

5.08.30 The following matters may be considered on directions:

(a) Affidavit(s) of means.

(b) Valuation(s) of property.

(c) Filing of copies of land registry entries.

(d) List(s) of documents and inspection (see **5.05.06-11**).

(e) Length of hearing.

5.08.31 Maintenance pending suit

A party may apply to the registrar for maintenance pending suit.

The hearing is on affidavit evidence (see **14.01.25-30**). A party may be permitted to give additional evidence.

An order made on an application for maintenance pending suit will last until the decree absolute or the hearing of the application.

PREPARATION

5.08.32   All affidavits and documents should be filed at least 14 days before the hearing.

Any document filed less than 14 days before the hearing may not be included in the court file. The advocate should therefore take extra copies to court.

5.08.33   Bundles

Where there is substantial correspondence and/or documents a bundle should be prepared (usually by the applicant) and agreed (see **5.06.16**).

5.08.34   Costs Estimate

The parties should prepare an estimate of any costs which should be taken into consideration in the court's assessment of the award. The estimate may include:

(a)   An estimate of the legal costs.

(b)   The costs of the sale or purchase of any properties.

(c)   The costs of discharging any mortgages.

5.08.35   Assessment of Tax Implications

If an award may have tax implications, the parties should be prepared to explain to the court the effect of any reduction (or increase) in a party's tax liability.

5.08.36   The Date of the Hearing

The hearing may be fixed by the court (in a simple case) or by application of the parties, on filing certificates of readiness and time estimates.

5.08.37   Referring to the Parties or Witnesses

The parties are advised to agree, before the hearing, how to refer to the parties or witnesses, particularly in the following situations

(a)   Where the parties have remarried.

(b)   Where the court is considering an application in which the respondent to the petition is the applicant.

A useful form of words is for the parties to refer to **the husband, the wife, the child** or **children**, and to the new spouse as **Mr** or **Mrs** (name).

PRACTICE

5.08.38   The conduct of the hearing of an application for ancillary relief varies greatly. One court may treat the hearing more informally than another.

The following is intended as a guide:

5.08.39   The hearing will be in chambers (see **5.08.16-18**) usually before a registrar. In both the High Court and the county court, the registrar may refer the case to a judge if he considers it complex.

5.08.40   Conduct

If the hearing is before the judge, it will usually be in a court room. The advocates or any party should stand to address the court. The judge may invite the advocates to sit but this is unusual.

If the hearing is before the registrar, it will usually be in the registrar's room. The advocates and parties will usually be seated at a table.

A party or witness taking the oath should do so standing.

5.08.41   Presence of Witnesses in Court

A judge (but not usually a registrar) may expect the witnesses to remain in court throughout the proceedings although practice varies.

5.08.42   Order of Presentation

The party having the burden of proof or, where both parties have an application before the court, the party who was first in time to make an application, will usually open.

5.08.43   The opening is important because it enables the party opening to predispose the court in his favour (see **14.02.03-06**).

5.08.44   The party opening may ask the court whether it has read the papers in advance, for example:

May I ask whether (the court) **has had the opportunity to read the papers?**

5.08.45 The party opening may also ask the court what papers are on the court file, for example:

May I ask whether you have the following affidavits (state name of person(s) making the affidavit and date sworn) **and reports** (state name of person(s) making the report and date).

5.08.46 If the court has read the papers, the party opening may omit **5.08.47(e)-(g)**.

5.08.47 The opening may contain:

(a) An explanation of the nature of the application, for example:

This an application for (state nature of relief sought).

(b) An explanation of the facts giving rise to the application.

(c) The names, ages and dates of birth of the parties.

(d) The names, ages and dates of birth of the children.

(e) The history of the marriage.

(f) A summary of any affidavit or part thereof.

(g) A summary of the evidence that the party is intending to call.

The party may also refer to any relevant law (if necessary).

5.08.48 The advocate must be prepared to adapt his opening to the requirements of the court.
If the court has not read the papers, after **5.08.47(a)-(d)**, the court may say:

Now that I know the basic issues, I shall read the affidavits.

5.08.49 Evidence on behalf of the Applicant

The evidence is usually on affidavit.

The party may read and/or call the evidence in any convenient order but will usually read the evidence of (and/or call) the applicant first.

The practice in **14.01.25-30** should be followed.

5.08.50   Order of Cross-Examination

The order of cross-examination follows the title order of the application (see **5.06.50**).

5.08.51   Close of the Applicant's Case

The party may say:

That is the case on behalf of the applicant (petitioner).

5.08.52   Submission of No Case to Answer

A submission of no case to answer is almost never made and is actively discouraged by the court.

It could be made where there is a technical defect in the case although, as a general rule, the submission should have been made as a preliminary issue.

5.08.53   The Case for the Respondent

As a general rule, the respondent does not make an opening speech (see **6.05.18A**).

The evidence on behalf of the respondent will follow the practice in **5.08.49**.

5.08.54   Speeches

The parties will make their speeches in such order as the court directs (or, as agreed between the parties and the court).

The usual order of speeches is that the party who opened the case will make his speech last, for example:

(a) Respondent.

(b) Applicant.

The parties may address the court on the facts and on any relevant law in their closing speeches.

5.08.55 Decision

The court will then sum up the case, and make such findings of fact and/or law as are appropriate.

The court may:

(a) Grant the application (in whole or in part).

(b) Refuse the application.

(c) Adjourn the case for further evidence and/or argument, usually after inviting the parties to address him further.

PART 3: CUSTODY AND ACCESS APPLICATIONS

INTRODUCTION

5.08.56 Custody and access applications, in relation to children of the parties, may be made at any stage in proceedings for divorce or judicial separation or within a reasonable time therafter.

The practice in **5.08.57-76** may also be used as a guide in applications under the Guardianship of Minors Act.

5.08.57 Custody

Custody may be awarded to one parent only or to both parents jointly. Where it is awarded to both parents jointly, the court will specify which parent has care and control of the child.

5.08.58 Access

Where an order for custody (or, care and control in the case of joint custody) of a child is made, the order will usually provide for the non-custodial parent to have access to the child.

5.08.59 The principles upon which the court will exercise its powers to make an order for custody of, or access to, a child and the orders which are available are complex and should be researched in the common practitioners' handbooks.

The overriding principle is that the welfare of the child(ren) will always come first.

5.08.60   The Child

An order for custody and access may be made in relation to:

(a) Any child of both parties.

(b) Any child who has been treated as a child of the family by both parties.

5.08.61   The Parties to the Application

Either party to the proceedings (or any 'linked' person, for example, a step-parent or guardian having custody or control of the child under a court order) may apply for custody of or access to a child.

5.08.62   Other persons may seek to become parties to the proceedings, for example, grandparents.

A person seeking to become a party must obtain the leave of the court on an application in writing to the registrar. The application should be accompanied by an affidavit setting out the person's reasons for wishing to be a party.

An appointment will be made for all parties to make representations.

5.08.63   The Court

All applications relating to custody of, or access to, a child are heard by a judge, except where:

(a) The application is unopposed.

(b) The order is to be made by consent.

(c) The application for access is agreed in principle, but the extent and frequency are in dispute.

5.08.64   Application for Custody and/or Access

The notice of application or summons is made on a standard form to the registrar of the court.

The party making the application should file:

(a) The notice of application (in duplicate).

(b) An affidavit in support of the application.

5.08.65   A copy of the notice of application and affidavit in support should be served as soon as possible after filing on the respondent(s).

Although postal service is acceptable, the party making the application may wish to effect personal service where the other party may attempt to avoid service.

5.08.66   Affidavit

See **5.02.05-06** and **5.08.25(a)-(c)**:

(d) Any relevant matters concerning the child (including his age and date of birth).

(e) Any proposals for the custody of, or access to, the child.

The affidavit should not contain:

(f) Unnecessary reference to the behaviour of the respondent, except where the applicant is claiming that such behaviour should be taken into account (see **5.08.68**).

5.08.67   Affidavit in Reply

Where the respondent to the application wishes to rely on an affidavit in reply, the affidavit should be served as soon as possible after receipt of the notice of application and affidavit in support. For the content of the affidavit, see **5.08.26** and **5.08.66**.

5.08.68   Welfare of the Child

The parties should always remember that the overriding principle in cases involving children is the welfare of the child (and not the alleged conduct of the parties).

5.08.69   Directions

The court will usually set a date for the hearing.

If a date cannot be arranged at the hearing for directions, a direction will usually be given that the case should only be listed on the court receiving certificates of readiness and time estimates from the advocates who are expected to conduct the case.

Where an affidavit in reply has not been filed, the court may treat the hearing as directions (see also **5.04.15** and **5.04.17**).

5.08.70   If both parties attend the hearing, the registrar will usually attempt to assess the issues between the parties and to consider the best way of resolving them.

In some courts, the hearing may have been arranged as a conciliation appointment with a court welfare officer. This can be very helpful as the court welfare officer (as an independent observer) can sometimes assist the parties to reach an amicable solution to their differences without a full trial. There may then be a consent order.

If the issues cannot be resolved, the court may treat the hearing as directions.

5.08.71   The following matters may be considered on directions:

(a)   The filing of further affidavits.

(b)   The preparation of reports by a court welfare officer.

(c)   Timing.

(d)   Interim arrangements for the children.

5.08.72   Reports

A report from the court welfare officer may be requested where either party and/or the court is of the opinion that the court will be assisted by the report in making a decision as to future welfare of the child.

The court welfare officer will not usually be present at court to be cross-examined on the report unless requested by the court or a party. A written request may be made to the reporting officer or an order may be made on directions.

PRACTICE

5.08.73   The conduct of the hearing of an application for custody and/or access varies greatly. One court may treat the hearing more informally than another.

The following is intended as a guide:

5.08.74 The hearing will be in chambers, see **5.08.16-18**.

5.08.75 The practice at the hearing will follow the practice in **5.08.40-55**.

5.08.76 If, in the decision, the court ignores the recommendation in any welfare report, the court should state its reasons for doing so.

CHAPTER 6

County Court

SECTION 1: INTRODUCTION

6.01.01   Mode of Address

His Honour Judge (name)   Your Honour.

Deputy Judge (name)   Your Honour.

Judge (name)	Your Honour.
Mr Recorder (name)	Your Honour.
Mr/Mrs Registrar (name)	Sir/Madam.
Mr/Mrs Assistant Registrar (name)	Sir/Madam.
Mr/Mrs Deputy Registrar	Sir/Madam.

6.01.02 A judge or registrar may sit in:

(a) Open court.

(b) Chambers (in the court room).

(c) Chambers (in the judge's or registrar's room).

6.01.03 Right of Audience

Barrister.

Solicitor.

A fellow of the institute of legal executives or an articled clerk (usually in uncontested or procedural matters).

An authorised local authority employee (usually in landlord and tenant actions where the local authority has brought the action).

Party in person.

Any person with the leave of the court.

6.01.04 Dress

Open Court:

Barristers	Robed.
Solicitor	Robed.
Party in person (or any other person)	Respectably dressed.

Chambers:

Barristers	Respectably dressed.
Solicitors	Respectably dressed.
Party in person (or any other person)	Respectably dressed.

6.01.05   Seating in Open Court and in Chambers (in the court room)

The advocates will sit in the rows and/or benches facing the judge.

The plaintiff will usually sit in the rows and/or seats on the left hand side of the court facing the bench.

6.01.06   Conduct in Open Court and in Chambers (in the court room)

Any person addressing the court should do so standing.

In chambers (in the court room), as a matter of courtesy the advocate and/or party should address the court standing. The court may invite the advocate and/or party to sit.

6.01.07   Conduct and Seating in Chambers (in the Judge's or Registrar's room)

If a hearing in chambers takes place in the judge's or registrar's room, the advocates and/or parties will usually remain seated to address the judge or registrar. The parties will usually be seated at a table.
The hearing is less formal than in open court.

6.01.08   Admission of the Public

When the court is sitting in open court, members of the public are usually admitted.

When the court is sitting in chambers (in the judge's or registrar's room), members of the public are almost always excluded.

6.01.09   When the court is sitting in chambers (in the court room), members of the public are usually excluded. If a party wishes to have other persons in court with him, for example, family or friends, that party should seek the leave of the judge or registrar.

6.01.10 Order of Presentation

The party having the burden of proof will usually address the court first.

In any other case the parties will usually address the court in title order of the case.

6.01.11 Witnesses

If the court is sitting in open court, witnesses will usually be present in court throughout the proceedings and/or the day, or part of the day, on which the witness gives evidence.

If the court is sitting in chambers (in the judge's or registrar's room), witnesses will very rarely be present in the room (except in small claims arbitrations, see **6.10.10**).

If the court is sitting in chambers (in the court room) practice varies although witnesses will not usually be present in the court room.

6.01.12 Standard of Proof

The civil standard of proof, 'on the balance of probabilities' applies, except **6.08.01:Committal Applications.**

6.01.13 Relationship to Practice in the High Court

The practice in the county court will usually follow the practice in the High Court.

Where no special procedure is laid down by the County Courts Act or the County Courts Rules, the Rules of the Supreme Court will apply.

6.01.14 Actions in the County Court

Actions in the county court may be commenced by:

(a) Summons.

(b) Originating application.

(c) Petition.

The action must be commenced either in the court for the district in which the defendant resides (or carries on business) or in which the cause of action arose.

6.01.15   Service of Proceedings

As a general rule, proceedings in the county court are served by the court by post.

SECTION 2: INTERLOCUTORY APPLICATIONS (METHOD)

PART 1: INTRODUCTION

6.02.01   An interlocutory application is any application made between the issue of proceedings and the final determination of the action, or part of the action, at trial.

6.02.02   Practice is more straightfoward in the county court than in the High Court.

The following sections should be read in conjunction with this section

5.02.01-47	**Interlocutory Applications (Method).**
6.07.23-47	**Family.**

6.02.03   Types of Interlocutory Applications

Interlocutory applications may be made *ex parte* or on notice.

6.02.04   Ex Parte Applications

An *ex parte* application is made by a party without giving notice to the other party or parties to the action.

The following applications are usually made *ex parte*:

(a) An application for leave to serve out of the jurisdiction (to a registrar).

(b) An application for an order restraining a party to a marriage from disposing of matrimonial assets (usually to a registrar, but sometimes to a judge).

(c) An application for the protection of a party to or child of a relationship (see **6.07.03-47**) (to a judge).

6.02.05 Applications on Notice

An application on notice is made by a party issuing and serving a notice of application (see **6.02.06**) on the other party or parties to an action. Interlocutory applications in the county court are usually on notice.

The following applications are usually made on notice:

(a) Summary judgment (see **6.03.01-10**).

(b) Pre-trial review (see **6.03.11-15**).

(c) Directions generally.

(d) Applications for injunctions (except in urgent cases).

6.02.06 Notice of Application

The notice of application is usually set out on a standard form available from the county court.

The notice of application must set out:

(a) The order sought.

(b) The reason(s) for the application.

6.02.07 An example of a notice of application:

> **The plaintiff's application is for an order that the defendant give further and better particulars of the defence in accordance with the plaintiff's request dated (date) and that in default the defendant be debarred from defending the action.**

6.02.08 Affidavits

An affidavit in support of the application must be prepared and served with the notice of application (except in simple cases) (see **5.02.05-06**).

The respondent may serve an affidavit in reply (see **5.02.07**).

6.02.09 Applications to the Registrar or Judge

An interlocutory application may be made to the registrar (see **6.02.10-20**) or the judge (see **6.02.21-26**).

PART 2: APPLICATIONS TO THE REGISTRAR

6.02.10 Most interlocutory applications are made to the registrar except where an injunction is sought (**6.02.04(b)** is the only exception).

The application is in chambers.

6.02.11 Right of Audience, Dress, Mode of Address & Conduct

See **6.01.01-07**.

6.02.12 Attendance of the Parties

As a general rule, if a party is represented at the hearing the party need not attend, although if the party is seeking to rely on an affidavit, the registrar may not allow its use if the maker is not present to be cross-examined (see **14.01.25-30**).

If the applicant does not attend, the application will usually be dismissed.

If the respondent does not attend, the application may be granted in his absence.

6.02.13 A party may consent to the application by letter (see, for example, **5.04.12&16**).

In a case where it would usually be expected for that party to attend, the party may apologise in the letter, as a matter of courtesy, for his non-attendance.

PREPARATION

6.02.14 The notice of application and affidavit must be served:

In most applications: two clear days before the hearing.

In applications for summary
judgment: seven clear days before the hearing.

6.02.15 In an *ex parte* application, the advocate should hand the affidavit (and notice of application) to the usher for him to give to the registrar (see, for example, **6.07.26**).

In an application on notice, the parties may hand any additional documentation to the registrar during the hearing if either party has not had the time to file the documentation in advance of the hearing.

6.02.16 The parties should attempt to file and serve all documents in advance. Late service of documents may lead to an adjournment of the application.

PRACTICE

6.02.17 The Appointment

Registrar's appointments are usually listed in blocks with time markings at, for example, 10.00, 10.30, 11.00, 11.30 and so on.

If a case is likely to last longer than half an hour, the court should be notified and an appropriate listing will be arranged.

6.02.18 On arrival at court, the party should give his name to the usher. The party will then wait to be called in to see the registrar.

6.02.19 The Hearing

The practice at the hearing varies greatly. Some registrars will allow the parties to conduct the application as they see fit, others will take over completely.

The parties are advised to follow the practice (with amendment) in:

5.02.17-20   *Ex Parte* **Applications**

5.02.22-36   **Applications on Notice**

The court draws up and posts the order made unless the party requesting it collects it for service.

6.02.20 Appeal

Appeal against a decision of the registrar in interlocutory applications is to the judge (see **6.06.01-13**).

PART 3: APPLICATIONS TO THE JUDGE

6.02.21 The application is usually in chambers (usually, in the court room).

6.02.22 Right of Audience, Dress & Mode of Address

See **6.01.01-07**.

6.02.23 Attendance of the Parties

See **6.02.12-13**.

6.02.24 Preparation

See **6.02.14-16**.

6.02.25 The Hearing

The parties are advised to follow the practice (with amendment) in:

| 5.02.17-20 | *Ex Parte* Applications |
| 5.02.22-36 | **Applications on Notice** |

The parties should note that, unlike the High Court, the court will have most of the documentation.

6.02.26 Appeal

Appeal is to the Court of Appeal (see **8.01: Civil Appeals** and especially **8.01.01-12**).

SECTION 3: PRE-TRIAL PROCEDURE

See **5.03: Summary Judgment**.

See **5.04: Directions**.

See **5.05: Discovery**.

PART 1: SUMMARY JUDGMENT

6.03.01 Introduction

Proceedings may be commenced by:

(a) Summons (with particulars of claim).

(b) Originating Application.

(c) Petition.

6.03.02 The defendant/respondent will be served with a document setting out the requirements for acknowledging service and lodging a defence (or other response).

The period of compliance is usually 14 days.

6.03.03 Judgment in Default

If the defendant fails to return the acknowledgement of service the plaintiff may apply for judgment in default (of acknowledgement of service) (see **5.03.05-10**).

6.03.04 Summary Judgment

If the defendant returns the acknowledgement of service and/or files a defence and the plaintiff considers that there is no real defence to the claim, the plaintiff may apply for summary judgment (see **5.03.11-14**).

6.03.05 An application for summary judgment is known as an Order 9, rule 14 application.

6.03.06 Summary judgment may be obtained in default actions only. A default action is one in which the only relief claimed is the payment of money (which can be quantified).

6.03.07 Summary judgment cannot be obtained where there is a claim for:

(a) General damages (for example, personal injury actions).

(b) An injunction.

(c) A declaration.

6.03.08 An application for summary judgment is made by issuing an application at the court returnable before the registrar.

6.03.09 Preparation for the Hearing

See **5.03.13-15-22**.

6.03.10 Practice

See **5.03.23-37**.

PART 2: PRE-TRIAL REVIEW

6.03.11 A Pre-Trial Review is the equivalent of a Summons for Directions in the High Court.

See **5.04:Directions**.

6.03.12 Directions as to the conduct of the action can be given at any time during the course of the pre-trial procedure (see **5.04.15**).

6.03.13 Directions

See **5.04.09**.

6.03.14 Practice

See **5.04.10-16**.

6.03.15 Non-Compliance

As a general rule, non-compliance will not be dealt with as severely in the county court as in the High Court especially where the parties are not represented (unless obvious gross default is proved).

PART 3: DISCOVERY

6.03.16   The principles of discovery are identical in both the county court and the High Court.

See **5.05:Discovery** (and especially **5.05.11-13**).

6.03.17   One of the problems in the county court is that cases are often badly prepared by people who are unqualified and do not understand the principles involved.

The court will often permit a party in person to refer to a document which is produced at court on the day of the hearing if it is relevant to the issues even if it has not been disclosed.

However, an adjournment (with costs thrown away) may be granted if a represented party produces a document on the day of the hearing.

6.03.18   If there is some evidence to show that a document has been wilfully concealed until the last moment (as opposed to overlooked) it is very unlikely that the court will permit its introduction and use at the hearing.

SECTION 4: SEEING THE JUDGE

INTRODUCTION

6.04.01   An informal discussion may take place between the advocates and the judge. It is called *seeing the judge*.

In any civil proceedings it is extremely unusual for the advocate(s) to ask to see the judge.

If it does take place, seeing the judge may be arranged as follows:

(a) The party wishing to see the judge should indicate informally to the other party or parties that he wishes to do so.

(b) The party or parties will ask the clerk if the judge will see them and state briefly the reasons for the request.

The judge will not see non-qualified persons in this way.

6.04.02   It is a matter for the discretion of the judge whether he will see the parties (see **3.03.03-04**). Many judges are not prepared to see the advocates privately.

In the county court, the judge is more likely to see the parties than in the High Court (except **6.04.09-11**), but less likely than in the crown court.

If the judge agrees to see the parties he will not usually see a party in the absence of the other party or parties (except see **6.04.10**).

6.04.03   Dress

Counsel and solicitors will usually remain robed in the judge's room. The judge may invite the parties to remove gowns (and wigs).

6.04.04   Mode of Address

High Court Judge:	Judge.
County Court Judge:	Judge.
Registrar	Sir.

6.04.05   Conduct

The party or parties should not sit down unless invited to do so by the judge.

The parties must be careful not to embarrass the judge or compromise the hearing of the case in open court.

6.04.06   Introduction of the Parties

The party asking to see the judge will usually introduce the parties:

Judge, I represent (name of party). **Mr** (name) **represents** (name of party). **It is my request to see you.**

REASONS FOR SEEING THE JUDGE

6.04.07   Conduct of the Hearing

The party may say:

The issues in this case fall into two distinct parts: liability and quantum. The evidence on quantum is almost entirely documentary. Would you agree to our dealing solely with liability to begin with.

6.04.08   Order on Breach in Committal Proceedings

The party should not ask the judge to indicate the actual order which he is minded to make on breach of an order in committal proceedings.

A potential order may be introduced as follows:

If the respondent were to admit breach of the order (state breaches admitted), **he is obviously anxious about the order you would make. He would be entitled to credit for his candour and** (state briefly best mitigating factor(s) or extenuating circumstance(s)). **Perhaps you could indicate your view?**

The judge may either give a definite indication or he may give no indication or he may simply say:

This is/is not a serious breach. I would make an order accordingly.

In this example, it is unlikely that the judge will give any better indication and counsel should not, as a general rule, press the judge to do so.

6.04.09   Matters which a party may not wish to raise in Open Court

There may be sensitive matters which a party does not wish to raise in open court, for example, for fear of aggravating problems that exist between the parties (in domestic proceedings).

For example, in an access dispute where an agreement has been reached, a party may say:

The proposed agreement may seem unusual. As a matter of courtesy we thought it would be best to explain the background without airing it in front of the parties as the situation is volatile.

The party may then explain the background to the agreement and (as required by the judge) how the agreement is likely to assist the situation.

6.04.10   Personal Problems of the Advocates

For example: listing problems; illness in the family.

6.04.11   Any other matter

The parties may raise any other matter which either party feels should be raised privately and not in open court.

For example, where it is suspected that there has been an improper communication between a party and a witness.

6.04.12   Leaving the Judge's Room

At the conclusion, the party making the request to see the judge will usually say:

Thank you for seeing us, Judge.

SECTION 5: TRIAL

6.05.01   Introduction

The trial of an action in the county court represents, in practice, the final decision of the issues between the parties which commenced with the issue of proceedings.

6.05.02 Issue of Proceedings

Proceedings may be commenced by:

(a) Summons.

(b) Originating application.

(c) Petition.

6.05.03 Interlocutory Applications

Applications made between the issue of proceedings and the final determination of the action, or part of the action, at trial are called interlocutory applications (see **5.02: & 6.02: Interlocutory Applications**).

6.05.04 Directions

The way an action proceeds is determined by the giving of directions (see **5.04 & 6.03.11-15**).

Orders made on directions are made on application to the court of any party or by the court of its own motion.

In preparation, the parties to the trial of an action should give consideration to any order made on directions or at the pre-trial review (PTR) (see also **5.04.09**).

PREPARATION

6.05.05 A party presenting a case should give consideration to the following:

(a) Formal documents (usually in the possession of the court), for example, pleadings and orders of the court.

(b) Evidential documents (not usually in the possession of the court), for example, correspondence between the parties, which tend to prove the facts alleged in the pleadings.

(c) Law.

6.05.06 Formal Documents: See **5.06.06-10**.

6.05.07 Evidential Documents: See **5.06.11-15**.

6.05.08   Presentation of Documents: See **5.06.16-19**.

6.05.09   Law: See **5.06.20-23**.

PRACTICE

6.05.10   Order of Presentation of Case

The plaintiff will usually present his case to the court first (except, see **5.06.24**).

ORDER OF PRESENTATION AND SPEECHES

6.05.11   Content and Purpose of Speeches

See **14.02.01-12**.

6.05.12   In the absence of any ruling by the court and/or agreement between the parties, the order of presentation and speeches is as follows:

6.05.13   Where the plaintiff and the defendant both call evidence:

Plaintiff opens.

Plaintiff's evidence.

See **6.05.18(A)**.

Defendant's evidence.

Defendant closes.

Plaintiff closes.

Defendant's response (if permitted).

6.05.14   Where the plaintiff calls evidence and the defendant calls no evidence:

Plaintiff opens.

Plaintiff's evidence.

See **6.05.18(B)**.

(Plaintiff closes).

Defendant closes.

Plaintiff's response (if permitted).

6.05.15 Where there are two or more defendants and/or parties:

The plaintiff calls evidence and the defendants and/or other parties call no evidence:

Plaintiff opens.

Plaintiff's evidence.

See **6.05.18(B)**.

(Plaintiff closes).

Defendants and/or parties close in order of title.

Plaintiff's response (if permitted).

6.05.16 Where there are two or more defendants and/or parties:

The plaintiff and the defendants and/or parties all call evidence:

Plaintiff opens.

Plaintiff's evidence.

See **6.05.18(A)**.

1st Defendant's evidence.

Continue in order of title.

Defendants and/or other parties close in order of title.

Plaintiff closes.

Defendants' and/or other parties' responses (if permitted, in such order as determined by the court).

6.05.17   Where there are two or more defendants and/or parties:

The plaintiff calls evidence and one or more but not all of the defendants and/or parties call evidence:

Plaintiff opens.

Plaintiff's evidence.

See **6.05.18(A)**.

Defendant and/or party calls evidence.

Continue in order of title.

Defendant and/or party calling evidence close in the order that they presented their cases.

See **6.05.18(B)**.

Plaintiff closes.

Defendant and/or party not calling evidence close in order of title.

Defendants' and/or other parties' response (if permitted, in such order as determined by the court).

6.05.18(A)   It is important to note that in the county court the defendant does not normally open, as of right. Different judges have different views on the matter and some are quite flexible.

The rule is said to be that the defendant has the right to one speech only and, therefore, if the defendant opens he does not close. Some judges will actually stop the defendant opening if he tries. Others, if asked, especially in complex cases, will permit both opening and closing.

If in doubt, the court practice should be checked in advance.

6.05.18(B)   Practice varies as to whether:

(a) The plaintiff gets a second speech.

(b) The defendant normally closes after the plaintiff if the plaintiff is permitted to close.

If in doubt, the court practice should be checked in advance.

PRACTICE

6.05.19   Open Court

The trial of an action is held in open court before a judge or registrar.

If the public are excluded and the court is sitting *in camera*, the conduct of the trial and mode of address are the same as in open court. The advocates are usually robed.

6.05.20   Calling the Case

The clerk of the court will read out the name of the case. If the parties are already in court, the parties should go to their seats.

If the parties are not in court, the usher will usually call the parties into court. The court clerk will then read out the name of the case.

6.05.21   Presence of Parties and/or Witnesses in Court

The parties and/or witnesses will normally be present in court throughout the proceedings or on the day or part of the day on which the party and/or witness gives evidence.

A party may make application to exclude a witness where, for example, there is an allegation of misconduct by that witness.

6.05.22   Jury Trials

See **5.06.34** (except defamation actions).

6.05.23   Introduction of the Parties

The plaintiff usually introduces the parties to the court:

In this action I appear for the plaintiff.
My learned friend, Mr (name of counsel) (or) **My friend, Mr** (name of solicitor) **appears for the** (name of defendant/party).

OR

The defendant, Mr (name) **appears in person.**

Where a party appears in person, the judge may ask if the unrepresented party is present and is content not to be represented.

6.05.24 Conduct of the Case

After the introduction of the parties, the trial proceeds in the same way as in the High Court (see **5.06.37-42**).

The parties should remember that a judge is addressed as **Your Honour** and a registrar as **Sir** or **Madam**.

THE CASE FOR THE PLAINTIFF

6.05.25 See **5.06.43-72**.

SUBMISSION OF NO CASE TO ANSWER

6.05.26 See **5.06.73-74**.

THE CASE FOR THE DEFENDANT AND/OR OTHER PARTY

6.05.27 See **5.06.75-82**.

SPEECHES

6.05.28 See **5.06.83-86**.

JUDGMENT

6.05.29 See **5.06.87-88**.

6.05.30 In the county court there is no court shorthand writer and the proceedings are not tape recorded. It is therefore important to try to obtain as accurate note as possible in order that the following matters are recorded for later consideration:

(a) Findings of fact.

(b) Rulings on the law.

(c) Method of applying the law.

The lack of a good note can hamper the chances of a successful appeal.

6.05.31 Judgment Order

See **5.06.89**.

6.05.32 Interest and Costs

See **5.06.90-92**.

6.05.33 Appeal

Appeal is to the Court of Appeal (Civil Division). The Notice of Appeal should be served within four weeks from the date on which the judgment or order was made (not drawn up) (see **8.01:Court of Appeal (Civil Division)** and especially **8.01.04(f)**).

SECTION 6: APPEALS FROM THE REGISTRAR TO THE JUDGE

INTRODUCTION

6.06.01 An appeal may be made from an order of the registrar to a county court judge.

The time limit for the service of the notice appealing an interlocutory application is five days.

The time limit for the service of the notice of appeal of a judgment or final order is 14 days.

6.06.02 The hearing is usually in chambers either in court or in the judge's room, or it may be in open court (see **6.01.05-11**).

6.06.03   Mode of Address & Right of Audience

See **6.01.01-03**.

6.06.04   Dress

The advocate is not usually robed. However, some judges may hear the appeal in open court when the advocate should be robed (except in family matters).

The practice in **6.10.03** does not apply.

APPEAL IN AN INTERLOCUTORY MATTER

6.06.05   The appeal is a re-hearing of the case before the judge.

6.06.06   The party appealing the order opens the case (whether he was the applicant or respondent before the registrar).

6.06.07   The party appealing the order may say:

> **I appear on behalf of the plaintiff/defendant, who appeals the order of Mr Registrar** (name) **made at this court on** (date).
>
> **The order was made on the plaintiff's/defendant's application for** (state nature of application).
>
> **The order made was** (state order appealed).
>
> **The plaintiff/defendant appeals against that order (or part of that order).**

6.06.08   The party appealing the order may then read any affidavit(s) used at the hearing before the registrar.

The party may also read and/or call any new evidence with the leave of the judge.

6.06.09   The party appealing the order may then say:
> **It is the appellant's/plaintiff's/defendant's contention that the appropriate order is** (state order sought) **for the following reasons** (refer to any relevant law).

6.06.10   The respondent may then read any affidavit(s) used at the hearing before the registrar.

The respondent may also read and/or call any new evidence with the leave of the judge.

6.06.11   If the parties have made an agreed note of the judgment of the registrar, either party may refer to that note although the judge is entitled to ignore it if he so wishes.

6.06.12   The parties will then be invited by the judge to address him (or the judge may give judgment without hearing either party).

6.06.13   Costs

Costs will usually be awarded to the party who is successful, although it is not unusual for costs to be in the cause or reserved to the trial judge (see **7.01.08-09&14-15**).

APPEAL FROM JUDGMENTS OR FINAL ORDERS

6.06.14   An appeal from a judgment or final order of the registrar to the county court judge may be made on a point of law only.

In this case, the appellate jurisdiction of the county court judge is comparable to that of the Court of Appeal.

6.06.15   The judge may only interfere with the order of the registrar if the registrar has erred in law or the registrar has acted unreasonably in the exercise of his discretion.

6.06.16   If the parties have made a note of the judgment of the registrar, the parties should agree the note and make a copy available to the judge.

The party or parties should submit the note to the registrar for authentication prior to the appeal. This is particularly important where the note is not agreed.

6.06.17   If no note is available, the registrar should be asked to state in writing his findings of fact and/or rulings on the law.

6.06.18   The practice is similar to the practice in appeals in interlocutory matters (see **6.06.06-12**), except that the judge is bound by the registrar's findings of fact (hence the need for an agreed note of judgment or authenticated transcript).

6.06.19   The party appealing the order may say:

I appear on behalf of the plaintiff/defendant who appeals the order of

Mr Registrar (name) **made at this court on** (date). **The order was made on the plaintiff's/defendant's application for** (state nature of application and order sought). **The order was** (state order appealed).

There is an agreed note/authenticated transcript of the judgment.

The (party) **appeals against the whole of the order/part of the order** (set out part of order appealed). **It is the appellant's contention that the Learned Registrar was wrong in law for the following reasons** (refer to any relevant law).

6.06.20 The practice in **8.01.39-54** (except **8.01.44**) is then followed with appropriate amendment.

6.06.21 Costs

Costs will usually be awarded to the successful party. However, it is not unusual for costs to be in the cause or reserved to the trial judge (where as a result of the appeal, there is to be a trial of the action) (see **7.01.08-09 & 14-15**).

APPEAL FROM THE REGISTRAR IN A SMALL CLAIMS ARBITRATION

6.06.22 There is no appeal from the registrar to the judge. An appeal may be made on a point of law only to the Divisional Court of the QBD (see **6.10.15-17**).

SECTION 7: FAMILY

INTRODUCTION

6.07.01 The jurisdiction of the county court in family matters includes claims affecting matrimonial property, maintenance, custody of and access to children, undefended divorces (in a county court designated as a divorce county court) and domestic violence.

6.07.02   The following sections are appropriate for use in the county court:

5.08.01-19	**Introduction.**
5.08.20-55	**Ancillary Relief Applications.**
5.08.56-76	**Custody and Access Applications.**

6.07.03   All county courts have jurisdiction to grant injunctions against molestation and/or to order a spouse or cohabitee to leave (or not return) to the parties' home.

6.07.04   For the purposes of **6.07.23-47** it is assumed that the applicant is the wife or female cohabitee in family proceedings.

6.07.05   Non-Molestation Order

A non-molestation order may be granted where the applicant is able to show that:

(a)   The other party has used actual violence against the applicant, and

(b)   The other party is likely to do so again.

6.07.06   The order will usually be granted *ex parte*. A return date may be fixed (see **6.07.36-37**).

6.07.07   The usual terms of the order are:

That the respondent do not assault, molest or otherwise interfere with the applicant/petitioner (state name) **or** (state names of children) **by himself, his servants or agents.**

6.07.08   Exclusion Order

An exclusion order may be granted in the same circumstances as a non-molestation order although the fear of future violence must be greater.

6.07.09   The order may be granted *ex parte*, usually where the judge is satisfied that the respondent has left the parties' home. A return date may be fixed (see **6.07.36-37**).

6.07.10   The usual terms of the order are:

That the respondent do not return to/approach enter or attempt to enter (address).

6.07.11 Ouster

An ouster may be granted where the applicant is able to show that the other party has caused actual bodily harm to the applicant or a child.

6.07.12   The order will only be granted *ex parte* in exceptional circumstances (see **6.07.28**). A return date will usually be fixed (see **6.07.36-37**).

6.07.13   The usual terms of the order are:

> **That the respondent vacate** (address) (or **the former matrimonial home at** (address)) **by** (date and time) **and do not return thereto (save as may be agreed in writing for the purposes of access to** (name(s) of children)).

6.07.14 Power of Arrest

A power of arrest may be attached to a non-molestation or exclusion order or an ouster, for the protection of the applicant, only where the application is made under the Domestic Violence and Matrimonial Proceedings Act (DVMPA).

It may be granted only where the applicant is able to show that:

(a) The other party has caused actual bodily harm to the applicant or a child, and

(b) The other party is likely to do so again.

PREPARATION

6.07.15   If the application is made other than under the DVMPA a plaint or petition should be issued.

6.07.16   In all applications the applicant should have:

(a) Notice of application.

(b) Affidavit in support.

(c) Draft order (optional).

6.07.17   If the application is *ex parte* (usually in an urgent case) the minimum practical requirement is an unsworn draft affidavit. In such a case, the applicant will have to give an undertaking to have the affidavit sworn and/or issue the appropriate proceedings within in a short period of time (which may be specified in the order) (see **6.07.29**).

The advocate is advised to check the practice of the court because some courts will not hear the application until all the documents are available however urgent the case.

PRACTICE

6.07.18   Right of Audience

Barristers.

Solicitors.

Qualified legal executives (in some courts).

6.07.19   Dress

Barristers and solicitors are not robed.

All parties should be respectably dressed.

6.07.20   Mode of Address

The hearing is before a judge only. The judge is addressed as **Your Honour**.

6.07.21   Conduct

The hearing is in chambers. It may take place in the judge's room or in the court room. In the judge's room the parties will sit. In the court room the parties will stand to address the judge.

6.07.22   Presentation of the Application

The advocate should always bear in mind that an order for non- molestation, exclusion or ouster affects both the liberty and property rights of the parties. It is therefore imperative that the court has all the information it needs to make a proper decision. This includes information which may not put the applicant in the best light.

EX PARTE APPLICATIONS

6.07.23 A party making an urgent *ex parte* application will usually telephone the court to find out when a judge can hear the application.

If a judge is available and the party is able to attend court, the hearing will usually take place at a convenient time at the beginning or end of the judge's morning or afternoon list.

6.07.24 If the party is able to attend the High Court, there is a divorce registry judge of the county court available on most days to hear *ex parte* applications. A party need not telephone in advance but is advised to do so.

6.07.25   Attendance of the Applicant

The applicant must attend court unless there is a good reason for her absence (for example, she is in hospital).

6.07.26   The Hearing

On arrival at court, the party should give his name to the usher or clerk and hand in any documentation (see **6.07.15-17**).

The party will then wait to be called in to see the judge.

6.07.27 The party making the application may say:

This is my application for (state order sought).

6.07.28 The party should make it clear what order is sought, for example:

The application is for a non-molestation order and ouster. However, I accept that today the court will not order the respondent to leave the matrimonial home. Therefore, the application is for a non-molestation order only.

6.07.29 If **6.07.17** applies, the party may then say:

At present, there is no formal application/proceedings have not yet been commenced. And I undertake to issue within (for example, 24 hours).

6.07.30 The party may then refer the judge to the affidavit (in such detail as required), for example:

There is a (draft) affidavit of (name of applicant).

6.07.31 The judge may indicate that he wishes to read the affidavit. He may then ask some questions to clarify matters.

6.07.32 The application will then usually proceed informally (often in the nature of a discussion between the advocate and the judge as to the merits of the application).

6.07.33 If there are matters which have arisen since the affidvit was drafted (or sworn), the advocate will usually call the applicant to give evidence (see **14.01.25-30**).

6.07.34 If the affidavit is defective, the advocate may be required to undertake to file an additional affidavit.

6.07.35 The Order

The judge may:

(a) Grant the application and make an order.

(b) Refuse the application.

(c) Adjourn the case for further evidence and/or argument.

If the judge makes an order and **6.07.17 & 29** apply, the order will have no effect until such time as any conditions (for example, the issuing of proceedings) have been complied with.

6.07.36 The Return Date

If the application is granted or adjourned, a return date may be fixed (which is the date on which the case returns to court *inter partes*). The return date may be seven days or (less frequently) up to three weeks.

6.07.37 In some courts which do not sit regularly, a return date is often not fixed. In which case, the respondent may apply for a date to be heard on the application. The terms of the order will be:

Liberty to apply.

6.07.38   Costs

If the applicant is legally aided, the advocate should ask for legal aid taxation and a certificate for counsel (if appropriate) (see **7.01.19-26**).

INTER PARTES

6.07.39   The hearing will be *inter partes*:

(a)   On the return date of an *ex parte* application (see **6.07.36-37**).

(b)   On the first hearing where the application has been made on notice.

(c)   On any subsequent hearing.

6.07.40   6.07.17 applies. **6.07.29** does not apply.

6.07.41   Attendance of the Parties

6.07.25 applies. The respondent should attend court unless he intends to submit to the application in full or his solicitors have negotiated an agreement with the applicant in advance.

6.07.42   Conduct

Applications for non-molestation, exclusion or ouster are often made at, or very soon after, the break-up of a relationship. The feelings of the parties are likely to be strong.

The advocates should therefore try to assist their respective parties to come to a settlement of their affairs that each can live with. If there is a trial of the issues, it can often make the situation between the parties worse.

The respective advocates should be ready to discuss the issues sensibly and, if possible, to negotiate an agreed order (or a party may give an undertaking to the court).

6.07.43   Undertakings

If a party gives an undertaking to the court, the undertaking is a solemn promise to the court. It has the same effect as if an order had been made.

Any breach of an undertaking can be punished by the court as a contempt (see **6.08**).

6.07.44 Agreed Orders

An agreed order may be put in writing in order that it can be handed to the judge for him to agree or amend. (It may be signed by the advocates.)

6.07.45 The following is a brief guide to assist in the drafting of consent orders:

Title of Case

Upon hearing counsel/solicitor for the (name of party) (**or** (name of party) **in person) and counsel/solicitor for the** (name of party) (**or** (name of party) **in person)**

And, upon the (name of party) **undertaking:**

(a) Copy **6.07.07** and/or

(b) Copy **6.07.10** and/or

(c) Copy **6.07.13**.

It is ordered, by consent, that:

(1) This application be adjourned generally.

(2) There be liberty to apply.

(3) There be no order as to costs save legal aid taxation and certificate(s) for counsel (or special allowance for solicitor).

6.07.46 Practice at the Hearing

Where there is a contested hearing, the practice will follow the practice in **5.08.38-55** (with appropriate amendments).

6.07.47 Order

An order may be made in the same terms as **6.07.45**. Any breach of an order can be punished by the court as a contempt (see **6.08**).

SECTION 8: COMMITTAL APPLICATIONS

INTRODUCTION

6.08.01 Breach of an order made by or of an undertaking made to the county court (or High Court) is punishable as a contempt. This can be by reprimand, fine or imprisonment. Therefore, the rules of evidence and procedure have to be strictly adhered to.

The standard of proof is 'beyond reasonable doubt' and not 'on the balance of probabilities'.

6.08.02 The party seeking to prove the contempt must prove:

(a) That the order was made.

(b) That the order was duly served upon the person against whom the committal is sought.

(c) That the person is in breach.

(d) That service of notice of the application to commit has been made.

PREPARATION

6.08.03 The advocate should prepare or ensure that he has the following:

(a) A copy of the order (see **6.08.04**).

(b) Affidavit of service of the order.

(c) Affidavit (of the applicant) of breach of the order.

(d) Affidavit of service of the application to commit.

6.08.04 The advocate should check that the court has a copy of the order on the court file.

If not, the advocate should ensure that he is able to prove the order (usually by affidavit).

6.08.05   Open Court

A committal application is always before a judge in open court (even though most committal applications relate to family, domestic or matrimonial matters).

The advocate is robed.

6.08.06   For the purposes of **6.08.07-13** it is assumed that the applicant is the petitioning wife or female cohabitee in domestic proceedings.

6.08.07   Presence of the Parties in Court

The applicant must be present in court to be cross-examined on her affidavit.

The respondent should be, but is often not, present in court or represented at the hearing.

If the respondent is not present it is essential that the applicant proves:

(a)   Service of the original order

(b)   Service of the Notice of the Committal hearing and affidavit(s).

If the respondent attends but is not represented, the Judge will usually warn him of the possible outcome of the case and ask him if he is content not to be represented.

PRACTICE

6.08.08   Opening

The applicant may open, as follows:

May it please Your Honour, I appear for the petitioner in this case on her application to commit the respondent for contempt. The respondent is represented by Mr (name)/**the respondent appears in person.**

On the (date) **His Honour Judge** (name) **made an order as follows** (state as fully as necessary).

The order was served on (date) **as proved by the affidavit of** (name) **sworn on** (date).

It is the petitioner's case that, in clear breach of that order, the respondent (state facts), **as proved by the evidence of the petitioner whose affidavit dated** (date) **is before the court and the affidavits of** (state others).

6.08.09   No judge actually wants to put a person in prison. The judge may interrupt at any stage to see if a committal is the only remedy sought or if the application can be dealt with in any other way.

6.08.10   Evidence of the Applicant

The applicant is called and sworn.

See **14.01.25-30**.

The applicant may be cross-examined in the usual way.

6.08.11   Evidence on behalf of the Applicant

The applicant may call and/or read (**14.01.25-30** applies) any other evidence to prove the breach of the order.

6.08.12   Close of the Applicant's Case

The advocate may say:

That is the case. And, it is upon that evidence that I would invite Your Honour to find the respondent to have breached the order and make an order for committal accordingly.

6.08.13   Evidence on behalf of the Respondent

The respondent and/or any witnesses on his behalf may be called, and any evidence read (**14.01.25-30** applies) to prove that he was not in breach of the order.

SPEECHES

6.08.14   Order of Speeches

The usual order of speeches is:

Respondent.

Petitioner.

Response (by respondent) if permitted.

6.08.15   Judgment

The judgment will usually contain:

(a) The judge's findings of fact.

(b) A finding as to whether there is a breach.

(c) The pronouncement of the order.

It may be that after having made his finding as to whether there is a breach, the judge will invite the parties to address him as to what order he should make.

6.08.16   Discharge

A person committed to prison may apply to the court for his discharge. He must show that he has purged or desires to purge his contempt.

The notice of application to discharge must be served on the committing party not less than one day before the application is to be heard.

SECTION 9: POSSESSION ACTIONS

INTRODUCTION

6.09.01   Possession actions are usually commenced by summons and particulars of claim, or may be commenced by originating application.

The date of the first hearing is usually given at issue and served on the defendant together with the summons or originating application.

6.09.02   Summary judgment is not available in possession proceedings in the county court.

It is therefore quite common, particularly in residential tenancy cases, that there will be no defence filed by the first hearing.

FIRST HEARING

6.09.03   At the first hearing the landlord should be in a position to prove the case by calling evidence.

The landlord must be able to prove:

(a)   Title to the property.

(b)   A tenancy (or the lack of one).

(c)   Service of notice of the proceedings.

(d)   A ground for possession.

(e)   That he is entitled to the order sought, for example, that it is reasonable to make an order for possession.

6.09.04   Adjournment

If the landlord does not have the evidence available and/or is not able to prove the case, and/or the tenant asks for an adjournment at the first hearing, the registrar will usually grant the adjournment and give directions (see **6.03.11-15**) for the filing of a defence, discovery (see **6.03.16-18**) and setting down for trial (except where an adjournment is sought in order to deliberately delay the case).

6.09.05   Order for Possession or Suspended Possession

If the parties attend and the tenant admits the allegations a possession order may be made, or a suspended possession order may be made (usually in a case of non-payment of rent).

The plaintiff opens:

> **In this action I appear for the plaintiff who is the landlord of** (address). **The defendant is Mr** (name) **who is the tenant of that property. I have had the opportunity of discussing the case with him and he admits the**

alleged arrears of rent which amount to £(-) up to the last rent date/
today/end of the week. He offers to pay the current rent together with
£(-) per week off the arrears which the plaintiff would be happy to
accept on the basis of a suspended possession order.

6.09.06   The registrar will usually ask the tenant if he agrees with the summary
made by the plaintiff and understands the nature of a suspended possession order.

6.09.07   The plaintiff may then ask for an order, as follows:

I therefore ask for an order for possession and judgment in the sum
of £(-), judgment to be suspended on payment of the current rent
together with £(-) per week as of the next rent date.

6.09.08   If the tenant admits the alleged arrears and, either makes no proposals
for the payment of the arrears and/or, offers to vacate the property, the plaintiff
may say:

I therefore ask for an order for possession and judgment in the sum
of £(-).

FULL TRIAL

6.09.09   If the action is adjourned, at the full trial of a possession action, the
practice in a trial in the county court should be used as a guide (see **6.05**).

SECTION 10:
SMALL CLAIMS ARBITRATIONS

INTRODUCTION

6.10.01   An arbitration is a less formal hearing of a trial in the county court before
a registrar.

The registrar is entitled to adopt any procedure he may consider to be convenient
and therefore practice will vary according to the methods of each registrar.

6.10.02   As the hearing is less formal the strict rules of evidence are not usually applied.

The parties are often not represented at an arbitration.

6.10.03   The advocates are not robed, although, if a judge has taken part or all of a registrar's list in his court, he may expect the advocates to be robed.

An advocate who has not taken his robes to court may address the judge as follows:

> **Your Honour, I apologise that I am not robed as this matter was listed as an arbitration before the registrar.**
>
> **Perhaps, Your Honour, would nevertheless allow me to be heard on behalf of** (name of party).

6.10.04   Arbitrations are held where there is a small claim (the advocate should check the appropriate financial limits) or where the parties agree.

6.10.05   Formal Documents: Pleadings and Orders (see **5.06.06-10**)

The claim is usually made on summons with particulars of claim.

The particulars of claim should set out the basis of the claim and specify the amount claimed with interest (if appropriate).

6.10.06   A party contesting the claim should file a defence and/or counterclaim.

There may be a defence to the counterclaim.

6.10.07   Directions (see **6.03.11-15**) are made by the court of its own motion or on notice by either party. The parties will have the orders made on directions and/or any other interlocutory order.

6.10.08   Evidential Documents (see **5.06.11-19**).

Copies of all documents on which a party intends to rely to prove his case are usually prepared by both parties and should be served on the court a reasonable time in advance of the hearing.

PRACTICE

6.10.09   The Hearing

The hearing is usually in the registrar's room. The parties and their advocates usually remain seated when addressing the registrar.

If the hearing is in a courtroom, the parties and their advocates may be required to stand when addressing the registrar. If an advocate has not had the opportunity of checking the practice of the registrar before the case, the advocate should stand to address the registrar until invited to sit.

6.10.10   Witnesses

The parties and/or witnesses will normally be present in court throughout the proceedings.

A party and/or witness taking the oath should always do so standing.

Some registrars do not require evidence to be given on oath. If an advocate has not had the opportunity of checking the practice of the registrar before the case, the advocate may say:

> **I now call** (name of witness). **I am unfamiliar with the practice in this court. Is it your practice to require witnesses to be sworn?**

6.10.11   Conduct of the Hearing

If both parties are represented the registrar may permit the advocates to conduct the hearing as a trial (see **6.05**).

If no party, or only one party, is represented, the registrar may conduct the hearing as a type of impartial inquisition or he may assist the parties to conduct the hearing as a trial.

If an advocate has not had the opportunity of checking the practice of the registrar before the case, the advocate should treat the hearing as a trial until the registrar indicates with what informality he may treat the usual rules of the court.

PRACTICE

6.10.12 The practice in a trial in the county court should be used as a guide (see **6.05.10-32**).

The advocate should always remember to treat matters briefly and to note with care any indications from the registrar to shorten the case.

6.10.13 Evidence

Strict rules of evidence do not usually apply although the advocate should present his case on the basis that strict rules of evidence will be applied.

Some registrars will accept bills, estimates, engineers' reports without the maker of the document being present at the arbitration.

6.10.14 Costs

Costs are only awarded for:

(a) The costs of the summons (issue fee).

(b) Witness expenses.

(c) Unreasonable conduct (usually dishonesty) of a party.

6.10.15 Appeal

There is no appeal on the facts from the finding of the registrar on a small claims arbitration.

6.10.16 The decision may be set aside by the judge (see **6.06**) on a matter of law only where it can be shown that either:

(a) There was an error of law, or

(b) The registrar's behaviour was such as to be considered misconduct.

6.10.17 If the finding and award are set aside there may be a rehearing.

CHAPTER 7

Costs

Section 1:   **Costs in Civil Proceedings**

Section 2:   **Costs in Criminal Proceedings**

SECTION 1: COSTS IN CIVIL PROCEEDINGS

INTRODUCTION

7.01.01   The Effect of an Order for Costs

In the civil courts, the costs of an action may often exceed the claim.

The parties should attempt to keep an approximate running total of the costs incurred to date for the purposes of considering settlement of the action.

7.01.02   The advocate should also be prepared to warn his client that civil litigation is not cheap; it is a gamble and, no matter how meritorious the claim, there is very rarely the certainty of winning.

THE GENERAL PRINCIPLES

7.01.03   Costs 'Follow the Event'

Costs are in the discretion of the court but will usually 'follow the event' (which means that the successful party will obtain his costs against the unsuccessful party).

7.01.04   Exceptions to 7.01.03

(a) Costs of an amendment to pleadings, without leave, are borne by the party making the amendment.

(b) Costs of an application to extend time limits are borne by the applicant.

(c) Costs of proving facts, where a party on whom a notice to admit Facts has been served (see **5.06.67**) has refused to admit the specified facts, are usually borne by the party refusing to make the admission.

(d) Costs of discovery before action against a party are borne by the applicant.

The general rule does not necessarily apply in the Family Division.

7.01.05   Costs are recovered by Order of the Court

A party is not entitled to recover the costs of any proceedings from any other party to the proceedings except by order of the court.

7.01.06   Exceptions to 7.01.05

A party is entitled to his costs without an order of the court, where:

(a) The action against that party is withdrawn without leave.

(b) The party accepts a payment into court in satisfaction of his claim.

(c) The party successfully defends a summons to set aside the proceedings on the ground of irregularity.

7.01.07   Costs in Interlocutory Proceedings

The issue of costs often arises in interlocutory proceedings because the proceedings are not a final determination of the issues between the parties.

See **5.02: Interlocutory Applications**.

See **5.03: Summary Judgment**.

See **5.04: Directions**.

See **5.05: Discovery**.

THE USUAL ORDERS FOR COSTS

7.01.08 Costs in the Cause

Costs in the cause means that on the final determination of the issues between the parties, the costs of the proceedings will follow the event.

7.01.09 An order for costs in the cause is usually made on an interlocutory application of an administrative nature or by agreement.

Either party may say, for example:

I ask for costs in the cause.

7.01.10 Costs in Any Event

Costs in any event means that the party in whose favour the order for costs is made, is entitled to his costs of the proceedings regardless of the final determination of the issues between the parties.

7.01.11 An order for costs in any event is usually made against a party to whom it appears to the court has incurred costs wastefully.

The successful party may say, for example:

I ask for the costs of this application in any event.

This application should never have been made/opposed.

7.01.12 Costs Thrown Away

Costs thrown away means that where proceedings (or any part of them) have been ineffective or set aside, the party in whose favour the order for costs is made, is entitled to his costs of the proceedings regardless of the final determination of the issues between the parties.

7.01.13   An order for costs thrown away is often made in similar circumstances to an order for costs in any event.

The successful party may say, for example:

I ask that the costs be costs thrown away.

The plaintiff/defendant refused to consent to this application and has now failed to attend for the hearing, I ask that the costs be costs thrown away.

7.01.14   Costs Reserved

Costs reserved means that the question of who should be liable for the costs of the proceedings will be determined on the final determination of the issues between the parties (although the costs will usually follow the event unless the court orders otherwise).

7.01.15   An order for costs reserved is often made on an interlocutory application.

Either party may say, for example:

I would ask that today's costs be reserved in order that they can be resolved at trial/on a later date.

7.01.16   No Order as to Costs

No order as to costs is frequently made in cases where both parties are legally aided and an apportionment of costs would be inappropriate.

Either party may say:

I would ask that there be no order for costs save legal aid taxation.

Both parties are legally aided with nil contributions.

7.01.17   Costs not to be Enforced Without Leave

A legally aided party is not normally liable for the other side's costs unless he can be shown to have assets.

7.01.18 If a party wins against a legally aided opponent he may obtain an order for costs not to be enforced without leave. This will enable him to return to court at a later date, if the legally aided party is found to have assets, to make an application for costs to be paid by that party.

The successful party may say:

> **The** (name of party) **having succeeded on all points, I would ask for judgment as prayed and costs.**
>
> **As the** (name of party) **is legally aided but is in employment, I would ask for costs to be awarded but not to be enforced without the leave of the court (after proper investigation of his means).**

7.01.19 Legal Aid Taxation

In order for a solicitor instructed by a client on legal aid to be able to have his fees paid out of the legal aid fund, it is necessary for him to have an order for legal aid taxation if the case is not finished.

7.01.20 A party may ask for legal aid taxation at each stage of the proceedings although the judge/registrar/master may decline to grant the order.

If in doubt, a party should ask for legal aid taxation, for example:

> **I ask that there be no order for costs save for legal aid taxation of the plaintiff's/defendant's/both parties costs.**

CERTIFICATE FOR COUNSEL

7.01.21 If counsel is instructed in certain interlocutory matters (but see **5.02.10(a)&24**), a certificate for counsel is required if his fee is to be allowed on taxation of costs.

As a general rule, a certificate for cousel is required for applications in chambers. It will only be given where the court is of the opinion that the expense of instructing counsel is justified.

7.01.22 A certificate for counsel is often thought to be needed for legal aid cases only. This is incorrect as it can be relevant on the taxation of costs between privately funded parties where one was represented by a solicitor and the other by a barrister.

7.01.23 A certificate for counsel is not presently required on the full trial of an action.

7.01.24   After an application for costs, a party may apply for a certificate for counsel as follows:

And I would ask for a certificate for counsel for the plaintiff/defendant/ both parties.

7.01.25   If the court is reluctant to grant a certificate for counsel, the party may draw the court's attention to:

(a)   The complexity of the case.

(b)   The issues of law.

(c)   Any matters (including (a) and (b)) which may have been raised but for agreement between the parties.

(d)   The time saved.

7.01.26   If it is not clear whether the application is an appropriate application on which to grant a certificate for counsel, a party may say:

I am unsure whether a certificate for counsel is required.

In order to avoid any doubt, perhaps I might have a certificate for counsel in any event?

FINAL ORDER

7.01.27   The final order for costs may be for costs to be taxed or costs to be taxed, if not agreed or costs may be assessed by the court in a specified sum if the parties agree.

   The basis and scope of the taxation of costs is complex and should be researched in the common practitioners' handbooks.

SECTION 2:
COSTS IN CRIMINAL PROCEEDINGS

INTRODUCTION

7.02.01   This section provides a brief guide to the award of costs in the courts of criminal jurisdiction, namely:

(a) Magistrates' Court.

(b) Juvenile Court.

(c) Crown Court.

(d) Court of Appeal (Criminal Division).

(e) Divisional Court of the QBD.

7.02.02   This section is divided into four parts:

Prosecution Costs out of Central Funds   7.02.05-08.

Prosecution Costs against the Defence   7.02.09-19.

Defence Costs out of Central Funds   7.02.20-30.

Defence Costs against the Prosecution   7.02.31-33.

7.02.03   As a general rule, the award of costs in the juvenile court follows the rules in the magistrates' court subject to certain procedural and financial limits which should be researched in the common practitioners' handbooks.

7.02.04   Central Funds

Central funds are maintained by the government.

As a general rule, a party making an application for costs will usually apply for costs out of central funds.

PROSECUTION COSTS OUT OF CENTRAL FUNDS

7.02.05   An order for the payment of the prosecution's costs out of central funds is rare (see **7.02.06(a)**).

A court may order that the prosecution's costs (or such amount as the court considers reasonable) be paid out of central funds in:

(a) Any proceedings before the magistrates' court, juvenile court, crown court, Court of Appeal (Criminal Division) or Divisional Court of the QBD in respect of an indictable offence.

(b) Any proceedings before the Divisional Court of the QBD in respect of a summary offence.

7.02.06   An order for the payment of the prosecution's costs out of central funds may not be made in favour of the following:

(a) The Crown Prosecution Service or other public authority.

(b) Any person acting on behalf of (or in his capacity as an official of) the CPS or other public authority.

7.02.07   The Amount

The amount may be:

(a) Specified (if agreed) by the court, or

(b) Assessed or taxed by the court.

7.02.08   The court has complete discretion in the award of costs out of central funds.

PROSECUTION COSTS AGAINST THE DEFENCE

7.02.09   Magistrates'Court, Juvenile Court and Crown Court

A magistrates' court, juvenile court or crown court may order that (a contribution towards) the prosecution's costs be paid by the defendant (or the parents of a juvenile defendant) where:

(a) The defendant is convicted by the magistrates' court or juvenile court.

(b) The defendant is convicted by the crown court.

(c) The crown court dismisses the appellant's appeal against conviction and/or sentence.

7.02.10   The prosecution may say (see **4.01.23**):

There is an application for costs of (amount) **made up as follows** (state how the amount is calculated).

OR

Would you/the court consider the question of costs?

7.02.11   Court of Appeal

The Court of Appeal may order that (a contribution towards) the respondents costs be paid by the appellant if the appeal or the application for leave to appeal is dismissed by the full court.

7.02.12   Divisional Court

The Divisional Court has the power to award costs *inter partes* on:

(a) An application for judicial review of a decision of the magistrates' court or the crown court.

(b) An appeal by way of case stated (from the magistrates' court).

7.02.13   The Amount

The amount of costs must be specified in the order.

Unlike **7.02.07&27** there is no provision for the taxation of costs against the defendant.

7.02.14   The court should take into consideration the nature of the case and/or defence when exercising its discretion to award costs against the defendant.

When considering the amount, the court will usually ask the question:

Has the defence, by its conduct, increased the costs of the case?

7.02.15   As a rough rule of practice, the court will not usually make an order for costs together with any other financial penalty which, in the opinion of the court, is more than the defendant could pay in one year.

7.02.16   Remission of Legal Aid Contribution

A defendant may be represented under a legal aid order accompanied by a contribution order (usually with periodic payments).

If the defendant is convicted, the court may remit any payments which have not fallen due, usually where a custodial sentence is imposed or where **7.02.15** applies.

The defence may say:

> **The defendant is on legal aid with a contribution of £(-), of which £(-) is still outstanding.**
>
> **Would you remit that sum?**

7.02.17   Appeal of Costs from the Magistrates' Court or Juvenile Court to the Crown Court

A defendant, against whom an order to pay part or all of the prosecution's costs has been made, may appeal against conviction and/or sentence to the crown court.

Where the appeal is allowed the crown court may also review the order for costs.

Where the appeal is dismissed, see **7.02.09(c)**.

7.02.18   A defendant may not appeal an order for costs against him on its own except where the court improperly exercised its discretion in making the order. In this case the appeal is to the Divisional Court of the QBD. The defendant must obtain leave (see **8.03.07-10**).

7.02.19   Appeal of Costs from the Crown Court to the Court of Appeal

A defendant against whom an order to pay part or all of the prosecution's costs has been made may appeal the order on its own to the court of appeal.

The defendant must obtain leave (see **8.02.16-19**).

DEFENCE COSTS OUT OF CENTRAL FUNDS

7.02.20 Defendant's Costs Order

A defendant's costs order is a payment out of central funds to a defendant of such amount as the court considers reasonably sufficient to compensate him for any expenses properly incurred by him in the proceedings.

7.02.21 A defendant's costs order is made in respect of expenses actually incurred by the defendant.

If the defendant is legally aided, payments made by the Legal Aid Fund are disregarded.

If the defendant is not legally aided, a defendant's costs order may also include the costs of his representation.

A defendant's costs order may be made (**7.02.22-26**):

7.02.22 Magistrates' Court (and Juvenile Court)

(a) Where the prosecution offer no evidence or otherwise discontinue the proceedings (see **1.06.13**).

(b) Where the defendant is discharged in committal proceedings (see **1.05.25**).

(c) Where the defendant is found not guilty of an offence tried in the magistrates' court (see **1.06.49-50**).

7.02.23 Crown Court

(a) Where the prosecution offer no evidence or otherwise discontinue the proceedings (see **3.04.07**).

(b) Where the defendant is acquitted following a trial (or re-trial) on indictment (even if he is acquitted on only one of several counts). The order may include the defendant's costs in the magistrates' court (or of the first trial) (see **3.04.96**).

7.02.24 Appeal against Conviction and/or Sentence from the Magistrates' Court or Juvenile Court to the Crown Court

(a) Where the conviction is set aside (see **3.05.16(a)**).

(b) Where a less severe punishment is imposed (see **3.06.07**).

The order in (a) or (b) may include the costs in the magistrates' court or juvenile court (although the order is still called a defendant's costs order).

7.02.25 Court of Appeal

(a) Where the appeal against conviction is allowed (see **8.02.45**).

(b) Where the court substitutes a verdict of guilty to another offence (see **8.02.44(c)**).

(c) Where the appeal against sentence is allowed (see **8.02.55**).

The order in (a)-(c) may include the appellant's costs in the court(s) below.

7.02.26 Divisional Court of the QBD

Where any proceedings in a criminal matter are determined by the court (see **8.03.26**).

The order may include the appellant's costs in the court(s) below.

7.02.27 The Amount

The amount may be:

(a) Specified (if agreed) by the court, or

(b) Assessed or taxed by the court.

7.02.28 The court has a complete discretion in making a defendant's costs order.

As a general rule, the court should make a defendant's costs order if the defendant is entitled to one except where:

(a) The defendant brought suspicion on himself. (The advocate should be prepared to argue this exception as it is often overworked).

(b) The defendant was acquitted on a technicality.

7.02.29 When making the application for a defendant's costs order, the defence may say:

Would you make a defendant's costs order?

The defendant is legally aided. He has incurred out of pocket expenses of £(-) namely (state nature of expenses) **in these proceedings.**

And I would ask for an order in that sum.

OR

The defendant is not legally aided. He has personally incurred the cost of his representation in these proceedings.

And I would ask that the costs be taxed.

7.02.30 Return of Legal Aid Contribution

A defendant may be represented under a legal aid order accompanied by a contribution order (usually with periodic payments).
If a defendant is acquitted or discharged, the court will usually:

(a) Remit any payments which have not fallen due.

(b) Remit any payments which have fallen due but not been paid.

(c) Order that some or all of the payments which have been made be returned.

The defence may say:

The defendant is on legal aid with a contribution of £(-). Would you order that his legal aid contribution be returned?

DEFENCE COSTS AGAINST THE PROSECUTION

7.02.31 Magistrates' Court, Juvenile Court, Crown Court, Court of Appeal

The defendant's costs will usually be paid out of central funds (see **7.02.04**).

However, the court may order either party to pay costs incurred as a result of an unnecessary or improper act or omission by another party to the proceedings.

7.02.32 The court will usually indicate whether it is of the opinion that an order for costs should be made against the prosecution, for example:

There is no reason that the prosecution should not pay the costs thrown away.

The prosecution may then address the court.

7.02.33 Divisional Court

See **7.02.12.** It is not necessary to satisfy the court of any impropriety.

CHAPTER 8

Appeals

Section 1:   **Court of Appeal (Civil Division)**

Section 2:   **Court of Appeal (Criminal Division)**

Section 3:   **Appeals to the High Court**

SECTION 1:
COURT OF APPEAL (CIVIL DIVISION)

INTRODUCTION

8.01.01   An appeal from a decision of a judge of the High Court or the county court may be made to the Court of Appeal, Civil Division.

8.01.02   If a party is intending to appeal a decision of the county court, the party should consider an application for a retrial. The county court has wide powers to order a retrial (for example, where there is new evidence). A retrial is quicker and cheaper than an appeal to the Court of Appeal.

8.01.03   An appeal to the Court of Appeal is often in two stages:

(a)   Application for leave to appeal.

(b)   Full hearing of the appeal.

APPLICATION FOR LEAVE TO APPEAL

8.01.04   Leave to appeal a decision of the High Court or county court is required in certain cases, namely:

(a)   Interlocutory judgments and orders, except no leave is required:

    (i)   Where an injunction is granted or refused.

    (ii)   Where the liberty of the subject is concerned.

    (iii) In other specified cases.

(b)   An order made by consent of the parties.

(c)   An order as to costs only.

(d)   An order of a judge in chambers in the Family Division or the Chancery Division.

(e)   A determination by a Divisional Court of an appeal (see **8.03.40**).

(f)   *County court only:* on a financial claim (but not the award) which is less than one half of its financial jurisdiction:

    For example, where the financial jurisdiction is limited to £5,000 and the claim was for £2,000, leave will be needed. If the claim was for £3,000 (even if the award was £2,000) leave will not be needed.

8.01.05   In most cases the party may (and in **8.01.04(b) & (c)** must) make the application for leave to the Judge whose order that party is appealing.

8.01.06   The party intending to appeal may say:

It is the plaintiff's/defendant's intention to appeal the order made against him.

It is clear that there is some conflict between the leading cases which should be resolved. And in the circumstances, I ask for leave to appeal.

8.01.07   If leave to appeal is refused or the application is not made to the judge whose order the party is appealing, the party must apply for leave to a single judge of the Court of Appeal.

8.01.08   The appellant must file a notice of appeal within four weeks (or any shorter period in an interlocutory appeal) of the judgment or order (although an application for an extension of time may be made to the Registrar of Civil Appeals).

8.01.09   The notice of appeal must state the grounds of appeal and the nature of relief sought on appeal.

No grounds can be raised at the hearing of the appeal that are not contained in the Notice of Appeal (although leave to amend may be sought).

8.01.10   The notice of appeal will not be effective until leave to appeal has been granted.

8.01.11   The notice of application for leave should be lodged with the Civil Appeals Office.

The following documents are usually filed with the notice:

(a)   The order which is the subject of the appeal.

(b)   The order refusing leave (see **8.01.05-07**).

(c)   Draft grounds of appeal.

(d)   Any affidavit(s) in support.

8.01.12   The application for leave is usually heard *ex parte* by a single judge of the Court of Appeal sitting in chambers (see **5.02.38-42**).

The registrar cannot give leave to appeal.

8.01.13   Practice on the Application for Leave

The appellant may say:

> **This is my application for leave to appeal the order of** (name of judge) **at** (name of court) (sitting in chambers) **on** (date). **Mr** (name) **now appears on behalf of the defendant/plaintiff** (if the proposed respondent is represented).

8.01.14   The appellant will then usually:

(a)   Outline the nature of the case.

(b)   Outline the facts as proved at the hearing.

(c) Outline the issues in dispute and/or any relevant law.

8.01.15 The single judge will:

(a) Grant leave to appeal, or

(b) Adjourn the hearing for the case to be argued *inter partes* (if appropriate), or

(c) Refuse leave to appeal. There is no appeal from that decision.

8.01.16 If leave to appeal is granted the party must serve notice of appeal, if this has not already been served (see **8.01.08-11**).

8.01.17 Service of the Notice of Appeal

The notice of appeal should be served on all parties within four weeks of the date of judgment or order being appealed and, if appropriate, on the registrar to the county court.

8.01.18 If a party has applied for legal aid, the legal aid application is unlikely to have been considered within the time limit of four weeks. An application for an extension of time is unlikely to be granted pending consideration of the application. The notice of appeal should be served.

8.01.19 Effect of Giving Notice of Appeal

A notice of appeal does not act as an automatic stay of execution.

8.01.20 The parties may agree to take no steps to enforce the judgment until the appeal is heard.

If the parties do not agree, the appellant must apply for a stay of execution to the judge of first instance and/or to a single judge of the Court of Appeal on notice (*inter partes*).

8.01.21 Leave to Call Fresh Evidence

An application to call fresh evidence may be made on summons (after leave to appeal is granted, if appropriate) to the Registrar of Civil Appeals. The application should be supported by affidavit.

If the application to call fresh evidence is granted, the court, at the hearing of the appeal, may order a new trial.

8.01.22 The party making the application must show special grounds, namely:

(a) That the evidence was not readily available at the trial.

(b) That, if the evidence had been available at the trial, it would have been likely to have influenced the decision.

(c) That the evidence appears to be admissible and truthful.

PREPARATION FOR APPEAL

8.01.23 Documents

The following documents must be deposited at the Civil Appeals Office within seven days of service:

(a) Copy of the judgment order (see **5.06.89**).

(b) Two copies of the notice of appeal.

(c) Office copy of list of exhibits.

8.01.24 Respondent's Notice

If the respondent wishes to contest the appeal or is seeking a variation of the order, he must serve a respondent's notice on the parties within 21 days (or seven days in an interlocutory appeal) of receipt of the notice of appeal.

8.01.25 The court will then set down the appeal in the appropriate list according to the court from which the appeal is made and the nature of the appeal.

The appellant must, within two days of setting down, give notice of setting down to the parties in **8.01.17**.

8.01.26 The case will eventually appear in the Daily Cause List.

The appellant must then within 14 days lodge at the Civil Appeals Office three bundles each containing copies of the following documents:

(a) Notice of appeal.

(b) Respondent's notice.

(c) Any further or amended notices.

(d) Judgment order appealed.

(e) All pleadings.

(f) List of exhibits.

(g) Any relevant affidavit.

(h) Any other relevenat documents (including correspondence).

(i) A note or transcript of the judgment and, if appropriate, of any relevant part(s) of the evidence (see **8.01.27**).

8.01.27 Agreed Note

There is no official shorthand note made of proceedings in the county court.

The parties will have a note of the evidence and the judgment. (Counsel is under a duty to take a note.)

The note should be agreed by the parties, if possible, and submitted to the judge who may agree the note (with or without comment). The judge may be asked to provide copies of his note.

If the note made by the parties and the judge's note of his judgment differ, the judge's note is final.

The note signed by the judge can be used in the appeal.

8.01.28 In an appeal from an interlocutory order in the High Court, **8.01.27** applies.

8.01.29 Transcripts

In the High Court the proceedings will have been tape recorded and there may also be a shorthand note.

The appellant must arrange (and pay) for the tape or shorthand note to be typed and certified. The typed copy will usually be sent direct to the Civil Appeals Office.

8.01.30 Law

The parties should exchange lists of authorities in advance of the hearing in order that each party can properly prepare his argument(s).

The parties should also hand to the court the lists of authorities in advance of the hearing (and not later than 10.00 am on the day of the hearing).

8.01.31   Skeleton Arguments/Chronologies

The Court of Appeal requires the use of skeleton arguments (see **8.01.33**).

A skeleton argument must be accompanied by a chronology of events relevant to the the appeal (except in urgent cases or where the court orders otherwise).

As a general rule, a skeleton argument should be lodged by all parties to the appeal.

8.01.32   Three copies of the skeleton argument and chronology of events must be lodged with the civil appeals office (and a copy each delivered to the other parties):

Fixed date appeals:	Not less than four weeeks before the date of the hearing.
Short warned list appeals:	Not less than 10 days before the case becomes 'on call'.

8.01.33   The skeleton argument should:

(a) Identify (not argue) any point of law, with reference to the principal authorities in support.

(b) Identify any finding of fact in the transcript or notes of evidence and state briefly the basis on which it is contended that the court can interfere with that finding of fact.

PRACTICE

8.01.34   **Right of Audience**

Barristers.

Litigants in person.

8.01.35 Dress

Barristers are robed.

Litigants in person should be respectably dressed.

8.01.36 Mode of Address

There will usually be three judges.

The court is addressed as My Lords/Your Lordships but where a party is responding to an individual judge, the judge is addressed as My Lord or My Lady.

8.01.37 Conduct

The hearing is in open court.

A party addressing the court should do so standing.

8.01.38 Calling the Case

The associate will stand and read out the name of the case.

The presiding judge will then indicate to the appellant that he may begin.

THE CASE FOR THE APPELLANT

8.01.39 Appellant's Introduction

The appellant may say:

My Lords, this is an appeal from the judgment/order of Mr Justice/ Judge (name) sitting in the (name of) **Division/**(name of) **Court. My Learned Friend Mr** (name) **appears for the respondent.**

8.01.40 The court will usually have read all the papers in advance. The presiding judge may say:

We have read the papers Mr (name).

If the court does not give any indication the appellant may say:

Before I present the appeal can I ask whether (the court) **has had the opportunity to read the papers?**

If the court has read the papers, the appellant may omit the introduction (**8.01.41**) and argue the main points of the appeal.

If the court has not read the papers, the appellant may introduce the case.

8.01.41   Content of the Introduction

The introduction should contain:

(a)   An outline of the nature of the case

(b)   A summary of the issues in dispute

(c)   Reference to the skeleton argument, (which will then form the basis of the argument).

8.01.42   Presentation of the Appeal

After opening the appellant may present the appeal in as much detail as the appellant feels is necessary (or as indicated by the court).

8.01.43   The appellant may:

(a)   Refer to the events leading up to the issue of proceedings with reference to the chronology (if appropriate).

(b)   Read or refer the court to any agreed note of evidence.

(c)   Read or refer the court to any relevant part of the transcript of evidence.

(d)   Read any relevant affidavit.

(e)   Read or refer the court to any part(s) of the agreed note or transcript of the judgment.

(f)   Refer the court (with reference to any document) to the issues in dispute and whether the issues in dispute are of law only or mixed law and fact.

(g)   Set out the law on which the appellant relies with reference to the skeleton argument and refer the court to any authorities.

The court may indicate that it has read any of (a)-(g). The appellant may then argue each point shortly.

8.01.44   The appellant may, either after introducing the case or when referring the court to the evidence, call or read any fresh evidence if leave has previously been obtained to call it (see **8.01.21-22**).

Leave to call fresh evidence will not be given at the hearing.

8.01.45   A party presenting his case to the court should never expect to do so without interruption or intervention from the court.

8.01.46   The court is very likely to direct the party's attention to certain areas of the case.

The court will usually indicate if it considers certain grounds of appeal to be without merit.

The party should note such indication carefully and be ready to move to another argument if necessary.

THE CASE FOR THE RESPONDENT

8.01.47   If the appellant has not established any of the grounds of appeal, the court may dismiss the appeal before hearing the respondent.

The usual form of words is:

We need not trouble you, Mr (name of respondent).

8.01.48   If the appellant has established any of the grounds of appeal the court will usually indicate to the respondent the grounds on which the respondent should address the court.

8.01.49   The respondent should note any indication of the court carefully.

8.01.50   The respondent may then present his case to the court in the same way as the appellant (see **8.01.39-46**).

8.01.51   The usual order of response is in the title order of the action (although this may be varied by the direction of the court of appeal or by agreement of the parties).

REPLY

8.01.52   The appellant may reply to any new matter raised by the respondent (or other party) or the court. The appellant should not (and will usually not be permitted to) repeat the arguments in **8.01.39-46**.

JUDGMENT

8.01.53   The court may:

(a)   Deliver a full judgment.

(b)   Deliver a short judgment with reasons to follow.

(c)   Reserve judgment.

8.01.54   In judgment the court may:

(a)   Allow the appeal in full (or in part)

(b)   Dismiss the appeal

(c)   Make any order which could have been made by the lower court

(d)   Order a new trial in the lower court (usually where fresh evidence has been admitted).

8.01.55   Costs

As a general rule, costs follow the event.

A successful legally aided party has an obligation to apply for costs (usually against a non-legally aided party) to indemnify the legal aid fund.

A successful non-legally aided party may apply for costs against a legally aided party although the court will usually order that costs not be enforced without leave of the court (see **7.01.17-18**).

If both parties are legally aided the usual order for costs will be no order for costs save legal aid taxation (see **7.01.16**).

SECTION 2: COURT OF APPEAL (CRIMINAL DIVISION)

PART 1: INTRODUCTION

INTRODUCTION

8.02.01 An appeal against conviction or sentence on indictment by the crown court is made to the Court of Appeal, Criminal Division.

An appeal against a decision of the crown court on any other matter is made to the Divisional Court of the Queen's Bench Division (see **8.03: Appeals to the High Court**).

8.02.02 Leave to Appeal

An appellant may appeal against conviction, as of right, to the Court of Appeal, Criminal Division

(a) If the ground(s) on which the appellant relies involves a question of law only, or

(b) If the trial judge has granted a certificate of fitness for appeal.

In all other cases the appellant must obtain the leave of the Court of Appeal.

8.02.03 As a general rule, an appellant to the Court of Appeal against sentence must obtain the leave of the court.

8.02.04 Time Limits

The appellant must serve notice of appeal or notice of application for leave to appeal (on a standard form) on the crown court within 28 days of the conviction, order or sentence appealed.

8.02.05   The notice must be accompanied by grounds of appeal (see **8.02.08**).

The effect of the time limit is that, if sentence is delayed for any reason, the appellant must nevertheless serve notice of appeal of the conviction.

If sentence is later appealed, the appeals may be consolidated.

8.02.06   The Decision to Appeal

It is the duty of the advocate instructed in the defence of a person, who is convicted or sentenced, to consider and advise on the merits of an appeal.

This should first be done by giving provisional advice immediately after conviction or sentence at court. As a general rule, counsel should not wait to be asked by the defendant for any provisional view on appeal.

8.02.07   Advice on Appeal

The initial advice on appeal should be followed by a written advice on appeal, if requested, and, where appeal is advised, signed grounds of appeal.

8.02.08   Grounds of Appeal

The grounds of appeal must identify the matters relied on and state reasons for the appeal. It is not sufficient for counsel drafting the grounds of appeal to state only that 'the conviction is unsafe and unsatisfactory'.

The advice on appeal (and grounds of appeal) should be sent to the solicitor, usually within 14 days, to enable the solicitor to consider the prospects of the appeal with the appellant.

8.02.09   Service of the Notice of Appeal

If counsel has advised an appeal, the solicitor should send the notice of application, the signed grounds of appeal and the advice on appeal to the crown court.

The crown court will forward these to the Registrar for Criminal Appeals.

Counsel may also draft a note to the registrar if he wishes to bring to the registrar's attention any additional matters, for example a request for a transcript of the evidence/summing up or other additional information.

8.02.10   Bail Pending Appeal

An application for bail pending appeal may be made to:

(a) A single judge of the Court of Appeal, sitting in chambers, on service of the grounds of appeal.

(b) The judge at first instance, where a certificate was issued by that judge.

See **4.02: Bail**, although the advocate should remember that the primary test for bail pending appeal is: What are the chances of the appeal being successful?

8.02.11   Transcripts

The registrar may order that a transcript be obtained of any part of the proceedings.

If the registrar is of the opinion that part or all of the transcript requested is not necessary, he may refer the request to a single judge of the Court of Appeal for his consideration.

8.02.12   Perfecting the Grounds of Appeal

If a transcript is obtained, the registrar will usually invite counsel to perfect his grounds of appeal in the light of the transcript.

When perfecting the Grounds of Appeal, counsel may alter or amend any drafted ground of appeal.

Counsel may also refer (usually in margin note), in respect of any ground of appeal, to:

(a) The appropriate page and section letter of the transcript.

(b) Any document.

(c) Any exhibit.

(d) Any authority on which he intends to rely.

8.02.13   Leave to Call Fresh Evidence

If the appellant wishes to call fresh evidence, he should apply on a standard form to the registrar enclosing the following documents (for the consideration of the single judge):

(a) A (section 9 CJA) statement from the witness.

(b) An affidavit (usually sworn by the appellant's solicitor) stating why the witness was not available at the trial.

Copies of the statement and affidavit should be served on the Crown.

8.02.14   The full court will consider the application for leave to call the witness.

8.02.15   At the hearing of the appeal, the appellant must show special grounds, namely:

(a) That the evidence was not available at the trial.

(b) That, if the evidence had been available at the trial, it would have been likely to have influenced the decision.

(c) That the evidence appears to be admissible and truthful.

8.02.16   Obtaining Leave

The (Perfected) Grounds of Appeal and any other relevant documents are then placed by the registrar before a single judge of the Court of Appeal for his consideration.

The single judge may grant the application for leave to appeal, refuse it or refer it to the court.

The registrar has no power to grant leave.

8.02.17   Leave Granted

If the single judge grants leave to appeal or refers the application to the court (or where the appeal is by certificate of the trial judge), the single judge will usually grant legal aid for the hearing.

The registrar will then assign counsel (who will usually be the counsel who appeared at first instance).

8.02.18   Leave Refused

If the single judge refuses leave, the registrar will send a notification of the refusal (and any observations made by the single judge) to the appellant and his solicitors.

If the appellant wishes to pursue the appeal further, he (or his solicitor) must give Notice of Intention to renew the application before the full Court of Appeal within 14 days.

The Court of Appeal will not usually grant legal aid to renew the application.

8.02.19   If the appellant wishes to pursue the appeal and he is serving a custodial sentence, he may be at risk of the full court ordering that the time spent in custody pending appeal not count against the sentence if it dismisses the application for leave.

8.02.20   Preparation for the Hearing of the Appeal/Renewed Application for Leave

The appellant (usually after consultation with the registrar) may provide to the court any additional material which he considers would be of assistance to the court when considering the appeal.

The appellant may also further perfect the grounds of appeal, if appropriate.

8.02.21   Case Law and Authorities

The appellant should provide a list of cases and/or authorities to the court and the other parties in advance of the hearing.

It is recommended that the list should be provided to the court and any other party to the appeal (at the very latest) by 4.00 pm on the day preceeding the hearing.

The court has extensive reports available but if the authority to be used is not a common work, it is recommended that the appellant have sufficient (photo) copies available for the court and any opponent(s).

8.02.22   Skeleton Arguments

In a conviction appeal, the appellant may provide to the court, in advance of the hearing, four copies of a note setting out the skeleton arguments upon which he intends to rely (see **8.01.31-33**). A copy should also be provided to any other party to the appeal.

PRACTICE

8.02.23   Right of Audience

Barristers.

Appellant(s) in person.

8.02.24   Conduct and Dress

The hearing of an appeal is in open court. Any person addressing the Court does so standing.

Barristers are robed.

Appellants in person should dress respectably.

8.02.25   Mode of Address

The court is addressed as My Lords/Your Lordships although when one judge addresses the advocate, the advocate should reply to that judge as My Lord/Lady.

8.02.26   Presence of the Appellant

If the appellant is in custody, he will usually be produced for the hearing of his appeal.

8.02.27   Role of the Crown

If the appeal is against conviction, the Crown will usually be represented.

If the appeal is against sentence, the Crown will not usually be represented.

It is the duty of the Crown to assist the court.

PART 2: APPEAL AGAINST CONVICTION

8.02.28   Calling the Case

The associate will stand and read out the name of the case.

The presiding judge will then indicate to the appellant that he may begin.

THE CASE FOR THE APPELLANT

8.02.29 Appellant's Introduction

The appellant may say:

This is an appeal/application for leave to appeal the conviction of (name) **before His Honour Judge** (name) **sitting at the** (name) **Crown Court on** (date).

My learned friend, Mr (name), **appears for the Crown.**

8.02.30 The advocate should assume that the court has read all the papers in advance.

8.02.31 Content of the Introduction

The introduction may contain:

(a) A statement of the offences of which the appellant was convicted.

b) A summary of the evidence against the defendant.

8.02.32 The appellant may then say:

I seek to persuade the court that the conviction is unsafe and unsatisfactory for the reasons set out in the grounds of appeal.

8.02.33 Consideration of Leave

On an application for leave to appeal, usually in a straightforward case or where the registrar has asked for the Crown to be represented, the court may say:

If we are minded to grant leave, do you have instructions to treat this as a full hearing?

The appellant is advised to obtain instructions before the hearing (see **8.02.43**).

8.02.34 Presentation of the Appeal

After the introduction, the appellant may present the appeal in as much detail as the appellant feels is necessary (or as indicated by the court).

8.02.35   The appellant may then refer the court to each ground of appeal in order of merit.

In respect of each ground of appeal, the appellant may:

(a)   Read or refer the court to any part of the transcript of evidence.

(b)   Read or refer the court to any part of the transcript of the judge's summing up.

(c)   Refer the court (with reference to any document) to the issues raised in that ground of appeal.

(d)   Set out the law on which the appellant relies and refer the court to any authorities.

8.02.36   Fresh Evidence

The appellant may, either after introducing the case or when referring the court to the evidence, apply for leave to call fresh evidence.

If the court grants leave, the appellant may call the witness (or read the evidence).

The usual rules as to the examination, cross-examination and re-examination of witnesses apply (see **14.01.01-24**).

8.02.37   Intervention by the Court

A party presenting his case to the court should never expect to do so without interruption or intervention by the court.

8.02.38   The court is very likely to direct the appellant's attention to certain areas of the case.

The court will usually indicate if it considers certain grounds of appeal to be without merit.

The appellant should note such indications carefully and be ready to move to another argument if necessary.

THE CASE FOR THE CROWN

8.02.39   If the appellant has not established any ground of appeal, the court will usually dismiss the appeal without hearing the Crown.

The usual form of words is:

We need not trouble you, Mr (name).

8.02.40   If the appellant has established any ground of appeal, the court will usually indicate to the Crown the grounds on which he should address the court.

8.02.41   The Crown may then present his case to the court in the same way as the appellant (see **8.02.34-35**).

REPLY

8.02.42   The appellant may reply to any new matter raised by the Crown or the court.

The appellant should not (and usually will not be permitted to) repeat the arguments in **8.02.31-38**.

JUDGMENT

8.02.43   Application for Leave to Appeal Conviction

The court may:

(a)   Dismiss the application for leave

(b)   Grant the application for leave and stand the case out for a full hearing

(c)   Grant the application and invite the appellant to address the court for a second time, for example:

Is there any other matter on which you would wish to address us?

If leave is granted after a full hearing, the court may be minded to allow the appeal and the appellant will often decline to address the court for a second time.

8.02.44   Appeal (where leave has been granted)

The court may:

(a)   Dismiss the appeal.

(b)   Allow the appeal in full and direct an acquittal.

(c)   Allow the appeal and substitute a conviction for another offence that would have been open to the jury.

8.02.45   Costs

The majority of appeals are legally aided and costs are not usually considered.

A successful appellant who is privately represented may apply for a defendant's costs order (see **7.02.25**).

PART 3: APPEAL AGAINST SENTENCE

THE CASE FOR THE APPELLANT

8.02.46   Appellant's Introduction

After the case has been called (see **8.02.28**) the appellant may say:

> **This is an appeal/application for leave to appeal the sentence imposed on** (name) **by His Honour Judge** (name) **sitting at the** (name) **Crown Court on** (date).

8.02.47   Introduction

See **8.02.30-31**.

8.02.48   The appellant may then say:

> **I seek to persuade the court that the sentence is excessive/wrong in principle, for the reasons set out in the grounds of appeal.**

8.02.49   Consideration of Leave

See **8.02.33**.

8.02.50   Presentation of the Appeal

The appellant may then refer the court to each ground of appeal in order of merit (see **8.02.34-35**).

If a transcript of the judge's remarks on sentence is available, the appellant may read or refer the court to any part of the transcript.

8.02.51   Mitigation

The appellant may, when referring the court to each Ground of Appeal, address the court in mitigation (see **4.01.29-33**).

8.02.52   Intervention by the Court

8.02.37-38 apply.

JUDGMENT

8.02.53   Application for Leave to Appeal Sentence

8.02.43 applies.

8.02.54   Appeal (where leave has been granted)

The court may:

(a)   Dismiss the appeal.

(b)   Allow the appeal and substitute any sentence which the crown court could have passed.

8.02.55   Costs

Where the appeal against sentence is allowed, the court may make a defendant's costs order (see **7.02.25**).

SECTION 3:
APPEALS TO THE HIGH COURT

PART 1: INTRODUCTION

8.03.01   An appeal to the High Court from a decision of a court of lower jurisdiction, tribunal or person (for example, an arbitrator or inspector) may be made to:

(a)   The Divisional Court of the Queen's Bench Division:

Where the decision is said by the relevant statute to be final.

(b)   A single judge of the High Court:

Where the relevant statute describes the manner in which an appeal may be made.

8.03.02   The preparation and practice in the following situations are considered in this section:

Part 2:   Application for Judicial Review.

Part 3:   Appeals to the High Court under Statute.

Part 4:   Appeals by Case Stated.

8.03.03   As a guide:

(a)   Judicial review is a review of the decision making process of a court, tribunal or person specified in **8.03.04(a)-(c)**.

(b)   Appeals to the High Court under statute are directed by the relevant statute.

(c)   Appeals by case stated are made where a court, tribunal or person specified in **8.03.41 (8.03.04(a)-(c))** has made a decision on the wrong principles of law.

PART 2: APPLICATION FOR JUDICIAL REVIEW

8.03.04 As a general rule, judicial review may be obtained against:

(a) A court of lower jurisdiction.

(b) A tribunal.

(c) A person or body of persons charged with a public duty.

8.03.05 As a general rule, judicial review may be obtained where the court, tribunal or person:

(a) Acted without jurisdiction or exceeded its jurisdiction.

(b) Acted in breach of the rules of natural justice.

(c) Acted unreasonably.

Or, where in respect of the court, tribunal or person

(d) There is an error of law on the face of the record.

Examples of cases in which judicial review may be obtained should be researched in the common practitioners' handbooks.

8.03.06 Orders

The applicant may apply for the following prerogative orders:

(a) Mandamus

An order directing a court, tribunal or person to do an act where it has refused or neglected to do so, for example, where a magistrates' court has refused, on demand, to state a case (see **8.03.48**).

(b) Prohibition

An order restraining a court, tribunal or person from exceeding its jurisdiction.

(c) Certiorari

An order removing the proceedings of the court, tribunal or person into the

Divisional Court for the purpose of quashing the proceedings (see **8.03.25(c)**).

AND/OR the following non-prerogative orders:

(d) A declaration.

(e) Damages.

(f) An injunction.

The law on this subject is complex and should be researched in the common practitioners' handbooks.

8.03.07 Application for Leave

An applicant for judicial review must first obtain leave.

An application for leave must be made as soon as possible after the decision complained of and, in any event, within three months.

This is an unusual time limit because, if the court is of the opinion that a period shorter than three months is sufficient, it may refuse leave on that ground alone even though the application is within the three month time limit.

8.03.08 The application for leave is made *ex parte* to a single judge by filing in the Crown Office:

(a) A standard form notice, stating:

(i) The name, address and description of the applicant.

(ii) The name and address of the applicant's solicitors.

(iii) The relief sought.

(iv) The grounds on which the applicant claims to be entitled to that relief.

(b) An affidavit (usually sworn by the applicant) verifying the facts in the notice (with any relevant exhibits).

8.03.09 The application for leave is usually determined on the documents by the single judge without a hearing (although a hearing may be requested; for the practice, see **5.02.38-42**).

The applicant is then notified of the decision of the single judge.

8.03.10   Renewing the Application for Leave

If leave is refused, the applicant may renew the application, to the court(s) described in **8.03.11(a)&(b)** on service of a standard form notice.

PREPARATION

8.03.11   Mode of Applying for Judicial Review

If the application for leave is granted, the applicant should make the application for judicial review by originating motion within 14 days:

(a) In a criminal case, to the Divisional Court.

(b) In any other case, to a single judge in open court.

8.03.12   Service

The applicant should then serve the standard form notice, the affidavit and originating motion (applying for judicial review) on the court, tribunal or person who made the decision a reasonable time before the hearing (which should be not less than 10 days).

8.03.13   Affidavit of Service

An affidavit of service of the documents must be served before the application can be entered for hearing.

8.03.14   Amendments and Further Affidavits

A respondent wishing to file evidence should do so by affidavit within 21 days of service on him of the originating motion.

8.03.15   The applicant should give notice (if appropriate) of his intention at the hearing of the application for judicial review to:

(a) Amend the notice in support of the application.

(b) Rely on further affidavits.

8.03.16   A party may make an interlocutory application (see **5.02**) to a master of the QBD, for example, for discovery (see **5.05**) or for leave to cross-examine the maker of an affidavit (see **14.01.25-30**).

8.03.17   Agreed Notes and Transcripts

Agreed notes and transcripts may be used (as appropriate). See **8.01.27-29**.

8.03.18   Law

See **8.01.30**.

8.03.19   Skeleton Arguments

See **8.01.31-33**.

PRACTICE

8.03.20   Right of Audience

Barristers.

Applicants in person.

8.03.21   Dress

Barristers are robed.

Applicants in person should be respectably dressed.

8.03.22   Mode of Address

There will usually be three judges.

The court is addressed as My Lords/Your Lordships but where a party is responding to an individual judge, the judge is addressed as My Lord or My Lady.

8.03.23   Conduct

The hearing is in open court.

A party addressing the court should do so standing.

A party should note that the prerogative orders are discretionary remedies. The application may be refused if there has been delay or misconduct.

8.03.24   The practice in **8.01.39-53** is then followed.

8.03.25   The Decision

In judgment, the court may:

(a)   Allow the application for judicial review and grant the prerogative order sought in the originating motion.

(b)   Dismiss the application.

(c)   Where certiorari is granted, quash the decision and remit the matter to the court, tribunal or person with a direction to reconsider it.

8.03.26   Costs

Costs are in the discretion of the court.

Criminal cases:	See **7.02.26.**
Non-criminal cases:	See **7.01.03.**

8.03.27   Appeal

Criminal cases:	From the Divisional Court to the House of Lords, with leave.
Non-criminal cases:	From the single judge or the Divisional Court to the Court of Appeal, as of right.

PART 3: APPEALS TO THE HIGH COURT UNDER STATUTE

8.03.28   Where the jurisdiction of a court, tribunal or person is founded on statute, the statute may set out the method of appeal of the decision of the court, tribunal or person.

The preparation, practice and conduct of the appeal should, in each case, be researched in the common practitioners' handbooks.

The following is intended as a brief guide:

8.03.29   Right to Appeal

The right to appeal will be set out in the relevant statute.

8.03.30   Leave

Leave may be required under the relevant statute.

8.03.31   Court to Hear the Appeal

(a) Where the decision of the court, tribunal or person is final, the appeal is heard by the Divisional Court.

(b) In all other cases, the appeal is heard by a single judge.

8.03.32   Commencement

The appeal is by originating motion, stating:

(a) The grounds of appeal.

(b) Whether the appeal is against the whole or part of the decision.

8.03.33   The originating motion should be served on:

(a) The court, tribunal or person against whose decision the appeal is made.

(b) Any other person affected by the appeal.

8.03.34   As a general rule, service and entry of the originating motion must be made within 28 days of the date of the decision.

8.03.35   At the hearing the court may reconsider any matter which, in the opinion of the court, is relevant.

8.03.36   Evidence at the Hearing

The court will usually decide the appeal on the basis of the findings of fact by the court, tribunal or person. The appellant should obtain an agreed note or transcript (see **8.01.27-29**).

The court may hear or read any other evidence in its discretion, but:

(a) Fresh evidence will not be heard if the appeal is on law only.

(b) Affidavits and/or signed notes of a person attending the hearing before the court, tribunal or person, will not be considered unless they have been submitted to the court tribunal or person whose decision is being appealed for signature and/or comment.

PRACTICE

8.03.37 The practice in **8.03.20-23** and **8.01.39-53** applies.

8.03.38 The Decision

In judgment, the court may:

(a) Give any judgment or decision which could have been made by the court, tribunal or person.

(b) Remit the case for rehearing.

The court is not bound to interfere unless a substantial wrong or miscarriage of justice has been occasioned.

8.03.39 Costs

The court's power to award costs will usually be set out in the relevant statute.

8.03.40 Appeal

A right of appeal to the Court of Appeal, with leave, may be set out in the relevant statute.

PART 4: APPEALS BY CASE STATED

8.03.41 Introduction

A decision, judgment or order of a court, tribunal or person may be challenged by any party affected by that decision on appeal by case stated, usually on the ground that it is wrong in law or in excess or jurisdiction.

The appellant will require the court, tribunal or person to state:

(a) The findings of fact.

(b) The principles of law applied.

8.03.42 Appeal by case stated is an appropriate form of appeal where the facts are not in dispute but the principles of law to be applied to the facts are in dispute.

If the facts are in dispute, the appellant should consider an alternative form of appeal where fresh evidence may be introduced (for example, an appeal from the magistrates' court to the crown court, see **3.05: Appeals against Conviction**).

8.03.43 The Court

(a) In criminal cases (except any case heard on indictment) the appeal is to the Divisional Court of the QBD.

(b) In any other case the appeal is to a single judge of the QBD, except

(c) In family cases (usually domestic proceedings heard by the magistrates' court, see **1.09.37**) the appeal is to the Divisional Court of the Family Division.

8.03.44 Appeal by Case Stated from the Magistrates' Court

The most common appeal by case stated is from the magistrates' court.

The application to state a case should be made in writing to the clerk to the justices (specifying **8.03.45(d)**) within 21 days of the decision or sentence.

8.03.45 The statement of case should contain:

(a) The statement of facts.

(b) Any submissions made by the parties.

(c) The decision of the court.

(d) The question of law or jurisdiction on which the opinion of the High Court is sought.

8.03.46 The appellent must, within 10 days of receiving the statement of case, lodge it in the Crown Office.

8.03.47 The procedure on case stated from the Crown Court (except, see **8.03.43(a)**) is similar to the procedure in **8.03.44-46**.

8.03.48 If the clerk to the justices refuses to state a case he may be compelled to do so by an order of mandamus (see **8.03.06(a)**).

8.03.49 Appeals by Case Stated from Ministers, Tribunals or Other Persons

The application to state a case will usually be made under statute which will prescribe the method and time limits for the application.

8.03.50 The party making the application will usually apply to the court by originating motion for a case to be stated, stating:

(a) The grounds of the application

(b) The question of law on which it is sought to have the case stated.

8.03.51 The appellant must, within 14 days of receiving the statement of case, issue an originating motion together with a copy of the statement of case.

8.03.52 Interlocutory Applications

See **8.03.16**.

PRACTICE

8.03.53 The practice in **8.03.20-23** and **8.01.39-53** applies.

8.03.54 The Decision

See **8.03.38**.

8.03.55 Costs

Costs are in the discretion of the court.

Criminal cases:	See **7.02.26.**
Non-criminal cases:	See **7.01.03.**

8.03.56 Appeal

Criminal cases:	None.
Non-criminal cases:	From the single judge or the Divisional Court to the Court of Appeal, as of right.

CHAPTER 9

Tribunals

Section 1:	**Industrial Tribunal**
Section 2:	**Social Security Appeal Tribunal**
Section 3:	**Immigration Appeal Tribunal**

SECTION 1: INDUSTRIAL TRIBUNAL

INTRODUCTION

9.01.01   Mode of Address

The tribunal is usually composed of a chairman and two lay members.

The chairman of the tribunal is addressed as **Sir** or **Madam**. The lay members of the tribunal may be addressed as **your colleagues** occasionally out of courtesy, for example, at the conclusion of re-examination:

Do you or your colleagues have any questions?

9.01.02   The Hearing

The hearing will usually take place in public although there may be an exception where the tribunal is hearing confidential information.

9.01.03 Right of Audience

Any person may represent a party in the proceedings. The representative may also be a witness.

9.01.04 Dress

All parties should be respectably dressed. Advocates are not robed.

9.01.05 Seating

The arrangement of the seating varies according to the facilities available, but the parties will usually sit facing the tribunal.

9.01.06 Addressing the Tribunal

Any party addressing the tribunal will usually remain seated (although witnesses taking the oath should do so standing). An advocate may stand if he prefers but should not do so if all other parties remain seated.

9.01.07 Witnesses

After the case has been called, the parties and their witnesses will usually enter the room together and remain in the roon until the conclusion of the case. After having given evidence, a witness may only leave the room with the permission of the tribunal.

9.01.08 Practice

Practice in the industrial tribunal is similar to practice in the county court although it is more informal. The law encourages parties to conduct their own cases.

9.01.09 Terms

The following list shows the correpondence between terms used in the county court and in the tribunal:

County Court	Tribunal
Trial	Hearing
Action	Application/complaint

Plaintiff	Applicant/complainant (usually the employee)
Defendant	Respondent (usually the employer)
Summons and particulars of claim	Originating application (Form IT1)
Defence	Notice of appearance (Form IT3)
Damages	Award
Further and better particulars	Further particulars.

PREPARATION

9.01.10   Application (Form IT1)

The applicant must apply in writing, on Form IT1, to the Central Office of the Industrial Tribunals (COIT).

The application must be made within three months from the date dismissal took effect. A late application will only be considered if it was not 'reasonably practicable' for it to be on time.

In some cases an employee may be awaiting a final decision of an appeal board or panel, or a criminal court, which relates to the dismissal. He should make the application and apply in writing (stating reasons) to the Tribunal to postpone the hearing.

9.01.11   Notice of Appearance (Form IT3)

The COIT will send a copy of the Form IT1 to the respondent. The respondent must enter notice of appearance on Form IT3 within 14 days stating whether he intends to resist the application.

9.01.12   The COIT will then send a copy of the Form IT3 to the applicant.

9.01.13   Further Particulars

A party may wish to apply for further particulars of another party's case. The application should be made in writing to the other party (with a copy to the tribunal) or to the tribunal where the other party does not reply or refuses the further particulars requested.

9.01.14   Further particulars should not be confused with discovery (see **9.01.17**). Further particulars reveal what the case is and discovery reveals the evidence that can prove the case.

For example, the respondent may state in Form IT3 that the reason for dismissal was misconduct. The applicant is entitled to know if a specific incident is being alleged (further particulars). If the incident is documented, the applicant will usually be entitled to see a copy of the document (discovery).

9.01.15   Documents

The applicant will usually have the following documents:

(a)   Letter of appointment.

(b)   Contract of employment/statutory written terms.

(c)   Employer's disciplinary rules and procedures.

(d)   Any written warnings/minutes of disciplinary hearings.

(e)   Letter of dismissal/written reasons for dismissal.

9.01.16   If the applicant does not have one or more of these documents he may ask to see (and require the respondent to produce) the documents in the respondent's possession on Discovery.

9.01.17   Discovery

If either party refuses to disclose a relevant document, a party may apply in writing to the Tribunal for an order for Discovery (see **9.01.13** and **5.05: Discovery**).

9.01.18   Presentation of Documents in a Bundle

The parties will usually assemble the documents in a bundle (see **5.06.16**).

If the bundle of documents is agreed, it is usually prepared (as a matter of practice) by the respondent. If the bundle is not agreed, both the applicant and the respondent should prepare a bundle.

The bundle may be divided into sections for ease of reference. The documents in the bundle should be numbered in date order with an index.

9.01.19   The party or parties should prepare three copies of the bundle for the Tribunal and one copy for the other party. An extra copy of the bundle should be made available for witnesses at the hearing.

The bundles should be served a reasonable time before the hearing.

9.01.20   Law

A party intending to raise a matter of law should serve a list of authorities on the other party and the tribunal a reasonable time before the hearing.
The party is advised to take sufficient (photo)copies of the authorities to the hearing wherever possible because many tribunals and parties have limited access to legal works at short notice.

9.01.21   Witness Orders

The applicant should approach any witness he intends to call at the hearing. If the witness is reluctant to give evidence against his employer, the applicant may apply in writing to the Tribunal for a witness order.

The tribunal may order that the witness gets paid for his time off work to attend the tribunal.

ASSESSMENT OF AWARD

9.01.22   The parties should give consideration to Conciliation and Settlement (see **9.01.26-28**).

Conciliation and settlement are impractical unless the parties have made an assessment of how much a successful applicant is likely receive.

At the full hearing, the parties may submit a reasoned estimate (written if complex) of the award (see **9.01.65(g)**). The tribunal may then correct or alter the parties' assessment of the award.

9.01.23   The assessment of the award should be researched in the common practitioners' handbooks. The following is intended as a brief guide.

The award has two separate elements:

9.01.24   Basic Award

The basic award:

(a) Is calculated according to applicant's age and length of service.

(b) Is subject to a statutory ceiling on length of service.

(c) Is subject to reduction for 'contributory fault'.

9.01.25   Compensatory Award

The compensatory award:

(a) Is the amount of purely financial loss and expense 'in consequence of the dismissal'.

(b) Is subject to a statutory ceiling expressed as a cash sum.

(c) Is subject to reduction for 'contributory fault'.

(d) Is subject to further reduction on failure to 'mitigate loss' (usually to find a new job).

(e) Is not an award for hurt feelings (unless sex or racial discrimination is involved).

CONCILIATION

9.01.26   Copies of the IT1 and IT3 forms together with other correspondence to the tribunal are usually forwarded to the Advisory Conciliation and Arbitration Service (ACAS).

ACAS has a statutory duty to effect a settlement of the case. Settlements made through ACAS have the effect that neither party can later apply or reapply to the tribunal.

If the case is not settled, anything disclosed to ACAS is privileged and will not be disclosed to the tribunal.

SETTLEMENT

9.01.27 The application can be withdrawn, with or without settlement, (usually by writing to the tribunal) at any time before the full hearing, although the applicant may be liable for costs.

9.01.28 The advantages to the applicant of settling and withdrawing a case are:

(a) Costs will be reduced, and

(b) State benefits received by the applicant after dismissal, which are liable to be recouped from an award made by the tribunal, are not refundable from money received as a settlement.

The disadvantage to the applicant is that he will not have a written decision from the tribunal that he was unfairly dismissed.

HEARINGS BEFORE THE FULL HEARING

9.01.29 The following hearings may take place before the full hearing of the application:

(a) Pre-hearing assessment.

(b) Preliminary hearing.

(c) Interim relief hearing (for trade union reasons). It is not considered here.

A request for a pre-hearing assessment or a preliminary hearing may be made by either party or may be ordered by the tribunal of its own motion.

9.01.30 Pre-Hearing Assessment

At a pre-hearing assessment (PHA) the tribunal will consider whether either party's case has any reasonable prospect of success.

The parties may make written submissions, or attend to make submissions orally. The party with the weaker case usually attends.

The tribunal cannot dismiss the case, but it may issue a warning to the party pursuing the weaker case that it does so at risk as to costs and witness expenses at the full hearing.

9.01.31 At the full hearing the tribunal:

(a) Must be differently constituted from the one at the PHA.

(b) Will have a copy of the tribunal's comments at the PHA, but is not bound to order costs (see **9.01.68(e)**).

9.01.32 Preliminary Hearing

At a preliminary hearing the tribunal will consider whether it has jurisdiction to hear the application.

It is usually the respondent who requests the hearing, if he considers that the applicant is not qualified to pursue the application where, for example:

(a) There has been a late application with no good excuse.

(b) The applicant has failed to meet the minimum period of continuous service to qualify for the right not be to unfairly dismissed.

(c) The respondent does not employ a sufficient number of staff for the Act to apply.

(d) The respondent is not based in the UK.

9.01.33 The practice at a preliminary hearing follows the practice at the full hearing but the issue(s) is limited to the preliminary point.

As the whole application stands or falls on this hearing, both parties usually attend, with witnesses (if appropriate).

The burden of proof is on the applicant, who will usually open the case.

PRACTICE AT THE FULL HEARING

9.01.34 The practice at the full hearing is similar to the practice in a trial in the county court. The hearing is open to the public.

9.01.35 Before the hearing, the applicant and respondent and their respective lawyers and witnesses usually wait in separate rooms until called into the room where the tribunal is being held.

9.01.36   Presence of the Parties and/or Witnesses

After the case has been called, the parties and/or witnesses will usually enter the room together and remain in the room until the conclusion of the case. After having given evidence, a witness may only leave the room with the permission of the tribunal.

9.01.37   Introduction of Case

The clerk to the tribunal will usually read out the name of the case. He will then identify the parties and their legal representatives, for example:

Are you (name of applicant)? **And are you represented by** (name)? **And are you** (name of respondent)? **And are you represented by** (name)?

9.01.38   Chairman's Introduction

The chairman will usually introduce himself and his colleagues.

The chairman may briefly explain the tribunal procedure. He may also state how much the tribunal knows about the case from the tribunal papers and the bundle(s) (if any). This will assist the party opening to know in how much detail he should open the case (see **9.01.50-51**).

9.01.39   Introduction of the Parties

The applicant, or the party who has the burden of proof (see **9.01.43**), may introduce the parties to the tribunal (if this has not already been done).

9.01.40   Attendance of the Parties

The parties should attend.

If either party fails to attend, the tribunal will usually adjourn the case.

If the tribunal does not adjourn the case, it may, either:

(a)   Hear the case in the absence of either party and treat the contents of Form IT1 or Form IT3 (as appropriate) as written representations, or,

b)   Dismiss the case.

9.01.41   The party attending may invite the tribunal to hear the case if he is of the opinion that the other party is unlikely to apply to the tribunal to review the case if it is determined in his absence.

9.01.42   The party attending may apply for costs (see **9.01.68**).

9.01.43   Order of Opening

The party who has the burden of proof usually opens (and also has the final closing speech). This is not a matter of law and the chairman may ask either party to open. The following are some instances of the burden of proof:

Case	Burden: Party Opening
(a) Unfair dismissal (where the dismissal is admitted but unfairness is denied)	The respondent, (to prove the fairness of the dismissal)
(b) Unfair dismissal (where the dismissal is denied, for example, where the Respondent claims the Applicant left of his own accord)	The applicant, (to prove dismissal)
(c) Sex or race discrimination (where no dismissal is alleged)	The applicant, (to prove dismissal).

9.01.44   The practice in example (a) is followed in **9.01.50-66.**

9.01.45   In a case where dismissal and unfairness are both denied the tribunal may order that the case should be heard in two stages:

(a) The applicant proves the dismissal.

(b) The respondent proves the fairness of the dismissal.

9.01.46   Preliminary Applications

The tribunal may hear preliminary applications by either party, including an application to amend the Forms IT1 or IT3 or an application which could have been made at a preliminary hearing (see **9.01.32-33**), although the tribunal may grant the other party an adjournment with costs.

9.01.47   Purpose of Opening and Closing Speeches

In practice, both parties may make an opening and closing speech.

9.01.48   The party opening should help the tribunal to understand the evidence it is about to hear, usually with reference to the bundle(s).

The opening is important because it enables the party opening to 'set the scene' and to pre-dispose the tribunal in that party's favour. If a party is intending to open the case, the opening should be carefully prepared (see **14.02.03-06**).

9.01.49   The party closing should sum up the basic points of that party's case and/or the weaknesses in the other party's case, in so far as those points will assist the tribunal to give judgment for that party (see **14.02.07-10**).

THE CASE ON BEHALF OF THE RESPONDENT

9.01.50   The Respondent's Opening

The respondent will usually open the case except where the tribunal indicates that it has read and will treat the Forms IT1 and IT3 together with any documents as a sufficient explanation of the issues.

9.01.51   The respondent's opening should contain:

(a)   An explanation of the nature of the case, for example:

This is a claim by (name of applicant) **for compensation for unfair dismissal on the grounds that** (state grounds). **The dismissal is not in dispute.**

(b)   A summary of the allegations in Forms IT1 and IT3.

(c)   An outline of the contents of the bundle(s) of documents (in such detail as necessary).

(d)   An outline of the evidence upon which the respondent intends to rely.

(e)   An explanation of the structure of the business (if appropriate).

(f)   An explanation of any specialised working practices/words (if appropriate).

9.01.52   Proof of Reasons for Dismissal

The respondent must prove:

(a)   That he had a reason for dismissal.

(b) That the reason for dismissal related to:

  (i)   Capability.

  (ii) Conduct.

  (iii) Redundancy.

  (iv) Illegality (for example, a driver dismissed for losing his driving licence).

  (v) Any other substantial reason.

(c) That he acted reasonably, for example:

  (i)   That he acted on reasonable evidence (and not mere gossip).

  (ii) That reasonable dismissal procedures were followed (including adherence to any relevant code of practice).

  (iii) That it was reasonable not to adopt any measure short of dismissal (for example, a final warning).

EVIDENCE ON BEHALF OF THE RESPONDENT

9.01.53 The respondent and/or any witness on behalf of the respondent is called and identified, as follows:

Are you (name)? **What is your address?**

The respondent and/or any witness will usually be asked to describe his relationship to the applicant, for example:

Are you the former employer of the (name of applicant)?

9.01.54 The usual rules as to the examination, cross-examination and re-examination of witnesses applies (see **14.01.01-24**) except a party may ask leading questions in examination in chief.

9.01.55 Admissibility of Evidence

Rules concerning the admissibility of evidence in proceedings before the courts of law do not apply in the tribunal.

As a general rule, all relevant evidence is admissible, although a party should be careful, for example:

(a) Where it is practicable to ask or compel a witness to attend, hearsay oral or written evidence will carry less weight, (for example, a letter 'to whom it may concern').

(b) Where it is practicable to produce an original document, a photocopy of the document will carry less weight.

9.01.56 The parties may make oral or written admissions, without formal notice, and/or agreements in the usual way (see **5.06.66-69**).

9.01.57 The parties may read the statement(s) (in any form) of a witness. The statement is usually read by agreement without formal notice.

9.01.58 Close of Respondent's Case

The usual form of words is:

That is the case for the respondent.

SUBMISSION OF NO CASE TO ANSWER

9.01.59 In practice, a submission of no case to answer is rarely made.

As a general rule, a submission of no case to answer may be made where the party having the burden of proof has failed in law to discharge that burden.

If a submission of no case to answer is rejected, the party making the submission is still entitled to call evidence in support of his case.

9.01.60 The tribunal sometimes expresses an informal view of the evidence called by the party having the burden of proof.

The other party should give consideration to the view expressed by the tribunal before making a submission of no case to answer.

For the practice on a submission of no case to answer, see **5.06.73-74**.

CASE ON BEHALF OF THE APPLICANT

9.01.61   Applicant's Opening

The applicant may make an opening speech (although this is often unnecessary). The opening speech should be concise and brief.

The applicant's opening may contain:

(a) An explanation of the nature of the case (if not fully explained by the respondent or made clear by the applicant in cross-examination).

(b) An explanation of the Form IT1 and/or any other document to which no previous reference has been been made by either party.

(c) An outline of the evidence upon which the applicant intends to rely (usually where the applicant is calling witnesses).

(d) An explanation of any specialised working practice where the applicant holds a different opinion to the respondent as to the operation of that practice.

EVIDENCE ON BEHALF OF THE APPLICANT

9.01.62   The evidence on behalf of the applicant is presented in the same way as the evidence on behalf of the respondent (see **9.01.53-57**).

9.01.63   Cose of the Applicant's Case

The usual form of words is:

That is the case for the applicant.

The tribunal may then say:

Do you wish to address us on behalf of (name of applicant).

SPEECHES

9.01.64   The party having the burden of proof will usually address the tribunal last.

In a case of unfair dismissal, where the dismissal is admitted but the unfairness is denied, the order of speeches is usually:

(a) Applicant.

(b) Respondent.

9.01.65 In closing, either party will usually:

(a) Sum up the basic points of his case in so far as those points will assist the tribunal to give judgment for him.

(b) Explain, in relation to the evidence, any weaknesses in his case.

(c) Refer the tribunal to any weaknesses in the other party's case.

(d) Compare the evidence of the parties and the character and motives of the witnesses (if relevant).

(e) Deal with the issues (if raised) of the applicant's contributory fault and/or mitigation of loss.

(f) Refer the tribunal to any relevant law (see **14.02.11-12**).

(g) Provide the tribunal with an assessment (written, if complex) of the award sought by the applicant.

It is not thought presumptuous to do this, but the party should nevertheless do it with care. The applicant may say, for example:

If you find in the applicant's favour, I am able to provide a calculation of the award sought, if that would be of assistance. I have made a copy available to (name of respondent).

9.01.66 Where the respondent has the burden of proof, he should explain to the tribunal, with reference to the evidence, how he has discharged that burden in relation to the reasons for dismissal (see **9.01.52**).

The respondent may also answer the applicant's submissions and/or provide his assessment of the award sought by the appplicant.

DECISION

9.01.67 The tribunal may retire (or ask the parties and their witnesses to leave the room) to consider their decision.

The tribunal may:

(a) Give a short judgment and issue written reasons later.

(b) Give a full judgment with reasons.

(c) Reserve judgment.

If a party intends to appeal, he must have full reasons. Certain types of case always have a fully reasoned decision (eg sex and racial discrimination).

9.01.68 Costs

The tribunal has no power to award costs to either party save in exceptional circumstances. These are:

(a) Frivolousness.

If it is felt that a party has brought a hopeless case without himself believing it had any hope.

(b) Vexatiousness.
If it is felt that a party has been improperly motivated (for example, an applicant whose principle motive is adverse publicity for the respondent).

(c) Otherwise unreasonable behaviour.
For example, prolonging the hearing unnecessarily.

(d) Occasioning avoidable adjournments and postponements.

(e) Where a warning has been issued at a PHA. (see **9.01.30-31**).

9.01.69 Time to raise the matter of Costs

The matter of costs should always be raised after judgment has been given. If judgment is reserved, the matter of costs may be considered by the tribunal at a future hearing or by written representation, except where **9.01.68 (c)-(d)** apply (where costs may be awarded against a successful party) when costs may be considered at the hearing.

9.01.70 Allowances

Allowances should not be confused with costs.

Allowances are usually paid to the parties and the witnesses (but not the representatives) out of public money. Any party or witness may claim up to a modest maximum, regardless of success or failure. The allowance compensates for the expense of attending the hearing.

The parties should note that:

(a) A party against whom costs are ordered may not claim.

(b) A party in whose favour costs are ordered may instead receive his own and his witnesses' expenses from the other party (not subject to any maximum).

9.01.71   Appeal

Appeal on a point of law only is to the Employment Appeal Tribunal (EAT) within 42 days of the date on which the full written reasons are sent to the appellant.

If the appeal discloses no point of law, it will be rejected by the EAT (without hearing either party). Appeal against rejection must be made within 28 days.

SECTION 2:
SOCIAL SECURITY APPEAL TRIBUNAL

INTRODUCTION

9.02.01   An adjudication officer (AO), appointed by the secretary of state, may consider a claim made by any person for benefit and determine whether that person is entitled to benefit.

In a complex case, the AO may refer the claim directly to a tribunal.

9.02.02   Any person who is dissatisfied with the decision of the AO may appeal to an independent social security appeal tribunal (SSAT) within three months by writing to the DSS office concerned.

An appeal to the SSAT can only be made against the decision of an AO. Other claims, for example, housing benefit or social fund payments, are reviewed internally and are not independently appealed.

9.02.03   The clerk to the SSAT will acknowledge receipt of the notice of appeal and fix a date for hearing.

9.02.04   The AO will deliver to the SSAT and the appellant a written statement of the facts, a summary of the decision and any relevant law and the appellant's grounds of appeal.

THE SOCIAL SECURITY APPEAL TRIBUNAL

9.02.05   The Parties to an Appeal

Appellant/claimant.

Adjudication Officer (AO).

A party preparing for a hearing before the tribunal should give consideration to the (more formal) practice in the industrial tribunal.

9.02.06   Mode of Address

The chairman of the tribunal (who is a lawyer) is addressed as **Sir** or **Madam** (**see 9.01.01**).

9.02.07   The Hearing

The hearing will usually be open to the public. However, the tribunal may hear the appeal in private in certain sensitive cases.

9.02.08   Rights of Audience

Any person may represent a party at the hearing. The representative may also be a witness.

It is unusual for either party to be legally represented (although the appellant may sometimes be represented by a trainee lawyer).

The AO's case is conducted by a presenting officer from the DSS. This is not usually the same person as the AO.

9.02.09   Dress

All parties should be respectably dressed. Advocates are not robed.

9.02.10 Conduct and Seating

The conduct of the hearing is informal, usually in an ordinary room.

The parties and/or their representatives will usually sit facing to the tribunal.

9.02.11 Addressing the Tribunal

Any party or witness addressing the tribunal remains seated. Witnesses may move forward to give their evidence. The oath is not administered.

9.02.12 Witnesses

After the case has been called, the parties and any witnesses will usually enter the room together and remain in the room until the conclusion of the hearing.

A party may ask the chairman to exclude the witness(es) from the room where the presence of the witness(es) would affect the conduct of the hearing.

PRACTICE

9.02.13 The practice of the tribunal is informal (and usually more informal than the practice of the industrial tribunal).

The chairman decides the procedure at the hearing, which will vary from case to case.

9.02.14 The hearing is in the nature of an enquiry. It is not a contest.

In practice, this means that the order of presenting cases is unimportant, provided both parties have the opportunity to address the tribunal on the issues.

The usual rules of evidence do not apply. All relevant evidence is admissible.

The hearing is a rehearing of the claim before the AO. Any new facts or arguments may be heard if relevant to the claim.

9.02.15 Chairman's Opening

The chairman will usually:

(a) Introduce the tribunal members by name.

(b) Emphasise the independence of the SSAT from the DSS.

(c) Describe the practice to be adopted at the hearing of the appeal.

9.02.16 Attendence of the Parties

The tribunal may determine the appeal in the absence of either party, although in the case of the appellant, the tribunal must be satisfied that he has been notified of the date of the hearing.

9.02.17 The appellant is usually expected to open, and often does so. However, the chairman will often ask the appellant if he would prefer the AO to open. In practice, the appellant, will often prefer the AO to open.

9.02.18 The Presenting Officer's Opening

In opening, the presenting officer (on behalf of the AO) will usually reiterate the AO's written statement (see **9.02.04**) and may expand upon it.

The presenting officer should not strive to persuade the tribunal to uphold the AO's decision (see **9.02.14**).

9.02.19 The Case for the Adjudication Officer

Often no further evidence may be given, although the presenting officer may call the AO and/or any visiting officer, medical officer or counter-staff.

9.02.20 The presenting officer may tender any documentary evidence (see **9.02.22**) to the tribunal.

9.02.21 No Submission of No Case to Answer

A submission of no case to answer is not made in the SSAT.

9.02.22 The Case for the Appellant

The appellant may make any oral representation or may tender a written statement made by him to the tribunal and/or call and/or read any other evidence or tender any document (see **9.01.55-57**) to the tribunal in the same way as the respondent.

9.02.23 If new matters are raised by either party, the other party is usually permitted to respond and/or call evidence, unless the chairman considers it would be unnecessary or unfair.

9.02.24 Addresses

Either party may address the tribunal, on either law or fact, in such order as invited to do so by the chairman.

9.02.25 Decision

The tribunal will usually ask the parties concerned in the case to leave the room in order to consider its decision.

The parties will be invited to return to hear the decision.

9.02.26 The tribunal may:

(a) Give a short judgment and issue written reasons later.

(b) Give a full judgment with reasons.

(c) Reserve judgment.

The decision of the tribunal must be recorded by the chairman, in practice on a standard form, which is made available to the parties (usually together with a note of the evidence).

9.02.27 Costs/Expenses

Costs are not awarded by the SSAT. However, parties, witnesses and representatives may claim their expenses from the clerk of the tribunal.

Expenses cover only attendance at the hearing (including travel, subsistence, loss of earnings and child minding).

9.02.28 Appeal

Either party may appeal to the Social Security Commissioners with the leave of the tribunal or the Commissioners on a point of law only.

Application for leave must be made orally at the end of the hearing or in writing within three months of being notified of the tribunal's decision.

SECTION 3:
IMMIGRATION APPEAL TRIBUNAL

INTRODUCTION

9.03.01   An appeal to an adjudicator or to the Immigration Appeal Tribunal may be made against an administrative decision of:

(a)   The Secretary of State.

(b)   An immigration officer.

(c)   An entry clearance officer.

9.03.02   The following decisions may be appealed:

(a)   Exclusion from the UK.

(b)   Any condition limiting leave to enter or remain in the UK.

(c)   Deportation from the UK.

(d)   Any direction for removal of an illegal immigrant from the UK.

(e)   Any decision to remove a person to a particular country.

9.03.03   Any person making a decision specified in **9.03.02** against which there is a right of appeal must inform the appellant of the decision and of his right to appeal, the address to which the notice of appeal should be sent and the time limit(s) for appeal.

A notice of deportation will be sent to a person's last known address. It will take effect whether or not the person has knowledge of it.

9.03.04   An appellant who is in the UK should ensure that the application to extend his leave to remain in the the UK is made in good time. If leave is refused, the appellant must appeal within 28 days of the refusal.

9.03.05   Time Limits

Time limits for appeal vary, although the time limit is not shorter than 14 days.

If an application for variation of leave is not made before the existing leave expires, the tribunal will not have jurisdiction.

9.03.06   Notice of Appeal

The notice of appeal signed by the appellant must be served on the immigration authority named in the notice of decision.

The notice of appeal must state:

(a)   The name, address, date of birth and nationality of the appellant.

(b)   The decision appealed against.

(c)   The grounds of appeal.

9.03.07   The status of the appellant is frozen pending appeal. For example, an appellant making an application for variation of leave may remain in the UK on the same conditions as before.

9.03.08   Statement of Reasons for the Decision

After service of the notice of appeal, the immigration authority will prepare a written statement of reasons for the decision which is served by the appellate authority on the appellant.

The date of the appeal to the adjudicator is usually fixed and the appellant is informed of the date.

9.03.09   Presentation of Documents in a Bundle

The parties (usually the appellant) may present any documents in a bundle.

The bundle may be divided into sections for ease of reference. The documents in the bundle should be numbered in date order, with an index.

Copies of the bundle should be served on the immigration authority and the appellate authority a reasonable time before the hearing.

PRE-HEARING PROCEDURES

9.03.10   Apart from the full hearing of the appeal by the adjudicator and/or immigration appeal tribunal, there may be:

(a) Pre-trial review.

(b) Preliminary hearing.

9.03.11 Pre-Trial Review

A request for a pre-trial review may be made by either party or may be ordered by the appellate authority of its own motion (usually in a complex case).

The adjudicator may give directions for the hearing of the appeal (see **5.04: Directions**).

9.03.12 Preliminary Hearing

At a preliminary hearing the adjudicator will consider whether he has jurisdiction to hear the appeal.

It is usually the immigration authority which requests the hearing if it considers that the appellant is not qualified to pursue the appeal, for example, where the notice of appeal is out of time.

9.03.13 A preliminary issue is often decided by the adjudicator without an oral hearing. If there is an oral hearing the practice at a preliminary hearing follows the practice at the full hearing but the issue(s) is limited to the preliminary point.

9.03.14 Adjudicator Appeals

The practice at the hearing of an appeal before the adjudicator is the same as the practice at the hearing of an appeal before the Immigration Appeal Tribunal.

THE HEARING

9.03.15 Right of Audience

Barrister.

Solicitor.

Presenting officer.

Advisory counsellor.

Party in person.

9.03.16 Dress

All parties should be respectably dressed.

9.03.17 Seating

The arrangement of the seating varies according to the facilities available, but the parties will usually sit facing the adjudicator.

9.03.18 Addressing the Tribunal

Any party addressing the tribunal will usually remain seated.

9.03.19 Witnesses

In practice, witnesses will usually wait outside the hearing room until called to give evidence and leave after having given evidence.

9.03.20 Conduct

The conduct of the hearing is informal.

PRACTICE

9.03.21 Before the hearing, the appellant and a representative of the immigration authority and their respective lawyers and witnesses usually wait in separate rooms until called into the room where the appeal is heard.

9.03.22 Wherever possible, the advocate on behalf of the appellant should ascertain from the presenting officer, before the hearing:

(a) How the presenting officer will put the facts.

(b) Whether the presenting officer is intending to call or adduce evidence in addition to the written statement (see **9.03.08**).

The presenting officer is likely to have all the relevant case law including any recent or unreported decisions (copies of which will usually be made available).

9.03.23 Introduction of the Appeal

The adjudicator will usually introduce himself and identify the parties and their legal representatives. He may also briefly explain the procedure.

The adjudicator may also ask the presenting officer to explain any matter in the written statement.

9.03.24   Attendance of the Parties

The parties should attend.

If either party fails to attend, the adjudicator will usually adjourn the case except where the appellant has not provided any explanation of his absence.

9.03.25   Burden of Proof

The appellant has the burden of proof and usually opens (and also has the final closing speech) except where the burden of proof is on the immigrations authority (for example, where a decision to deport is made on the ground that it is conducive to the public good).

If in doubt, the advocate should seek the guidance of the adjudicator.

9.03.26   Standard of Proof

The standard of proof is on the balance of probabilities.

9.03.27   Preliminary Applications

The adjudicator may hear an application for additional documentary evidence or any application which could have been made at a preliminary hearing (see **9.03.12-13**) and, if appropriate, grant the other party an adjournment.

9.03.28   Appellant's Opening Speech

The appellant will usually open the case except where the adjudicator indicates that he does not require to be taken through the documents.

The appellant's opening should contain:

(a)   An explanation of the nature of the case, for example:

> **This is an appeal against a decision of** (name of immigration authority) **for** (a refusal to vary the conditions of leave to stay in the UK) **on the grounds that** (state grounds).

(b) An outline of the written statement of reasons for the decision.

(c) An outline of the evidence on which the appellant intends to rely, with reference to the contents of the bundle(s) of documents (if appropriate).

EVIDENCE ON BEHALF OF THE APPELLANT

9.03.29   The appellant is called first.

The appellant and/or any witness on behalf of the appellant is called and identified, as follows:

Are you (name)? **What is your address?**

The usual rules as to the examination, cross-examination and re-examination of witnesses apply (see **14.01.01-24**) except a party may ask leading questions in examination in chief.

9.03.30   Admissibility of Evidence

Rules concerning the admissibility of evidence in proceedings before the courts of law do not apply in the tribunal.

As a general rule, all relevant evidence is admissible, although a party should be careful, for example:

(a) Where it is practicable to ask or compel a witness to attend, hearsay oral or written evidence will carry less weight, (for example, a letter 'to whom it may concern').

(b) Where it is practicable to produce an original document, a photocopy of the document will carry less weight.

9.03.31   The parties may make oral or written admissions without formal notice, and/or agreements in the usual way (see **5.06.66-69**).

9.03.32   The parties may read the statement(s) (in any form) of a witness. The statement is usually read by agreement, without formal notice.

9.03.33   Close of the Appellant's Case

The usual form of words is:

That is the case for the appellant.

SUBMISSION OF NO CASE TO ANSWER

9.03.34 In practice, a submission of no case to answer is not made by the presenting officer.

THE CASE ON BEHALF OF THE IMMIGRATION AUTHORITY

9.03.35 Respondent's Opening

The presenting officer may draw to the attention of the adjudicator any matter in the written statement of reasons for the decision, in particular, where any matter has been established in cross-examination of the appellant and/or his witnesses.

9.03.36 It is unusual for the presenting officer to call or adduce evidence in addition to the written statement of the reasons for the decision. If he does so, the evidence on behalf of the respondent is presented in the same way and subject to the same rules as the evidence on behalf of the appellant (see **9.03.29-33**).

SPEECHES

9.03.37 The order of speeches is usually:

(a) Respondent.

(b) Appellant.

This is not a matter of law and the adjudicator may ask the appellant to address him before the presenting officer (for example, if no oral evidence has been called by either party).

For the purpose and content of speeches, see **9.01.47-49** and **14.02.07-10**.

DECISION

9.03.38 The adjudicator may:

(a) Give a short judgment and issue written reasons later.

(b) Give a full judgment with reasons.

(c) Reserve judgment.

If a party intends to appeal, he must have full reasons.

9.03.39 Costs

The adjudicator and/or the tribunal has no power to award costs to either party.

9.03.40 Appeal

Appeal from the decision of the adjudicator is, with leave, to the immigration appeal tribunal.

The application for leave should be made to the adjudicator as soon as he has given a full judgment.

CHAPTER 10

Planning Inquiries

INTRODUCTION

10.01.01   A developer who is aggrieved by a decision made against him by a planning authority may appeal against that decision to the Secretary of State for the Environment.

The appropriate office will provide the proper notice of appeal form.

10.01.02   The Secretary of State will appoint an inspector to hear the appeal. This will be at a public inquiry, unless both the appellant and the local planning authority agree to waive the right to such a hearing and have the arguments presented by way of written representations instead.

10.01.03   The inspector will usually be delegated by the Secretary of State to make the decision on the appeal in all but very significant development issues.

PRE-INQUIRY PROCEDURE

10.01.04   The aim of the procedure is to identify the principal issues upon which the public inquiry should concentrate.

A Department of Environment circular states that 'at a local inquiry there should be no place for surprise tactics'.

10.01.05   Relevant Date

At the pre-inquiry stage a 'relevant date' will be set to which the pre-inquiry timetable is tied.

10.01.06   Statements of Case

Within six weeks of the relevant date, the local planning authority must serve on the appellant, the Secretary of State and any person holding an interest in the land concerned who wishes to be informed, a written statement of its case (a Rule 6 statement).

At the same time the appellant must also serve a written statement of his case on the other parties.

The written statements must contain full particulars of the arguments and a list of any documents, photographs, maps and plans that it is intended to refer to or put in evidence at the inquiry.

10.01.07   Date and Location of the inquiry

A date will be fixed for the inquiry which must be within 20 weeks of the relevant date.

The inquiry will usually be held in a public room or hall in the locality of the proposed development.

PRACTICE AT THE INQUIRY

10.01.08   Conduct

The inquiry is a formal hearing. An advocate addressing the inspector should do so standing.

10.01.09   Mode of Address

The inspector is addressed as Sir or Madam.

10.01.10   Right of Audience

Barrister.

Solicitor.

Interested party (see **10.01.16**).

10.01.11   Dress

Advocates are not robed. All parties should be respectably dressed.

10.01.12 Opening the Inquiry

The inspector will open the inquiry.

He will introduce himself and state his qualifications. He will inform the parties whether he will determine the appeal or merely pass on a recommendation to the Secretary of State for his decision.

He will ask that an attendance sheet be circulated, that all persons at the inquiry (including advocates) should sign. He will also ask if the press are present.

10.01.13   The inspector will then take a note of the appearances.

10.01.14 The Appellant

The inspector will ask who appears for the appellant.

The advocate on behalf of the appellant should give his name and legal status (barrister or solicitor). If the advocate is a barrister, he should state the name and address of the solicitor instructing him.

The advocate should then list the number and names of the witnesses he proposes to call, with a brief description of their professional qualifications (if appropriate) and the type of evidence they will be giving, for example:

I appear on behalf of the appellant. My name is (name).

I am counsel, instructed by (name of solicitors).

I shall be calling (-) **witnesses. They are** (give the names of the witnesses and brief descriptions, as appropriate).

10.01.15 The Local Planning Authority

The appearance of the local planning authority will be taken in the same way.

10.01.16 Interested Parties

The inspector will ask if there are any other persons present who wish to be heard and who, at his discretion, may ask questions of witnesses.

He will take their names and addresses and ask if they wish to be notified of the decision in due course.

10.01.17   Opening Remarks by the Inspector

The inspector will outline the procedure he intends to follow and may make any other remarks to facilitate the good conduct of the inquiry.

THE CASE FOR THE APPELLANT

10.01.18   Appellant's Opening Address

The appellant may make an opening address. The appellant should outline his case.

The appellant's opening should contain:

(a) A brief description of the proposed development.

(b) A short history of the application, giving relevant dates and events.

(c) A summary of any environmental assessment of the proposed development (if favourable).

(d) A summary of the reasons why the development should be allowed.

(e) A summary of the reasons why the objections of the planning authority (or any objectors) should not be allowed to stop the development.

(f) A summary of any relevant law.

The opening is an excellant opportunity to deal with, and reduce the impact of, any anticipated objections before they are made by the parties relying on them.

10.01.19   Witnesses on behalf of the Appellant

The witnesses for the appellant will then be called. They are usually allowed to be seated to give their evidence.

The witnesses may read their evidence from written proofs. The advocate should ensure that the inspector, the local planning authority and, if possible, other persons asking to be heard, have copies of the written proofs before the evidence is given.

The inspector may require the evidence to be given on oath.

10.01.20   Each witness for the appellant may be cross-examined by the local planning authority, any person given permission by the inspector and the inspector himself. The witness may then be re- examined by the advocate for the appellant (see **14.01.01-24**).

10.01.21   Documentary Evidence

Documentary evidence may be adduced.

As a general rule, a document is admissible if it is relevant. Where documents, plans, drawings or reports are to be relied upon, copies should be made available to the other parties.

THE CASE FOR THE PLANNING AUTHORITY

10.01.22   The local planning authority may call witnesses and present documentary evidence in the same way (see **10.01.19-21**).

10.01.23   Closing Speech on behalf of the Planning Authority

The advocate on behalf of the local planning authority may make a closing speech.

The closing speech may contain:

(a)   A summary of the authority's case.

(b)   The reasons for objecting to the proposed development.

(c)   The basis upon which the authority states that the reasons are valid reasons.

10.01.24   The Case for the other Interested Parties

The inspector may hear from any person requesting to be heard in the same way (see **10.01.19-21**).

If the appellant or the local planning authority disagree with the case of an interested party, they can, at the inspector's discretion, ask questions of that party.

10.01.25   Closing Speech on behalf of any Interested Party

Any interested party may make a closing speech (see **10.01.23**).

10.01.26   Closing Speech on behalf of the Appellant

The appellant may make a closing speech.

The appellant's closing speech should contain:

(a) A summary of the points in favour of the proposed development.

(b) A description of any environmental or social benefits attendant upon the proposed development.

(c) Argument against the objections raised (both law and fact).

10.01.27   Inspection of Site

At the close of the inquiry, the inspector will announce his intention of inspecting the site at a specific time (if an inspection has not already been made).

The inspector will invite each party to send one nominated representative to accompany him on the visit. That person will be there to observe and assist the inspector, if he so requires. The representative is not entitled to give further evidence (see **5.06.71**).

DECISION

10.01.28   The decision will be sent at a later date to the parties to the appeal and to any other interested party requesting it.

The decision will be in writing. It will also indicate how any appeal may be made (see **10.01.31**).

10.01.29   Costs

As a general rule, each party bears its own costs of the appeal but if either the appellant or the local planning authority consider that the other party has acted unreasonably in the conduct of its case, they can ask for costs to be awarded against that party.

The law on this subject is complex and the parties should consult the current circular on costs from the Department of Environment.

10.01.30   Costs may be awarded against.

(a) A planning authority which refused planning permission with no reasonable grounds for doing so.

(b) A planning authority which imposed conditions on a grant which were found to be unreasonable.

(c) An appellant making an appeal with no reasonable prospect of success, for example, where the appeal was against published policy.

10.01.31 Appeal

An appeal from the decision of an inspector can only be made on the grounds that the decision was outside the powers given by statute or that a procedural requirement was not complied with.

The appeal is to the High Court (see **8.03.28-40**).

The appeal should be made within six weeks of notification of the inspector's/ secretary of state's decision.

CHAPTER 11

Coroner's Court

INTRODUCTION

11.01.01 Function of the Coroner's Court

The main function of the Coroner's Court is to inquire into the death of a person who has:

(a) Suffered a violent or unnatural death, or

(b) Suffered a sudden death and/or from an unknown cause, or

(c) Died in prison.

11.01.02 Purpose of Inquest

The purpose of the inquest is to determine how, when and where the deceased died.

The inquest is an inquiry into the *cause* of death. It is not an inquiry to determine blame. The advocate should always bear this in mind and be careful to address his questions towards the issue of causation rather than blameworthiness.

11.01.03 Nature of Inquest

The hearing is inquisitorial, not accusatorial. Therefore, there are no actual *parties* to an inquest.

11.01.04 Persons Appearing at the Inquest

Persons having an interest in questions of civil or criminal liability may ask questions (either in person or by legal representative) at the inquest, for example:

(a) The parent, child, spouse or personal representative of the deceased.

(b) Any beneficiary under a policy of insurance on the life of the deceased.

(c) The insurer who issued such a policy of insurance.

(d) Any person whose act or omission or that of his servant or agent may in the opinion of the coroner have caused or contributed to the death of the deceased.

(e) Any person appointed by a trade union to which the deceased belonged, if the death of the deceased may have been caused during the course of his employment or by industrial disease.

(f) An inspector appointed by, or a representative of, an enforcing authority or any person appointed by a government department to attend the inquest.

(g) The chief officer of police.

(h) Any other person who, in the opinion of the coroner, is a properly interested person.

The advocate will probably represent someone (who may also be a witness) from one of the above categories.

11.01.05 Mode of Address

Any person addressing the coroner does so standing and addresses him as Sir.

11.01.06 Dress

Any person appearing at the inquest and their legal representatives should be respectably dressed. Advocates are not robed.

11.01.07 Seating

There are no guide rules about seating in the Coroner's Court, although the person likely to have the most cross-examination should be seated prominently. The advocates should seek the guidance of the coroner's officer.

11.01.08   The Hearing

The coroner usually sits alone. For the circumstances in which a jury is required, see **11.01.13**.

Unless there is an application for evidence to be heard in camera, an inquest takes place in open court.

Inquests are often tape recorded and the evidence and any argument transcribed. The advocate should therefore prepare his cross-examination with special care.

11.01.09   Conduct of the Inquest

The usual rules of evidence do not apply and the coroner has the final say over what questions may or may not be asked. The advocate should bear this in mind before making an objection to evidence (see **11.01.24** and **27**).

The coroner determines what witnesses will be called and the order in which they will be called (except, see **11.01.30-31**).

The advocate has no right to the statements of the witnesses.

PRACTICE

11.01.10   Preliminary Hearing

There will often be a brief preliminary hearing at which the coroner:

(a) Opens the inquest.

(b) Takes evidence of identification. (See **11.01.18**).

(c) Issues the order for burial.

(d) Adjourns to a convenient time and place.

The advocate will usually be instructed to attend the resumed hearing.

11.01.11   Resumed Hearing

The following paragraphs deal with practice at the resumed hearing.

11.01.12 Opening

The court is formally opened by the coroner's officer (who may also act an as usher) calling Silence or by Proclamation.

11.01.13 The Jury

A jury (numbering between seven and 11 jurors) is required in the case of death occurring in prison, police custody or in circumstances which are likely to be prejudicial to the health or safety of the public.

11.01.14 If there is a jury the coroner's officer calls the names of the jurors.

The jurors are then sworn in by the coroner's officer either individually or *en masse*.

11.01.15 Challenging Jurors

There is no right to challenge jurors although an advocate is entitled to raise proper objections (usually in the absence of the jury), for example:

With your leave, Sir, I would like to raise objection to (name of juror) **being empanelled on this jury on the grounds that:**

(a) **He is an employee in the factory where** (name of deceased) **died, or**

(b) **He is related to the driver of one of the vehicles involved in this accident,** or

(c) **He is** (in some other way) **partial.**

The advocate should give reasons for the objection. The coroner is under an obligation to take note of a proper objection.

11.01.16 Introductory Remarks by the Coroner

This is the resumed inquest into the death of (name and address of deceased) **who died on** (date of death) **aged** (state age in years). **The inquest was adjourned to this date on** (state date).

The coroner may then:

(a) Introduce the advocates present.

(b) Give a brief introduction to the facts of the case.

(c) Give the names of the witnesses he intends to call (as to fact and/or medical evidence).

WITNESSES ATTENDING COURT

11.01.17   The coroner calls witness(es) to the witness box to be sworn. The oath is usually administered by the coroner's officer.

11.01.18   Evidence of Identification

It is customary for evidence identifying the body of the deceased to be given first (unless this was done at the preliminary hearing).

The coroner may say:

I call (name of witness).

Then, after the oath:

Your full name is (name of witness) **and your address is** (address of witness).

You are the (relation of witness) **of the deceased?**

(The deceased) **was** (-) **years of age and I believe that on** (date) **at about** (time) **you attended at the** (name of hospital) **where you saw and identified his** (the deceased's) **dead body?**

Thank you, Mr (name of witness). **Now, does anyone have any questions they would like to ask Mr** (name of witness)?

In practice, it is rare that any cross-examination arises out of formal identification evidence.

11.01.19   Witnesses of Fact

The coroner may say:

Next I will call (name of second witness).

The witness is sworn and identified.

The coroner will then lead the witness through his statement (although, in practice, he will not lead on controversial matters). The coroner will usually adduce evidence of the witness's:

(a) Address.

(b) Relationship to the deceased.

(c) Occupation.

(d) The events leading to or including the incident leading to death.

(e) The deceased's general state of health, etc.

The coroner may conclude by saying, for example:

> **Thank you Mr** (name of second witness). **Now has anyone got any questions they would like to ask?**

11.01.20 Cross-examination of Witnesses

If there is an invitation from the coroner to cross-examine, the advocate may say:

> **With your leave, sir, there is/are** (number of) **questions I would like to put to** (name of witness).

If there is no invitation from the coroner to cross-examine, the advocate may say:

> **With your leave, sir, I would be grateful if you would allow me to ask some questions of this witness.**

11.01.21 Order of Cross-examination

There is no rule as to the order of cross-examination.

The persons attending the inquest and their legal representatives will either, by agreement or, by application to the coroner determine the order of cross-examination.

If there has been no agreement and/or no other person wishes to cross-examine, the advocate should make an application (see **11.01.20**).

The advocate representing the witness will usually examine last.

11.01.22 The advocate should be ready to defend the relevance of his questions if challenged by the coroner, and should always bear in mind the rule in **11.01.02**.

11.01.23   Excluding the Jury

Where there is a jury, an objection to evidence is usually made in the absence of the jury.

A person objecting to evidence may say:

> **At this point there is a matter of law on which I would seek leave to address you and I feel it would be more appropriate if it were canvassed in the absence of the jury.**

11.01.24   Objecting to Evidence

An objection may be made as follows:

(a)   The party identifies the evidence to which an objection is taken.

If the coroner indicates that he is prepared to hear the objection (see **11.01.09**):

(b)   The party gives reasons for the objection and refers to any relevant law.

(c)   Reply by any other party at the invitation of the coroner, (see also **11.01.20**).

(d)   Response by the party, dealing with any new points raised by the other parties or the coroner but not repeating the submissions in (b).

(e)   Decision by the coroner.

(f)   Jury recalled (if excluded).

11.01.25   Police Evidence

The coroner will usually be assisted in the inquiry by the police. The police may prepare and distribute plans and/or photographs (if appropriate) or attend court as witnesses (see **11.01.19**).

The attendance of police witnesses does not, of itself, indicate that the inquest is an inquiry into criminal liability.

11.01.26   The coroner may also call evidence from eye witnesses to the incident, for example:

(a) Factory death.

(b) Death during hospital treatment.

(c) Death on holiday.

(d) Death whilst in police custody, etc.

11.01.27 Documentary Evidence

The coroner may admit documentary evidence (for example, a written statement).

The coroner will usually introduce the evidence in order that any party may object to its admission before it is read (see **11.01.24**).

11.01.28 Medical Evidence

The coroner will usually call medical evidence after evidence of fact (although the distinction between expert evidence and evidence of fact is blurred in cases involving death in hospital or whilst undergoing treatment).

However, there may be some cases where it is preferable to call the medical evidence first or where, as a matter of convenience to professional witnesses, the order is changed.

The extent of the medical evidence, other than that of the pathologist, will depend upon the nature of the case. For example, different considerations will apply between:

(a) Cases of immediate death.

(b) Serious injury subsequently followed by death.

(c) Industrial disease or other long standing illness followed by death while being treated.

(d) Suicide (where psychiatric evidence might be called).

Basic research into the areas of expertise involved will assist in cross-examination.

11.01.29 The coroner may call the pathologist, who is sworn:

Your full name is (name) **and your address is** (address). **You are a con-**

sultant pathologist at (name of hospital) **hospital and on the** (date) **you carried out a post mortem examination on the body of** (name of deceased)?

And do you now produce exhibit (-) **which is your report on the findings of the post mortem examination in which you found the cause of death to be** (state cause)?

The pathologist may then set out his findings as to the physical condition of the body and expand upon his reasons as to the cause of death.

11.01.30 Applications may be made after the conclusion of the evidence, or at any appropriate time during the inquest. The following are examples (see **11.01.31-33**).

11.01.31   Application to Call Evidence

Although it is usually expected that the coroner will have gathered together all relevant information and made use of it at the inquest, an advocate may wish to apply to the coroner to call further evidence, for example:

With your leave, sir, I would ask that Mr (name) **be called to give evidence in relation to the circumstances of the** (state cause of death).

11.01.32   Application to Adjourn

For example:

With your leave, sir, I would respectfully make application that in the light of the evidence of Mr (name)**, and the implications thereof, the inquest be adjourned whilst further evidence is sought (and that it is thereafter reconvened to be heard with a jury).**

11.01.33   Application for a View

For example:

Sir, at this stage, I would respectfully make application for an order that there be a view of (state place of death, for example, factory).

11.01.34   Conclusion of Evidence

On completion of the evidence and any applications, no one is permitted to address the coroner or jury on the facts in evidence at the inquest.

11.01.35. Address on Law

An interested person may address the coroner on relevant matters of law.

Where there is a jury, it will be excluded during legal submissions (see **11.01.23**), particularly if the submissions concern the summing up to the jury and the law on any appropriate verdict. For example:

If it please you, Sir, there are certain matters of law on which I would seek leave to address you before:

(a) **You sum this case up to the jury, and I feel it would be more appropriate if these matters were canvassed in the absence of the jury.**

(b) **You give your decision in this matter** (if the coroner sits alone).

11.01.36 It is unusual for the coroner to invite submissions if he is sitting alone but an advocate may seek leave to address the coroner on the law, whether or not there is an invitation to do so (see also **11.01.20**).

11.01.37 Summing Up (With Jury)

On completion of the evidence and any legal submissions, the coroner will, if sitting with a jury, sum up the evidence to the jury and direct them on any points of law. The coroner should:

(a) Warn against adding any riders to the verdict.

(b) Explain the scope of the inquest.

(c) Warn against any comments exceeding the scope of the inquest.

(d) Advise the jury to limit themselves to the facts of the case.

(e) Advise the jury only to answer the questions in the inquisition (see **11.01.42**).

(f) Advise the jury as to the various verdicts that they are entitled to return.

(g) Advise the jury that they are free to return any verdict available to them, subject to their obligation not to frame their verdict in a way which attributes civil or criminal liability to any named person.

(h) If there is a likelihood of an open verdict, the jury should be asked to agree as far as possible on the registrable particulars (see **11.01.42(e)**).

11.01.38 Summing Up (Without Jury)

If the coroner is sitting alone, it is not necessary for him to sum up the evidence although, in practice, the coroner may refer to it briefly. The coroner must state in public the verdict he has reached.

11.01.39 Returning the Verdict

After summing up, if there is a jury, they will retire to consider their verdict with any plans, photographs or exhibits.

The coroner's officer will take the appropriate jury oath.

11.01.40   The jury may return any verdict available to them.

If, after 'a reasonable period' the jury cannot agree, the coroner should direct, in open court that, if after a further attempt the jury cannot agree, he will accept a majority verdict (maximum of two dissenters).

11.01.41   The coroner is not obliged to accept a majority verdict but he must accept a unanimous verdict, however unreasonable, if, after suitable explanation, the jury persist in their view. In any other case the coroner will discharge the jury and hold a new inquest.

11.01.42 Questions in the Inquisition

The coroner or jury return a verdict by answering the questions in the inquisition, namely:

(a) The name of the deceased.

(b) The injury or disease causing the death.

(c) The time, place and circumstances in which the injury was sustained/disease contracted, etc.

(d) The conclusion as to death, see **11.01.43**.

(e) The registrable particulars of the deceased:

    (i) Date and place of death

    (ii) Full name of the deceased

    (iii) Maiden name of a married female

(iv) Date and place of birth

(v) Occupation and usual address.

11.01.43 Verdict

The conclusion as to cause of death is usually the most important finding at an inquest. The following standard verdicts are available:

(a) Natural causes.

(b) Accident/misadventure.

(c) Suicide.

(d) Open verdict.

(e) Unlawful killing.

(f) Lawful killing.

(g) Dependence on drugs/non dependent abuse of drugs.

(h) Industrial disease.

(i) Attempted/self induced abortion.

(j) Stillbirth.

(k) Want of attention at birth.

11.01.44 Recommendations

The jury/coroner might make recommendations to the appropriate authorities so as to avoid future fatalities.

11.01.45 After the verdict it might be appropriate for the advocate to express condolences or sympathy to the family of the deceased on behalf of his client(s) (without admitting liability).

11.01.46 Costs

Applications for costs are not made in the coroner's court.

11.01.47 Conclusion

The inquest is formally closed. Usually the coroner's officer will call for silence and ask those present to stand as the coroner leaves court.

If the coroner is to start immediately with another inquest, the coroner's officer may simply advise those present that the inquest is over and that those connected with it may depart (see **14.03.08-10**).

CHAPTER 12

Court Martial

Section 1:	Introduction
Section 2:	Practice before the Hearing
Section 3:	Practice at the Hearing
See also:	4.01: Sentencing

SECTION 1: INTRODUCTION

12.01.01   Court Martial

A court martial is a court which is convened to try any person subject to service law and who it is alleged is in breach of service (army, naval or air force) and/or civil criminal law.

12.01.02   Army, Royal Naval and Royal Air Force Court Martials

This chapter explains the practice in an army court martial.

There is little difference between an army court martial and a Royal Air Force court martial or a Royal Naval court martial.

12.01.03   There are three types of court martial:

(a)   A General Court Martial (in which the total sentence is open).

(b)   A District Court Martial (in which the the total sentence available to the court should not exceed two years imprisonment).

(c) A Field General Court Martial (which is convened only during times of war or states of emergency).

12.01.04   General Court Martial

At a General Court Martial, the court will consist of a president who is usually a brigadier or a full colonel. The other members are usually either lieutenant colonels, majors or captains.

A judge advocate must sit with a general court martial.

12.01.05   District Court Martial

At a District Court Martial, the court will consist of a president who is usually a major. The other members are usually captains or lieutenants.

A judge advocate may sit with a District Court Martial depending on the complexity of the case.

An officer may not be tried by a district court martial.

12.01.06   The Judge Advocate

The role of the judge advocate is very similar to that of a crown court judge. He will advise upon all matters of law and will sum up the evidence at the end of the case.

His advice on the law will almost certainly be followed by the court. He may be asked to deal with certain matters such as the admissibility of evidence in the absence of the court (see **3.04.40**).

The judge advocate takes no part in reaching a decision on the facts.

12.01.07   The Court

The court are the sole judges of law and fact. The court also decide upon and deliver sentence.

12.01.08   The Advocate

An advocate wishing to appear before a court martial on legal aid should apply to the MOD to have his name enrolled on the Army, RAF or Royal Naval courts martial lists.

12.01.09   Whether an advocate is instructed to appear before a court martial will depend largely upon the nature of the offence(s) and likely plea(s).

For example (**12.01.10 & 11**):

12.01.10   A soldier charged with, for example, the purely military offence of absence without leave and who is likely to plead guilty, would usually appear before a District Court Martial (sitting without a judge advocate).

The prosecutor would usually be the Regimental Adjutant.

The accused would be represented by an officer of his choice also from the regiment.

12.01.11   A soldier charged with a more serious offence, especially where the plea is likely to be not guilty, would usually appear before a General or District Court Martial (sitting with a judge advocate).

The prosecutor would be a legally qualified officer from the army legal corps.

The accused would be represented by either an officer from the army legal corps or a civilian counsel or solicitor appointed under the legal aid scheme (or privately instructed).

SECTION 2:
PRACTICE BEFORE THE HEARING

12.02.01   Investigation of the Offence

Where a soldier is suspected of having committed a (military or civil) offence, the matter may be investigated by the Royal Military Police.

During the investigation, the soldier may be held either in open or close arrest or not at all.

There is no provision as to bail.

12.02.02   A private soldier in close arrest, or an NCO in any form of arrest, hands over his duties and does not attend parades.

A private soldier in open arrest may be ordered to perform all duties and attend parades.

12.02.03   Once the investigation has been concluded, the statements, records of interview and any documentary exhibits are fowarded to the local office of the Army Legal Service (ALS) who will advise on the appropriate charges.

12.02.04   Election for Trial by Court Martial

The commanding officer may deal summarily with certain less serious charges and hear the evidence himself or he may order a summary or abstract of evidence.

The commanding officer must give the accused the choice of being tried by court martial where the punishment is other than a severe reprimand, reprimand, admonishment, any other minor punishment or a (usually small) forfeiture of pay. The offence may be, for example, failing to attend for duty or common assault.

12.02.05   If the accused accepts the commanding officer's jurisdiction, he is also agreeing to accept his award (if found guilty).

The commanding officer may say:

Will you accept my award, or do you wish to be tried by court martial?

12.02.6   If the commanding officer has no jurisdiction to try the offences, the accused will be remanded for trial by court martial (see **12.02.08**).

12.02.07   Summary Dealing

If the accused is dealt with summarily by the commanding officer, the practice is similar to a summary trial (see **1.06**) in the magistrates' court.

12.02.08   Summaries of Evidence and Abstracts of Evidence

The commanding officer must order a summary or abstract of evidence if the accused has elected to be tried by court martial. The practice is similar to an old style committal (see **1.05.03**).

The summary or abstract of evidence is usually prepared on the advice of the ALS.

A summary of evidence is taken by an officer on behalf of the commanding officer. Witnesses give their evidence on oath and are subject to cross-examination by the accused or his defending officer.

An abstract of evidence is the collection of written statements. A copy is served on the accused.

The evidence, once completed in either abstract or summary form, is then submitted together with the charge sheet to the commanding officer.

12.02.09   Documents

The accused should be given:

(a)   A copy of the charge sheet.

(b)   A copy of the summary or abstract of evidence.

(c)   The names of any witnesses upon whom the prosecution does not intend to rely.

(d)   Notice of any additional evidence.

(e)   The names of the president and members of the court martial (if requested).

12.02.10   The Right to Legal Advice

Once the accused has been remanded by his commanding officer for trial by court martial, he has the right to seek legal advice from an army legal officer who is not concerned in the prosecution.

12.02.11   An interview with an army legal officer will be arranged by the accused's unit.

The accused will attend together with his defending officer (usually an officer from the regiment, appointed by the commanding officer).

12.02.12   The purpose of the interview is:

(a)   To provide the accused with some general advice about the charges and the evidence against him.

(b)   To make a preliminary assessment as to the likely plea(s).

(c) To ascertain whether the accused requires representation by a barrister or solicitor and, if so, whether the accused wishes to apply for legal aid.

12.02.13 Representation

The accused may be represented by:

(a) A civilian barrister or solicitor (nominated by the accused or appointed by the Ministry of Defence, see **12.01.08**):

   (i) Under the legal aid scheme.

   (ii) At his own expense (usually where legal aid is refused).

(b) An officer of the army legal corps or a legal officer from another service.

(c) The accused's unit defending officer (usually where the offence is not a serious one and the plea is guilty).

12.02.14 Application for Legal Aid

If an accused decides to apply for legal aid, the application is submitted by the interviewing army legal officer to the Ministry of Defence who may:

(a) Grant the application (with or without a contribution).

(b) Refuse the application.

12.02.15 Appointment of Counsel

If the accused is unable to nominate a barrister or solicitor, the MOD will appoint one on his behalf (see **12.01.08**)

12.02.16 The legal officer who conducted the interview will usually prepare and foward to the MOD for counsel:

(a)-(d) See **12.02.09(a)-(d)**.

(e) A note to assist counsel.

(f) Any other relevant information.

12.02.17 The MOD will prepare the brief and formally instruct counsel.

12.02.18 If counsel requires further evidence (including the evidence of any witness for the defence) or any other assistance he should contact the unit defending officer.

Counsel may approach the MOD if he requires a conference with the accused. In practice, counsel will prepare the case on the papers and will have a conference with the accused on the day before the court martial.

SECTION 3: PRACTICE AT THE HEARING

INTRODUCTION

12.03.01   Right of Audience

Barristers.

Solicitors.

Serving officers.

Accused in person.

12.03.02   Dress

Barristers and solicitor advocates are robed.

Serving officers and soldiers taking part in the proceedings will be in full Number 2 Dress military uniform. In the case of an officer, this is Number 1 Dress hat, Sam Brown and cross belt and medals.

Military personnel, other than the accused, wear head-dress until the court has been convened. It is then removed and not worn again during the proceedings (until the court is about to rise).

If ordered, officers (except the accused) will also wear a sword.

12.03.03 Mode of Address

Judge advocate	Sir.
Any officer of the court:	Sir.
The advocate may also say:	Mr President and gentlemen of the court.

12.03.04 Conduct

The conduct of the hearing is formal.

12.03.05 Seating

At a District Court Martial, the three members of the court (and in some cases, the judge advocate), and at a General Court Martial, the five members of the court and the judge advocate, will sit at a table facing the court room.

12.03.06   The prosecuting officer will sit at a table on the left hand side of the court room.

Witnesses will sit beside the table, facing the court, to give evidence (unless a witness box is provided).

12.03.07   The defending officer and/or advocate will sit at a table on the right hand side of the court room.

The accused and his escort will sit beside the table, facing the court.

12.03.08 Addressing the Court

A party addressing the court or examining or cross-examining a witness should do so standing.

12.03.09 Burden and Standard of Proof

The burden of proof is on the prosecution.

The standard of proof is 'beyond reasonable doubt'.

12.03.10   Order of Presentation

The order of presentation and speeches follows the title order of the case.

12.03.11   Witnesses

Witnesses should remain outside court until called to give evidence. After giving evidence, a witness may be released and/or be required to remain outside the court.

12.03.12   The Names of Members of the Court Martial

The accused or the advocate may obtain a list of the names of the members of the court martial (see **12.02.09(e)**).

12.03.13   The Advocate at the Court Martial

If the court martial is taking place outside the United Kingdom, the advocate will usually be accommodated by the regiment of the accused.

12.03.14   On the day of the court martial, the advocate will be conveyed to the court martial centre, usually by the defending officer.

The defending officer will usually remain in attendance throughout the proceedings.

12.03.15   At the court martial centre, the advocate will be provided with robing accommodation and a room in which to interview the accused.

PRACTICE

12.03.16   The Members of the Court

The court will be seated in the court martial room.

12.03.17   Entering the Room

The parties will be asked to enter the court martial room by the court orderly.

The advocate will walk in together with the prosecuting officer. He will be followed by the defending officer. The officers will be wearing head-dress.

12.03.18   The prosecuting officer will salute, and the advocate will bow to, the court.

The prosecuting officer and the advocate will then walk to their respective tables and be seated.

12.03.19 Attendance of the Accused

The president will then tell the court orderly to bring in the accused.

The accused will be marched in together with his escort. The accused will not be wearing head-dress.

The accused will be halted in front of the court and told to be seated.

12.03.20   During the proceedings, the accused will be in close arrest and in the custody of an escort (but not handcuffed). The convening officer may direct that he be in open arrest while the court is not actually sitting.

If the case is not concluded on the first day, the court adjourns in the usual way.

12.03.21 Evidence of Fitness to be Tried

The accused will have had a medical examination on the morning of the first day of the trial.

The prosecutor will produce the medical certificate showing that the accused is fit to be tried.

12.03.22 Convening the Court

The president (or judge advocate) will read out the names of the officers appointed to form the court from the convening order. The accused will be asked if he objects to any of them.

The court is then sworn. The judge avocate will usually administer the oath to the president and members.

Where there is no judge advocate, the president will usually administer the oath to the members and the senior member will administer the oath to the president.

All military personnel will then remove their head-dress.

12.03.23 Preliminary Applications

Either party may make any preliminary application(s) to the court (for example, a plea to the jurisdiction) before the accused is arraigned (see **3.04.09-11**).

The party may say:

Before the accused is arraigned, there is a preliminary matter upon which I would seek to address the court.

12.03.24 The Arraignment

The judge advocate or the president will then read the charge sheet to the accused.

The accused will plead guilty or not guilty.

12.03.25 If the accused pleads guilty and the court is satisfied that the accused understands the nature and consequences of his plea the court will formally find him guilty.

The court will then proceed to sentence (see **12.03.31-32**).

12.03.26 Conduct of the Trial

If the accused pleads not guilty, the court will proceed to hear the evidence.

The conduct of the trial will follow a trial on indictment in the crown court. A submission of no case to answer may be made.

The practice in **3.04.26-90** should be followed.

12.03.27 Summing Up

At the conclusion of the case, the judge advocate will sum up the case (see **3.04.83**).

The Judge Advocate then withdraws from the court room and the court will be closed, or the court will retire in order to consider its verdict.

12.03.28 The Verdict

After considering its verdict the court will return to the court room. The verdict is announced by the president.

As a general rule, if the court is wearing head-dress, the verdict is likely to be not guilty. The reason for this is that the court will only again wear head-dress at the conclusion of the case.

12.03.29   If the verdict is not guilty, the accused is discharged. The accused may apply to the MOD for a refund of defence costs.

12.03.30   If the verdict is guilty, the court will then proceed to sentence.

SENTENCE

12.03.31   Prosecution Opening (Plea of Guilty)

The prosecution will open the facts from the summary or abstract of evidence in as much detail as is thought necessary.

The prosecution will read or summarise any statement made by the accused.

The prosecution may then offer to read any other matter from the summary or abstract of evidence requested by the defence (see **4.01.04-05**).

12.03.32   Plea in Mitigation (Plea of Guilty)

Where the accused has pleaded guilty the defending advocate will mitigate before **12.03.33-34**.

The defending advocate may apply to mitigate after **12.03.33-34** if he is able to satisfy the court that the mitigation is consistent with a plea of guilty (see **12.03.35**).

12.03.33   Evidence of Service Record and Antecedent History

The prosecution will call an officer to give evidence of the accused's service record and to produce his conduct sheets.

The prosecution will then call an officer (usually the adjutant of the accused's unit) to tender to the court a statement of evidence under RP71(3) which includes all the accused's details, his family background and any relevant reasons which point to his commission of the offence.

The statement is usually concluded with the words:

His commanding officer does/does not wish to retain him in the unit.

The prosecution will then read or call evidence of any previous civil convictions not recorded against the accused on his army conduct sheets.

12.03.34   The defence may cross-examine any officer called by the prosecution.

12.03.35   Plea in Mitigation (Plea of Not Guilty)

The advocate may make a plea in mitigation (see **4.01.29-33**).

In a court martial, the contents of the plea may be taken down by the members of the court. The advocate should be prepared to take the plea in mitigation slowly.

12.03.36   Sentence

At the conclusion of the plea in mitigation, the court will retire or the court may be closed to consider sentence. If a judge advocate is present, he will usually remain with the court to advise them.

12.03.37   Confirmation of Sentence

Every finding of guilt and sentence by a court martial is subject to confirmation by the confirming officer. This may take some weeks especially if the proceedings need to be transcribed.

12.03.38   Petition to confirming officer

An accused may petition the confirming officer against a finding of guilt and/or sentence.

The form of the petition is similar to the draft grounds of appeal (see **8.02.08**).

12.03.39   Appeal

If the finding of guilt and/or sentence is confirmed, the accused may petition the army board.

If the appeal is against conviction and an appeal to the Army Board has been unsuccessful, the accused has the right to appeal to the Court Martial Appeal Court.

A civilian convicted by a court martial may appeal to the Court Martial Appeal Court against sentence.

Appeal from the Court Martial Appeal Court is, with leave, to the House of Lords.

CHAPTER 13

Consistory Court

INTRODUCTION

13.01.01 Each diocese of the Church of England (and the Church in Wales) has a court of the bishop, which is known as the consistory court. The judge of this Court is appointed by the bishop and is known as the Chancellor of the Diocese.

In the Diocese of Canterbury the court is known as the Commissary Court and the judge as the Commissary General, but his jurisdiction is the same as that of a chancellor in any other diocese.

13.01.02 The Chancellor

The chancellor is appointed by the bishop of the diocese by letters patent.

It is possible, in the letters patent, for the bishop to reserve to himself the right to hear causes alone or with the chancellor. This is considered a regrettable anomaly and there are no current examples of such letters patent.

13.01.03 Faculty Applications

The consistory court deals with all matters of canon law at first instance but its main business and purpose is dealing with faculty applications.

Church buildings are exempt from ordinary planning and listed building legislation but changes in their use or ordering may not be made without a faculty granted by the Consistory Court.

13.01.04 In effect, a faculty hearing in the consistory court is like a planning application. However, the consistory courts are a regular part of the judicial system and the proceedings in them follow the traditional adversarial pattern and are not, generally, inquisitorial except that the chancellor has wider powers than any other judge to summon witnesses (see **13.01.28-31**).

13.01.05   Mode of Address

The chancellor is addressed as Worshipful Sir or Sir and is referred to in the third person as the Worshipful Chancellor.

The court itself is referred to as the Venerable Court.

Most dioceses have a mace for the chancellor to symbolise his authority. It is carried in and out of court in front of the chancellor and placed before him during the hearing. The officer who carries the mace is known as the apparitor.

13.01.06   The Registrar

Each diocese will also have a registrar of the consistory court who is also the bishop's legal secretary.

The registrar is very similar to a High Court master, in that he deals with all proceedings in ecclesiastical matters up to the hearing.

He is normally present in court for the hearing (unlike a master), sitting as a court clerk or associate.

He is also responsible for providing the necessary staff to administer the consistory court.

13.01.07   Parties

A person may be a party to proceedings before the consistory court if he has a personal interest in the faculty application or if he is a parishioner of the parish concerned or a member of its electoral roll.

13.01.08   Right of Audience

Barrister.

Solicitor.

Interested party or parties in person.

13.01.09   Dress

Barristers and solicitors are robed.

An interested party should be respectably dressed.

Church representatives should be respectably dressed but do not have to wear the robes of their orders.

PREPARATION

13.01.10   A great deal of preparation and prior consultation is necessary before a faculty hearing. This should be researched in the common practitoners' handbooks.

13.01.11   The Petition

The petition is the first pleading. This is lodged by the party or parties seeking the grant of a faculty who have a sufficient interest in the subject matter of the suit.

A petition could cover anything from a simple memorial plaque on a wall to the entire renovation, refurbishment or reordering of the church.

The party or parties presenting the petition are known as the petitioners.

13.01.12   The Citation

Once the petition has been lodged with the court, the registrar lays it, together with any plans or other supporting documents, before the chancellor, who will then issue a general citation.

13.01.13   The citation means that the petition and any necessary and supporting plans must be publicly displayed by the incumbent and church wardens in various places in the parish for a continuous period of not less than 10 days including two Sundays.

13.01.14   The citation announces the works to be done in the petition. It cites all persons who have (or claim to have) a lawful interest in the subject matter of the petition to send to the registrar a notice of objection within a required time limit if that person wishes to object to any of the proposed works.

13.01.15   Notice of Objection

The process described in **13.01.12-14** then produces the second set of pleadings in a faculty hearing, namely the notice of objection.

The service of a notice of objection is the equivalent of entering an appearance in High Court proceedings.

13.01.16   Act on Petition

To pursue his objection an objector must subsequently serve, within the required time limit, particulars of his objection. This pleading is known either as the particulars of objection or act on petition.

By lodging this pleading an objector becomes a party to the proceedings and is known as a party opponent and becomes liable for an order for costs.

13.01.17   In some cases where no objection is lodged, but the chancellor thinks it appropriate that there should be a hearing and that the petitioners should be put to proof of their case, he may invite the archdeacon to enter an appearance, either to put the petitioners to proof or, by way of outright opposition to their petition.

When this course is adopted the archdeacon has to enter an act on petition which may be a neutral pleading or may make points of objection.

13.01.18   Answer

After an act on petition has been lodged the petitioners have the right to a further pleading called the answer which should be lodged within 14 days.

13.01.19   Further Pleadings

Further pleadings may be necessary but are unusual and are regulated by the registrar.

13.01.20   Summons for Directions

All contentious hearings will require a summons for directions and this can either be heard by the registrar or by the chancellor himself in chambers.

THE HEARING

13.01.21   Introduction: Burden and Standard of Proof

The burden of proof is on the petitioners, but strictly speaking there is no particular standard of proof in an ecclesiastical case.

The chancellor gives such weight as he considers appropriate to individual items of evidence. The grant or withholding of a faculty is in his discretion (which must be judicially exercised).

13.01.22   The Petitioners' Opening

At the hearing of the case, the petitioner(s) opens the case in exactly the same way as in a trial in the High Court (see **5.06.43-46**).

13.01.23   Evidence in Support of the Petition

The petitioner then calls evidence in support of the petition.

The evidence must be given orally, although the chancellor has power of his own motion to direct that all or some of the evidence may be given before an examiner or by affidavit.

13.01.24   The usual rules of evidence apply and witnesses called to give evidence for the petitioner(s) are then subject to cross-examination by the party (or parties) opponent or archdeacon, if he has intervened (see **13.01.17**), (see **5.06.47-59**).

13.01.25   A written statement may be admitted in evidence under the Faculty Jurisdiction Rules.

13.01.26   The petitioner then closes his case (see **5.06.72**).

13.01.27   The Case for the Party Opponent or Archdeacon

The party (or parties) opponent, may then open the case to the court and call witnesses who will be subject to cross- examination in the same manner as the petitioner.

JUDGE'S WITNESSES

13.01.28   Thus far, the proceedings are almost identical to High Court civil proceedings but before the evidence is closed there is one very important difference in the consistory court and that is that the chancellor may call judge's witnesses.

13.01.29   Quite often judge's witnesses are representatives of the Central Council for Churches or the Diocesan Advisory Committee or some other diocesan official whom the chancellor thinks can assist in the proceedings.

13.01.30   The judge has to give seven clear days notice in writing of his intention to call a witness and the sort of evidence that the witness is being called to adduce.

13.01.31   Any witness called by the judge is liable to cross- examination by all the parties and then to re-examination by the judge.

13.01.32   A View of the *Locus in Quo*

Hearings of the consistory court usually take place in the church in question. This has obvious advantages for the parties to view the *locus in quo.*

However, some chancellors, either through age or infirmity or other indisposition, prefer not to sit in church but at some other location. This course almost inevitably means that a view of the *locus in quo* will be necessary (see **5.06.70-71**).

SPEECHES

13.01.33   When the evidence is completed, the parties may make submissions to the court on the law and the evidence as follows:

(a)   Party (or parties) opponent.

(b)   Petitioner(s).

JUDGMENT

13.01.34   The chancellor will then give his judgment. In most cases this will be reserved for him to consider the matters he has heard and seen and to view the church, if he has not already done so.

13.01.35   If the chancellor allows the petition, he will direct the issuing of a faculty which is the court order allowing for the particular works to be carried out.

13.01.36   Costs

The chancellor also provides in his judgment for the costs to be paid.

Unlike other courts, one of the parties is also ordered to pay the costs of the court.

13.01.37   Appeal

An unsuccessful party is entitled to appeal as of right.

Appeal lies in the Province of Canterbury to the Court of the Arches or in the Province of York to the Chancery Court of York unless proceedings are certified by the chancellor (on the application of either party) to involve a matter of doctrine, ritual or ceremonial, in which case the appeal lies to the Court of Ecclesiastical Causes Reserved.

13.01.38   The time limits and provisions for appeals can be found in the Ecclesiastical Jurisdiction (Faculty Appeals) Rules.

The time limits for appeal are 28 days after the date of judgment of the consistory court or 14 days after the date of the chancellor's certificate, whichever period last expires.

CHAPTER 14

General Court Practice

SECTION 1:
EXAMINATION OF WITNESSES

INTRODUCTION

14.01.01   The purpose of examination (asking questions) of a witness is to obtain answers.

As a general rule, a party should not ask a witness questions if he does not need the witness' answers.

14.01.02   The party examining a witness should:

(a)   Ask short, straightforward and easily understood questions.

(b)   Ask the witness only questions which are relevant to the issues between the parties.

The party examining a witness should not, as a general rule:

(c)   Ask the witness questions of which that party has little or no idea of the answer.

EXAMINATION IN CHIEF

14.01.03   The purpose of examination in chief is to obtain evidence from a witness in support of the case of the party calling that witness.

14.01.04   The witness should be asked questions in such a way that, without the answer being suggested to him, the witness tells the court what the party calling that witness wants the court to know.

14.01.05   The party calling the witness should:

(a)   Examine the witness only on matters relevant to the purpose of calling the witness.

(b)   Examine the witness from a statement or proof of evidence made (and preferably signed) by the witness before the witness is called to give evidence.

The party calling the witness should not, as a general rule:

(c)   Ask leading questions unless all parties agree this may be done (except see, for example: **9.01.54-55; 9.02.14; 9.03.29-30**).

Even if a party is permitted to lead, the evidence of a witness will usually sound better if it is unprompted. As a general rule the essential part of the evidence of that witness is better adduced in the usual way.

For examples of leading questions, see the common practitioners' handbooks.

CROSS-EXAMINATION

14.01.06   The purpose of cross-examination is to test the accuracy of evidence given by the witness against the party who has not called the witness and/or to obtain evidence from the witness favourable to that party.

14.01.07   The party cross-examining a witness may ask leading questions.

The party should:

(a)   Put his case on the relevant issues to the witness.

If it is the party's case that the witness is either mistaken or untruthful he should make either allegation clear.

(b)   As a general rule, cross-examine only on the issues which are in dispute between the parties.

(c)   Elicit from the witness any other material which may be useful to that party.

The party cross-examining a witness should not:

(d) Ask repetitive questions, either to emphasise an answer made by the witness which is favourable to that party, or to persuade the witness to change an answer made by the witness which is unfavourable to that party.

RE-EXAMINATION

14.01.08   The purpose of re-examination is to attempt to reinstate any part of the evidence of the witness rendered less cogent by cross-examination and to clarify any points raised in cross- examination that were not raised in examination in chief.

14.01.09   The general rule in **14.01.01** should be carefully considered by a party considering re-examination.

14.01.10   The party re-examining a witness should:

(a) Ask questions only on matters arising out of cross-examination. The party is not permitted to introduce new matter.

The party re-examining a witness should not:

(b) Ask leading questions.

(c) See **14.01.07(d)**.

REFRESHING THE MEMORY

14.01.11   A witness (usually a police officer) may wish to refresh his memory from a document made at the time.

The party calling the witness may say:

Do you wish to refresh your memory from (state nature of document)?

When did you make (the document)?

AND/OR

How long after the events recorded in (the document) **did you make** (the document)?

When you made (the document) **were the events still fresh in your mind?**

The party may then say to the court:

Could (name of witness) **be allowed to refresh his memory from** (the document)?

14.01.12   The document should be made available to the party or parties against whom the witness is called.

14.01.13   'Refreshing the memory' means what it says. The witness should not (but, often does) read *verbatim* from the document.

14.01.14   The document will usually have been made by the witness. If it was not made by the witness, the party may say:

Did you check the contents of (the document)?

AND/OR

Did you sign (the document)?

When you checked the contents of (the document) **were the events recorded in** (the document) **still fresh in your mind?**

14.01.15   A witness may refresh his memory before giving evidence from a document which may not have been made at the time.

The party calling the witness should:

(a)   Inform the other party or parties that the witness has refreshed his memory from the document, and

(b)   Make available the original or a copy of the document.

EXPERT EVIDENCE

14.01.16   An expert witness is a person with expert knowledge, whose opinion on any matter in which he has expert knowledge will be admitted in evidence.

It is for the court to decide whether the witness is an expert witness.

14.01.17   The party calling the witness should establish the witness' expert knowledge and/or qualifications, after the witness has been identified, as follows:

Are you (state occupation of witness and/or area of expertise, for example: a consultant toxicologist or a person who studies handwriting)?

How long have you been a (repeat above)?

What are your qualifications?

Do these qualifications/Does your (state area of expertise) **enable you to give evidence of** (state purpose of calling witness, for example: the effect of alcohol in the body or the author of a handwritten document)?

14.01.18   The party may then address the court, as follows:

Unless there is any objection I intend to ask (name of witness) **about** (state purpose of calling evidence).

14.01.19   The party should then establish the manner in which he intends to adduce the expert evidence, for example:

How do you determine (state purpose of calling witness)?

14.01.20   The party will then examine the witness in the usual way.

PRODUCING EXHIBITS/DOCUMENTS

14.01.21   A party may, during the course of examination in chief or cross-examination (but not in re-examination) invite a witness to produce an exhibit, for example:

Could the witness be shown (state nature of exhibit)?

Do you recognise (the exhibit)?

What is it?

Do you now produce (the exhibit)?

14.01.22   The party may then say to the court:

Could (the exhibit) **be marked Exhibit Number** (-)?

OR

(The exhibit) **is at page** (-) **in the bundle.**

TENDERING A WITNESS

14.01.23   If a witness gives corroborative evidence the party calling him may tender that witness for cross-examination on all or part of his evidence (as appropriate).

14.01.24   After identification of the witness the party may say:

> **Were you present with** (name of witness) **and are you therefore able to give evidence of** (state nature of corroborative evidence)?

> AND/OR

> **Did you make notes of this incident with** (name of witness)?

> See **14.01.11-15.**

> **Were there any occassions when** (name of witness) **was not present?**

> **I tender this witness for cross-examination.**

AFFIDAVIT EVIDENCE

14.01.25   A party wishing to rely on affidavit evidence should serve the affidavit and exhibits on the parties and the court (depending on the nature of the hearing) a reasonable time before the hearing.

14.01.26   A party will not usually be permitted, except in interlocutory proceedings, to rely on an affidavit (in the absence of agreement between the parties) unless the witness attends court to be cross-examined on it.

14.01.27   The witness giving affidavit evidence is sworn and identified.

The party may then say:

> **Do you recognise this as an affidavit that you swore on** (date) **for use in these proceedings?**

> **Did you read it through before you signed it and check that the contents were true?**

14.01.28   The party may then say to the court:

> **Have** (the court) **read the affidavit?**

The court will either require the party to direct it to the relevant passages or read the affidavit.

14.01.29   The party will then usually say:

I intend, with your leave, to tender this witness for cross-examination on his affidavit, but first, there are certain matters on which I would seek to examine this witness.

The party may then examine the witness on:

(a)   Any matter that has arisen since the affidavit was sworn.

(b)   Any matter which was not material at the time the affidavit was sworn (for example, if the affidavit was served for the purpose of an interlocutory application).

14.01.30   The witness may then be cross-examined and re-examined on his affidavit and other evidence in the usual way.

SECTION 2: SPEECHES

INTRODUCTION

This section considers:

(a)   The content and approach to speeches in civil cases.

(b)   The content and approach to speeches in criminal cases.

(c)   The standard phrases used in speeches to the judge and submissions.

14.02.01   Purpose of Opening and Closing Speeches

As a general rule, in a hearing before any court, tribunal or inquiry:

The opening speech prepares.

The purpose of opening is to assist the court, tribunal or inquiry to assimilate and understand the evidence it is about to hear.

The closing speech persuades.

The purpose of closing is to win the support of the court, tribunal or inquiry for that party on the basis of the evidence it has heard.

14.02.02   The advocate should always measure his speech to the court, tribunal or inquiry that he is addressing.

For example, a High Court judge will not need to be reminded of the standard of proof in civil cases, or the chairman of a tribunal of his jurisdiction (usually defined under the same statute under which the chairman was appointed).

SPEECHES IN CIVIL CASES

14.02.03   Opening Speech

The party having the burden of proof will usually be entitled to make an opening speech.

14.02.04   As a general rule, the party having the burden of proof is the party who has brought the case or is making the application.

That party will have done so for a reason.

Therefore, a party opening the case, in addition to explaining the nature of the case, should also explain the reason(s) why he is entitled to the order or judgment sought.

14.02.05   The party making an opening speech should prepare it carefully. It is that party's opportunity to pre-dispose the court, tribunal or inquiry in his favour.

14.02.06   The opening speech will usually contain:

(a) An explanation of the nature of the case.

(b) An outline of the evidence upon which that party intends to rely.

(c) A brief statement of the order or judgment sought.

(d) The reason(s) why that party is entitled to the order or judgment sought.

14.02.07   Closing Speech

As a general rule, a closing speech may be made by either party.

14.02.08   The closing speech will be that party's last opportunity opportunity to persuade the court why he is (or, the other party is not) entitled to the order or judgment sought.

14.02.09   The party should not repeat the evidence, although he should draw the court's attention to any important and relevant part(s) of it.

14.02.10   The closing speech will usually contain:

(a)   A summary of any important and relevant part(s) of the evidence.

(b)   A summary of any relevant agreed facts (if appropriate).

(c)   An explanation of any relevant evidence in dispute which is consistent with that party's case.

(d)   The reason(s) why that party is (or, the other party is not) entitled to the order or judgment sought.

14.02.11   Law

A party may refer to any relevant law during the course of his opening or closing speech (see also **14.02.32**).

14.02.12   A court, tribunal or inquiry may need to be persuaded on the law but, in most cases, it will need to be persuaded on the facts.

As a general rule, the advocate should address the court, tribunal or inquiry on the facts before referring to the law.

It is often an indication that the party has a weak case on the facts if he addresses the court, tribunal or inquiry on the law first or refers to numerous and/or obscure authorities.

SPEECHES IN CRIMINAL CASES

14.02.13   Prosecution Opening Speech

The prosecution is entitled to make an opening speech.

The prosecution should prepare his opening speech carefully. It is the prosecution's opportunity to pre-dispose the court and/or jury in his favour.

14.02.14   In many respects, the speech of the party opening the case is similar in both civil and criminal cases, although it would be considered bad practice for the prosecution to seek to persuade the court and/or jury that he is entitled to a verdict of guilt (see **14.02.15(e)**).

14.02.15   The prosecution's opening will usually contain:

(a)   An explanation of the nature of the case.

(b)   An explanation of the nature of the charges (in jury trials and, where appropriate, in the magistrates' court, for example, where the offence alleged is technical or complex).

(c)   An outline of the evidence upon which the prosecution intends to rely.

(d)   An explanation of the burden and standard of proof (in jury trials).

(e)   An invitation to the court or jury to draw the inference, on the evidence, that the defendant is guilty.

14.02.16   Defence Opening

For the circumstances in which the defence are entitled to open the case, see **3.04.62-66**.

14.02.17   The defence will usually confine the opening speech to an outline or explanation of the defence case although this is not strictly necessary and the defence may criticise the prosecution's case.

14.02.18   As a general rule, the defence opening speech prepares the court or jury for:

(a)   The defence evidence, and/or

(b)   Any observations the defence intends to make in his closing speech.

14.02.19   The defence opening speech may also be used to explain to the jury the purpose of questions put in cross-examination of the prosecution witnesses if it is not, at that stage, obvious or apparent.

14.02.20   Prosecution Closing

In a trial on indictment, the prosecution will usually make a closing speech (except **3.04.80**).

14.02.21   The purpose of the closing speech is to draw together the relevant evidence in the case to demonstrate to the jury how, on that evidence, the jury are entitled to draw the inference that the defendant is guilty of the offences charged (see **14.02.15(e)**).

14.02.22   Defence Closing Speech

The defence closing speech is often the only opportunity that the defence has to address the court or jury.

14.02.23   Despite the literature on the subject of defence speeches to the jury (or court), the defence should not feel intimidated by a closing speech.

14.02.24   The defence advocate should feel comfortable with his style. Although style will come with experience, a good rule is to 'be natural'. If the advocate is not accustomed to illustrating his day to day conversation with anecdotes or jokes, he should not do so in his speech to the jury.

14.02.25   The defence advocate should also remember that a jury (or the magistrates' court) is made up of individual people. He should consider what he would say to each one of them individually if he addressed them on behalf of his client.

14.02.26   The defence should prepare his closing speech carefully.

The speech should be properly ordered in a series of simple points and propositions which are relevant to the defendant's case.

The defence may find it useful to write down each point and proposition in advance for ease of reference.

14.02.27   The defence should address the court on each point (see **14.02.31**), explaining the significance of the evidence, the proposition the defence makes on that evidence and how it will assist the court in finding the defendant not guilty of the offences charged.

14.02.28   If the defence follows these simple points and propositions, he will avoid making an unstructured speech.

14.02.29   The defence may conclude by explaining the burden and standard of proof.

The defence is advised to give a positive explanation of the burden and standard of proof, for example, (where the prosecution have told the jury that, if they are not sure, they should acquit), the defence may say:

On the evidence you have heard, I would suggest that you cannot be sure of the defendant's guilt. And you should therefore acquit.

SPEECHES TO THE JUDGE AND SUBMISSIONS

14.02.30   Presentation

In speeches to the judge and submissions, the advocate should take care not to express his own opinion.

An expression of opinion can be avoided by the use of the following phrases:

I would submit that:

I would seek to persuade (the court) **that:**

The use of the phrase **I think that** should be avoided.

14.02.31   In a speech to a jury, an expression of opinion can be avoided by the use of the phrase:

You may think that:

14.02.32   Submissions on the Law

In a submission on the law, if the advocate is aware of a legal authority against him, he should draw the authority to the attention of the court, tribunal or inquiry and attempt to distinguish it (usually on the facts), for example:

There is an authority which is against me, namely (state authority).

I would submit that it does not apply in this case for the following reasons (state reasons).

14.02.33   Submissions of No Case to Answer

The advocate is often confused by what is or is not in evidence.

The advocate may have put certain matters in cross-examination (which he will later prove in evidence) with which the witness has not agreed. Only the answers made by a witness in cross-examination are evidence. The questions put in cross-examination are not evidence (although the advocate may make the mistake of thinking it is evidence because he is aware of the evidence to come).

The advocate must submit on the evidence as it is and not as it will be, although, in a trial on indictment, the submission may be renewed (see **3.04.78**).

SECTION 3: ETIQUETTE

14.03.01 Convening the Court, Tribunal or Inquiry

When the judge, magistrates, tribunal, inspector or coroner (person(s) hearing the case) enter the room in which the hearing is to be held, all the parties should stand (and will usually bow).

The parties should not sit until the person(s) hearing the case are seated.

14.03.02 During the Hearing
When the court, tribunal or inquiry is sitting, a party should enter and leave the room without causing a distraction and, in particular:

14.03.03 A party should not walk immediately in front of the person(s) hearing the case if any other route is available.

14.03.04 A party should not walk between the person(s) hearing the case and the party addressing them.

14.03.05 A party in criminal proceedings should not walk between the defendant and the judge or magistrates when pleas are being taken or the defendant is being sentenced.

14.03.06 Witnesses taking the Oath

All parties should observe silence and avoid any act which may distract the witness or the court, tribunal or inquiry when a witness is taking the oath.

14.03.07   Recalling a Witness or Party

If a witness (or party to the proceedings) is being cross-examined and the court adjourns, the advocate who called the witness may recall the witness when the court resumes (although this rule is now considered old fashioned), for example:

Mr (name), **could you return to the witness box, please.**

The advocate will then sit down and the opposing advocate will continue his cross-examination.

14.03.08   After the Hearing

An advocate should never leave the person(s) hearing the case sitting unattended by an advocate in open court.

If the advocate's case is the last case in which any party attending before the court, tribunal or inquiry is represented:

14.03.09   Before a Judge:

The advocate should sit in court until released.

The judge may say:

Please don't wait/There's no need to stay, Mr (name).

OR

The advocate may say:

There are no other represented cases before you today/this morning/ this afternoon. Could I have your permission to leave?

14.03.10   Before the Magistrate(s), Tribunal, Inspector:

The magistrates' court or the advocate appearing in the magistrates' court is often not aware of this rule (or, if aware, the rule is honoured in the breach).

In some tribunals and inquiries, the chairman or inspector often does not expect the rule to be observed.

The advocate should sit in the hearing room until released, or he may say

There are no other represented cases before you today/this morning/this afternoon. Could I have your permission to leave?

Common Practitioners' Handbooks

Magistrates' Court/ Juvenile Court	Stone's Justices' Manual (annual) (3 volumes) Butterworths
Road Traffic	Wilkinson's Road Traffic Offences (14th Edition) (1989) Longman
Licensing	Paterson's Licensing Acts 1989 (97th Edition) (1989) Butterworths
Crown Court	Archbold, Criminal Pleading (43rd Edition) Sweet and Maxwell
Sentencing	Current Sentencing Practice (1989) Sweet and Maxwell
High Court	Supreme Court Practice 1988 (+ 1989 Service) (The White Book) Sweet and Maxwell
	Butterworths Company Law Handbook (6th Edition) (1987)
County Court	County Court Practice (annual) Butterworths (The Green Book)
Costs	Butterworth's Costs Service (1987) (+ service to date)
	Greenslade on Costs 1986 (+ service) Services to Lawyers
Industrial Tribunal	
Social Security Appeal Tribunal	The appropriate pamphlets can be obtained from the relevant government department
Immigration Appeal Tribunal	
Planning Inquiries	Encyclopaedia of Planning Law and Practice (1989 service) Sweet and Maxwell

Coroner's Court	Jervis, Coroners (10th Edition) (1986) Sweet and Maxwell
	Thurston/et al, Law and Practice on Coroners (3rd Edition) (1985) Longman
Court Martial	The Manual of Military Law
Consistory Court	The Faculty Jurisdiction Rules
General Court Practice	Du Cann, The Art of the Advocate (Revised Edition 1980) Pelican
	Napley, The Technique of Persuasion (3rd Edition) (1983) Sweet and Maxwell